LAWRENCE & WISHART LTD.
LONDON

Freedom in Arms
A Selection of Leveller Writings
Editor A. L. Morton

BY THE EDITOR

A People's History of England
Language of Men
The English Utopia
Socialism in Britain
The Matter of Britain
The Life and Ideas of Robert Owen
The World of the Ranters

With George Tate:
The British Labour Movement
1770–1920

FREEDOM IN ARMS

*A Selection
of Leveller Writings*

Edited and
with an Introduction by
A. L. MORTON

Foreword by
Christopher Hill

1975
Lawrence and Wishart
London

Published simultaneously by
Lawrence & Wishart, London,
International Publishers, New York and
Seven Seas Books, Berlin, 1975
SBN 85315 3140

The portrait of Lilburne on the cover was originally a frontispiece to his *The Christian Mans Triall* (Dec. 1641). When Lilburne was again in prison in June 1646 it was re-used, with new captions and the addition of prison bars, as frontispiece to Overton's *Remonstrance of Many Thousand Citizens*.

The Printer
to the Reader.

I Desire thee to amend with thy pen,
one fault escaped in the printing, by negligence,
and the Authors absence,
which is in the 3. page and 10. line,
namely secretaries for sectaries:
And if there be any more faults
(as none liveth without some)
I also desire that thou wilt shew thy patience
by thy silence, and that thou may rather
make a profitable use of the sence,
then anywise strive about words;
even as thou wouldest except the like
favour of me or any other in thy absence,
if thou be one that shewest thy selfe
thus carefull and zealous for
the publike: especially now
in such extreme need.
Farewell.

From Walwyn's
The poore Wise-mans Admonition
Published June 10th, 1647.

Contents

Foreword
by
Christopher Hill

EACH generation rewrites history, they say, because each generation asks its own questions of the past. In the century of the common man, the Levellers have come into their own; and their historian, appropriately, is the author of *A People's History of England*. When that epoch-making book first appeared in 1938 it was a revelation to many of us; it told us things about our own past that we had never learnt at school. Some of its most exciting pages dealt with those seventeenth century democrats, the Levellers. Since then A. L. Morton has pursued the history of ordinary English men and women in *Language of Men, The English Utopia, The Matter of Britain* and in his latest and perhaps best book, *The World of the Ranters*.

Mr. Morton has also written about nineteenth and twentieth century working-class history, and he has always been concerned to stress the relevance of Leveller ideas for our own day – in addition to their intrinsic historical interest. "They were civilised in a new way," he wrote of the Levellers. "They wrote effectively not merely because they were exceptionally gifted or technically well equipped . . . but because they wrote with a purpose clearly understood and deeply felt, and for an audience which they knew to be close and immediately responsive . . . They can fairly claim to be the fathers of the tradition of plain English writing dedicated to the service of the plain man."

The claim is substantiated in this volume. The Levellers speak to us direct across three centuries. "Posterity, we doubt not", one of them wrote in the bitter hour of defeat, "shall reap the benefit of our endeavours whatever shall become of us." Many of the changes which the Levellers wanted to make in their unequal society have been achieved, mostly as a result of working-class struggle. But we have still a long way to go before we achieve their end of "freedom for all manner of people", a really equal society. William Walwyn indeed was alleged to have said that "it would never be well until all things were common," and being asked, "Will that ever be?" he answered, "We must endeavour it." The advice does not seem any the worse three and a quarter centuries later.

Balliol College, Oxford
October 1974

Editor's Preface

THE selection of one small volume from the mass of Leveller writings poses some real problems. The first is merely what to take from the sheer bulk available. Lilburne alone wrote over a hundred pamphlets. Overton and Walwyn were only slightly less prolific. There are many of doubtful or composite authorship. Yet one must try to make a representative selection of a dozen or twenty. Some of the most interesting are of substantial length. I would have liked, for example, to include *Walwyns Just Defence,* Wildman's *Putney Projects,* Overton's *The Hunting of the Foxes* and Lilburne's *Legall Fundamentall Liberties,* but these four would have just about filled my available space. So I decided, with some regrets, to give preference to shorter pamphlets in order to make possible a greater variety.

Again, a number of these pamphlets are available in existing collections, but these include the main basic documents without which a volume of this kind would be of little value to the student. So I have tried to include what seemed really essential, even if it has already been reprinted, but also a number of less familiar items. I have also tried to keep a balance between programmatic documents, theoretical writings and narratives of important events.

In any volume of this kind Lilburne is likely to come off badly. He was the most important political figure but a clumsy, long-winded and legalistic writer; the many good things in his pamphlets tend to be lost. After much thought I decided to let him be represented by the autobiographical *The Just Defence of John Lilburn.*

In my Introduction I have tried to give a short general account of the Leveller movement related as closely as possible to the documents selected. References to particular items are given by Roman figures in square brackets, as: [VI]. In giving references I have used the following abbreviations:

Haller –   *Tracts on Liberty in the Puritan Revolution.* Ed. William Haller.

H. and D. – *The Leveller Tracts 1647–1653.* Ed. William Haller and Godfrey Davies.

Wolfe –   *Leveller Manifestoes.* Ed. Don M. Wolfe.

Woodhouse – *Puritanism and Liberty.* Ed. A. S. P. Woodhouse.

I owe an immense debt to my wife Vivien for the way she has coped with my disorderly manuscripts.

A. L. M.
Clare, August 1974

Introduction

ONE of the outstanding historical developments of our century has been the reappraisal of the Levellers and the part they played in the English Revolution. To the classical Whig historians, down to Gardiner and even Trevelyan, they were little more than vulgar and irrelevant disturbers of the noble drama played out by the great statesmen, and their writings remained unreprinted and largely unread in the great Thomason Collection in the British Museum. The first signs of a better understanding came with C. H. Firth's edition of the Clarke Papers (1891–1901) and the useful biographies of Leveller leaders which he contributed to the Dictionary of National Biography. This did not, however, lead him to a new general estimate, as can be seen in his *Oliver Cromwell and the Rule of the Puritans in England* (1900). The first signs of such a change came with the pioneer studies of G. P. Gooch[1] and T. C. Pease.[2]

The real break came with the political ferment which followed the First World War and the Russian Revolution of 1917. The opening of a revolutionary age gave a new dimension to the study of the bourgeois revolutions of the past, and the rise of fascism led to important discussions about the nature and value of democracy, in which the Leveller contribution could be seen to have an unsuspected relevance. A feature of this period was that many of their basic writings were made accessible for the first time. William Haller's *Tracts on Liberty in*

[1] *English Democratic Ideas in the Seventeenth Century.* 1898.
[2] *The Leveller Movement.* 1916.

the Puritan Revolution (1933–1934) was followed by A. S. P. Woodhouse's *Puritanism and Liberty* (1938) in which the debates of the Army Council in 1647 were reprinted with a wealth of illustrative material. In 1944 Don M. Wolfe produced *Leveller Manifestoes* and William Haller and Godfrey Davies *The Leveller Tracts 1647–1653*, two volumes largely complementary. The parallel development of the Diggers or True Levellers was also receiving considerable attention.

Alongside these a number of studies have appeared by D. W. Petegorsky,[1] William Schenk,[2] Joseph Frank,[3] H. N. Brailsford[4] among others, as well as biographies of Lilburne and Wildman. More recently still the ground has been enlarged by a number of books in which the Levellers are placed in a background of subversive plebeian thinking. These include K. V. Thomas' *Religion and the Decline of Magic* (1970), Christopher Hill's *The World Turned Upside Down* (1971) and A. L. Morton's *The World of the Ranters* (1970). And Christopher Hill's *God's Englishman* (1970) was the first biography of Cromwell in which the central role of the Levellers in the crucial years from 1647 to 1649 was fully recognised.

I

Civil War

Christopher Hill suggests that "there was a greater background of class hostility in England before 1640 than historians have normally recognised."[5] There can be no doubt that the first half of the seventeenth cen-

[1] *Left-wing Democracy in the English Civil War.* 1940.
[2] *The Concern for Social Justice in the Puritan Revolution.* 1948.
[3] *The Levellers.* 1955.
[4] *The Levellers and the English Revolution.* 1961.
[5] *The World Turned Upside Down*, p. 16.

tury was a time of great stress and economic difficulties. Population was growing rapidly, more rapidly, probably than food production. So that the inflation, continuing from the previous century if perhaps at a slower pace, affected particularly food prices. The result was a continued fall in real wages. The population growth produced large numbers of rootless and masterless men, many squatting on commons and wastes and scratching a living on the edge of subsistence. It was to such people that Digger propaganda was later to be directed. The pressure of population on land made it profitable to enclose forests, commons and fens, increasing production but driving many of these squatters on to the already overcrowded labour market and further depressing wages. Many were driven into rapidly expanding London, where they formed a large, irregularly employed slum population. The same thing was true, to a less extent, in many provincial towns.

To these long term trends the century added its own specific causes of distress. The Thirty Years' War which devastated Europe from 1618 disrupted trade and depressed the export market. And the economic policies of the Stuart governments, with the continuation of what Christopher Hill has called "industrial feudalism", by which the cream of industrial profits were skimmed off for the benefit of a small parasitical section of the upper classes, imposed growing restraints on economic development. Finance by the sale of monopolies, for example, cost the population many times the revenue which the state received. If the government was sometimes blamed for more economic damage than it actually caused, that damage was still considerable and was widely resented. Again, while the grosser forms of feudal coercion in the relations between landlord and peasant had gone, plenty remained to be a constant source of irritation at local levels.

The whole period before 1640 was one of great

change and instability, in which many old established features were vanishing and old ideas seemed to be losing their relevance. This often reflected itself in hatred of the gentry and a growth of plebeian egalitarianism. Walwyn is alleged to have said:

"What an inequitable thing it is for one man to have thousands, and another want bread, and that the pleasure of God is, that all men should have enough, and not that one man should abound in this worlds good, spending it upon his lusts, and another man of far better deserts, not be worth two pence, and that it is no such difficulty as men make it to be, to alter the course of the world in this thing, and that a few diligent and valiant spirits may turn the world upside down, if they observe their seasons, and shall with life and courage ingage accordingly."[1]

We do not know if Walwyn actually did say this, but there is plenty of evidence that such ideas were widespread throughout the century.

No less subversive ideas were abroad in the matter of religion, which at this time can never be separated from politics. The Established Church taught social obedience, acceptance of a hierarchical structure in Church and State, reverence for authority. The Reformation had been at bottom a challenge to all these ideas, but the English Reformation aimed at retaining them as far as possible. It is not surprising that those who wanted to complete the work of the Reformation saw in Anglicanism the mark of the Popish Beast. The challenge came at a number of levels. Calvinism, the most "respectable" form of Puritanism, allowed the right of rebellion, but only if it was led by the properly appointed magistrates. Under English conditions this meant a rebellion against the King led by Parliament. Indeed, al-

[1] *Walwins Wiles.* H. and D., p. 301.

most to the last, the right-wing Parliamentarians to whom we have given the name Presbyterians, insisted that they were not fighting against the King, but merely to rescue him from evil advisers. For them, as for him, the people had nothing to do with the laws but to obey them.

But to the left of Calvinism were many groups who stood for "Reformation without tarrying for the Magistrate". If Parliament would lead them in the way they wanted to go, well and good. If not, as Overton said, the people themselves were the supreme power:

> "Wee are well assured, yet cannot forget, that the cause of our choosing you to be Parliament-men, was to deliver us from all kind of Bondage, and to preserve the Common-wealth in Peace and Happinesse: For effecting whereof, we possessed you with the same Power that was in our selves, to have done the same; For wee might justly have done it our selves without you, if we had thought it convenient; choosing you ... for avoiding some inconveniences ... Wee are your Principalls, and you our Agents; it is a Truth which you cannot but acknowledge."[1]

There were also many degrees of anti-clericalism. All Puritans hated Bishops. But many hated no less the Presbyterian ministers who replaced them. And to the left again were those who would have no ministerial office at all, but wished every man, and sometimes every woman, to have the right to expound the truth that was in them. And finally there were frank materialists who declared religion a deceit, denied that the Bible was the word of God and declared heaven and hell to be merely states of mind. Such was the London cobbler, who, we are told,

"when he heard any mention of God, he used to

---

[1] *A Remonstrance of Many Thousand Citizens.* Wolfe, p. 113.

laugh, and in a disdainful manner say that he believed money, good clothes, good meat and drink, tobacco and merry company to be Gods: but he was little beholding to any of these: for his God allowed him but eight pence or ten pence a day, and that he made him work for."[1]

We find that such ideas tend to coincide with a vigorous political radicalism.

With such a background, with passions aroused by the political crisis, it is understandable that on the eve of the Civil War many men felt that they were on the edge of a volcano. A Royalist wrote in 1642:

"The countenances of men are so altered, especially of the mean and middle rank of men, that the turning of a straw would set a whole country in a flame, and occasion the plundering of any man's house or goods."[2]

It was such fears that led many who had supported the early measures of the Long Parliament to come down in the end upon the side of the King. It was necessary for both parties (but especially for Parliament as the revolutionary body) to enlist the support of the masses, but the enthusiasm of these dangerous allies had to be contained. And, generally speaking, contained it was, though not without difficulty. Thus we find that when the Long Melford mansion of the Catholic Lady Rivers was sacked, the Parliamentarian Sheriff of Suffolk brought out the county militia, rather against their inclination, to disperse the rioters. And that great Puritan nobleman, the Earl of Warwick, sent his own servants to conduct her Ladyship to a place of safety. As compared with the Thirty Years' War in Germany or the French wars of religion it was a very civil war which

[1] *Arraignment and Tryall . . . of the Ranters.*
[2] Hill, op. cit., p. 19.

20

the leaders on both sides were anxious to keep within bounds. But the tensions continued to exist and were presently to erupt in more clearly political forms.

II

Classes and Parties

Even the most civil war has to be fought and won, and the first internal conflict arose between those (the Presbyterians) who did not wish to defeat the King outright but to patch up a compromise as quickly as possible and those (the Independents) who meant to fight the war to a victorious conclusion even if it meant enlisting the active support of the masses. Of this group Cromwell presently became the leader, and out of his struggle with the Earl of Manchester came an army of a kind never before seen – the New Model.[1] At first Parliament, despite its advantages in wealth and resources, fared badly. Its troops were of poor quality and badly led. Cromwell set out to enlist "men of a spirit . . . that is likely to go as far as gentlemen will go". Men, as he said on another occasion, that know what they fight for and love what they know. His troopers, including many officers, were drawn from the small farmers and artisans of Eastern England. Such enthusiasts were naturally, at first, in a minority and found mainly in the cavalry. But in time they set the tone of the Army as a whole. In June 1645 a decisive victory was won at Naseby and by the spring of the next year the war was over and the Army had time to sit down and think. It found plenty to think about and soon became a veritable school of politics.

[1] Confusion is sometimes caused by the names Presbyterian and Independent. They are commonly used to describe political parties of the right and centre respectively. These overlapped, but were by no means identical with, the religious groupings with the same names.

The great question, for the Army as for the whole people, was what should be done with this victory? What sort of society would emerge from the war? It was a time when unlimited expectations were balanced against increasing misery. War had accentuated the economic problems already referred to. Trade, industry and even agriculture had been disrupted, prices rose sharply, as did unemployment. The situation was made worse by a series of cold, wet summers, bringing bad harvests and scarce and dear food.[1] Yet for many the ending of the war seemed about to usher in a new age of justice and freedom. Sometimes these expectations took a fantastic and millennial shape, but most involved at least some democratic advance and an easing of economic burdens.

The Presbyterians, dominating what was left of the Long Parliament, shared neither the misery nor the expectations. Most of them had done very well out of the war in cash, estates or contracts. What they wanted was a speedy agreement with the King which would consolidate their authority. The Army, which seemed the only obstacle, was to be partly re-enlisted under new and more "reliable" officers, and packed off to a reconquest of Ireland from which more rich pickings might be expected. The plan failed, partly because of the obstinacy of the King who refused to do what was required of him but continued to behave as if he had won and not lost the war, but more because of the obstinacy with which the Army refused to disband, all the more because Parliament proposed to rob them of arrears of pay which in all cases amounted to many weeks and in most to many months. To this struggle between Army and Parliament we shall return later.

Meanwhile, to the two parties, Presbyterians entrenched in Parliament and Independents in control of

[1] There seems some evidence that the whole period suffered from weather much worse than average.

the Army, there was added a third – the Levellers.[1] Before outlining their history it may be worth looking briefly at some of their leaders.

First, by any reckoning, must be John Lilburne whose name comes at once to the mind whenever Leveller is mentioned. Born about 1615, younger son of a gentry family in Durham, he came early to London where he was apprenticed to a trader in cloth. He was arrested in 1637 for circulating an attack on Bishops, was brought before the Star Chamber, flogged and imprisoned. His courage made him a popular figure and he was released by the Long Parliament. Much of his later history will be found in the pamphlets [see especially I and XVI]. "Martyr, folk-hero and demagogue" as Professor Haller calls him,[2] he was the prime driving force behind the Leveller movement and its undisputed leader.

His colleague William Walwyn, born about 1600, also came from a gentry family in Worcester. His grandfather was a Bishop who annoyed Queen Elizabeth by the length of his sermons. Like Lilburne he too came to London where he was apprenticed to a silk merchant, but there the resemblance ends. While Lilburne was always prominent at the centre of struggle Walwyn was a quiet family man, successful in business, widely read, philosophical, a born committee-man and the possessor of a lucid style which infuriated his enemies because its smooth texture offered them nothing on which they could get a grip. He came to the Levellers by way of radical city politics and the struggle for religious toleration and the freedom of the press. His early pamphlet *The Power of Love* anticipated some of the thinking of Milton's *Areopagitica*.

---

[1] The name was given by their opponents, probably first during the debates at Putney, and never accepted by them. Often they referred to themselves as "Levellers, falsly so called". But it has been accepted by history and will be used here.

[2] *Liberty and Reformation in the Puritan Revolution*, p. 262.

Richard Overton came from a different and more obscure background. Some years older than Walwyn,[1] he was nominally a Baptist but in later life became increasingly rationalist. His world was that of the underground, illegal printer and bookseller. Of all the Leveller writers he was the most brilliant and lively, with an irreverent wit that sometimes shocked even his own supporters. He, too, began as a tolerationist and defender of the amateur preacher. His pamphlet *The Arraignment of Mr. Persecution* is sometimes thought to have given Bunyan (another Baptist) ideas for *A Pilgrim's Progress*. For all his courage and polemical ability he does not seem to have carried so much weight in the movement as Lilburne or Walwyn.

Other leading figures were John Wildman, Thomas Prince, Samuel Chidley and William Larner. Wildman, a younger man than the rest, had a university and legal education, helped the Army Levellers to put their case at Putney and wrote some of their most effective pamphlets, notably *The Case of the Armie Truly Stated* (at least in part) and *Putney Projects*. About the beginning of 1649 he deserted the party and had a long and chequered subsequent career of intrigue and conspiracy. After playing a dubious role in Monmouth's rebellion he ended in a comfortable government post under William III. Thomas Prince was a cheese merchant who fought in the campaign for the relief of Gloucester in 1643. His writings suggest a man of quiet dignity. With Chidley he acted as treasurer of the Leveller Party. Chidley was a prominent itinerant preacher whose mother Katharine was perhaps the most famous of the woman preachers of the time.[2] Larner was another

---

[1] Marie Brack has recently suggested he was considerably younger than was previously believed.

[2] H. N. Brailsford calls her "the recognised leader" among Leveller women. She may have been, but there is no real evidence for it. The wives of Lilburne and Overton were both active in the cause,

printer who published many of their pamphlets. All these three were arrested over the presentation of the Petition of November 1647 [VII]. Larner's trade, of course, brought him into frequent conflict with the authorities.

All these were civilians, for Lilburne left the Army rather than take the Covenant[1] and Wildman's title of Major can hardly be treated seriously. The Army Levellers form a different group, closely allied with the others, but, so far as one can judge, outside the closely knit collective leadership group. Outstanding was Colonel Thomas Rainborough, since he was the only officer of really high standing to identify himself completely with the Leveller cause, and the only man who could conceivably have challenged Cromwell for the leadership of the Army. His assassination during the siege of Pontefract (October 29th, 1648) was a crushing blow at Leveller hopes in the Army. His father had been a distinguished sailor whose capture of Sallee in 1637 had made him something of a national hero. There was also a close connection with New England: two of his sisters married Winthrops and his regiment had many New Englanders in its ranks.

The next most senior Leveller officer was Lt. Col. William Eyres. He shared with Henry Marten the command of a specially raised and extremely radical regiment and was with the Burford mutineers. For some reason he was not given or did not take any position of command. While in prison at Oxford he was concerned with another attempt at mutiny. Many junior officers also supported the Levellers. Among them were Major William Rainborough, Thomas' brother and later a

and a feature of the movement was its involvement of large numbers of women.
[1] The Solemn League and Covenant, which embodied the conditions insisted on by the Scots as the price of their entry into the war. It had to be signed by all persons holding official posts.

Ranter, Major Thomas Scott, Captain Francis White, who was to play a somewhat equivocal part at Burford [XV] and Captain William Bray, prominent both at Ware and Burford. Younger men included Lieutenant Chillenden and Cornet Chisman.

The list might be greatly extended. What is clear is that a large number of officers were convinced Levellers and a still larger number sufficiently sympathetic to give substantial support from time to time. When the tide was flowing in their direction, as it was in the summer of 1647, the Army seemed almost unanimous and the higher commanders were so isolated that they were forced to go along with the rest.

Finally, there was immense support among the rank and file. Here we have less information, though a number of names appear in lists of Agitators or Agents, appointed by their regiments to the Army Council. They include William Allen, Edward Sexby, William Everard and Richard Clarke. The first two later reached high rank, and Allen became an establishment figure. Sexby, a Lt. Col. by 1651, then had an extraordinary career, apparently acting as a double agent, persuading the Bordeaux radicals to adopt the Leveller programme and becoming involved in a plot to assassinate Cromwell which led to his death in prison in 1658. He justified his attempt in a famous pamphlet, *Killing No Murder*. The Army Levellers had also their martyrs: Richard Arnold, shot after the Ware mutiny, Robert Lockyer, shot in London in April 1649, Church, Perkins and James Thompson, shot at Burford. Rather apart from the rest is his brother "Captain" William Thompson (his military rank was self-awarded) a lone wolf with an immense admiration for Lilburne, who led an irregular force in a desperate outbreak which ended with his death near Northampton.

One more name requires noting, that of Henry Marten, the most consistent Republican in the Long Parliament. While probably never formally a member of the Leveller Party he was closely associated with many of its activities and was able to use his position in the House of Commons to assist them in a number of ways. Despite occasional differences he remained on close and friendly terms with Lilburne and with Walwyn, who called him "a true Englishman . . . always manifesting a most zealous affection to his Countries liberties".

These, then were some of the leading figures. What of the Leveller Party itself? Who composed it and whom did it represent?

It was a radical but not a working-class party: indeed, how could it be at a time when the working class as we know it was only beginning to exist? Still less was it a "socialist" party in the sense of advocating the type of egalitarian and agrarian communism which was widespread at this time and was most articulately expressed by Winstanley and his Diggers or "true Levellers". In a number of their statements the Levellers expressly repudiated such objectives:

> "We profess therefore that we never had it in our thoughts to Level mens estates, it being the utmost of our aime that the Common-wealth be reduced to such a passe that every man may with as much security as may be enjoy his propriety." [XII]

Such a statement may today be misunderstood. At this time they rightly saw the small property of the small man menaced not by the poor but by the rich – by monopolists, greedy entrepreneurs and enclosing landlords. It was against these that security was needed.

The Levellers, I think, represented and appealed in the main to the small and medium producers in town and country, and their perspective was that the small producer, thus protected, would prosper and increase till great wealth and excessive poverty would disappear or be greatly reduced. In Walwyn's words:

27

"And where you charge me, that I find fault that some abound, whils't others want bread; truly, I think it a sad thing, in so fruitfull a land, as, through Gods blessing, this is; and I do think it one main end of Government, to provide, that those who refuse not labour, should eat comfortably."[1]

They did at times advocate the restoration of recent enclosures for the benefit of the poor, but this was not stressed and their main appeal seems always to have been to the literate and politically conscious independent producers. At the same time, a pamphlet like *The Mournfull Cryes of Many Thousand Poor Tradesmen* (January 1648) was aimed at the poor and miserable, and their programme, in its various forms, did contain, alongside democratic political demands (annual or biennial Parliaments, wider franchise, equal constituencies), a wide variety of points to benefit the broadest strata of the people, including the abolition of tithes, legal and prison reform, abolition of conscription and abolition of taxes on food and other necessities [II, VII, IX, XIII].

The two great centres of Leveller power were London and the Army. If in London they probably recruited their members among the artisans and small or medium tradesmen, the vast demonstrations that took place on such occasions as the funerals of Rainborough and Lockyer or Lilburne's acquittal on a treason charge in October 1649, indicate massive support among the whole of the poorer population. From London they spread their influence first into the Home Counties and then beyond. Their newspaper *The Moderate* reports numerous and influential petitions in support of their programme from places as far apart as Newcastle, York, Hull, Bristol and Cornwall. As late as the summer of 1649, when the movement was already in de-

[1] *Walwyns Just Defence*. H. and D., p. 384.

cline, the Derby Levellers were active enough to give substantial support to the lead miners who were engaged in an industrial dispute with the Earl of Rutland. The miners, *The Moderate* reported, were issuing a declaration of their rigths "which they will maintain with their lives and fortunes and likewise the Agreement of the People and the Petition of 11th September 1648."[1] Like the Chartists two centuries later, the Levellers had great and widespread support, overwhelmingly among those outside the traditional political nation. What defeated both was their failure to find forms in which these new forces, set in movement one by the Revolution, the other by the Industrial Revolution, could make their desires effective.

In the Army there was a similar problem. From the spring of 1647, when the cavalry regiments began to elect Agitators, to the crisis of June with the formation of the Council of the Army [III], Leveller influence grew rapidly, especially among the cavalry who were almost entirely volunteers and drawn from a more educated and politically aroused strata than the infantry. Many of them came from freeholder or citizen families accustomed to political activity. Among them the ideas in the Leveller pamphlets which circulated freely among the troops found a ready response, all the more when these ideas were reinforced by the attempts of the Presbyterian majority in the House of Commons to disband the Army under wholly unacceptable conditions. But here, too, the problem was to turn this generalised support into a readiness, at the point of crisis, on the part of these highly disciplined soldiers to defy Fairfax and Cromwell, generals who had built up the Army and led it to victory. The struggle for the leadership of the Army lies at the heart of the Leveller story.

[1] H. N. Brailsford, *The Levellers and the English Revolution*, pp. 353 and 565–567.

III

The Rise and Fall of the Leveller Party

1. Formation

Lilburne had a distinguished record in the war, becoming Lt. Col. of dragoons. In the struggle for the efficient conduct of the war he was one of Cromwell's main assistants in his battle with the Earl of Manchester, against whom he had also a private grievance. At this stage a close personal friendship existed between Lilburne and Cromwell, creating feelings which no later differences could entirely destroy. In April 1645 Lilburne left the Army and began his career as a civilian agitator, pouring out a string of pamphlets. In July a dispute with another former friend, William Prynne, began a complicated train of events which led finally to his imprisonment by the House of Lords.

In the course of all this he met, probably in the summer of 1645, Walwyn, already an old campaigner for religious toleration and leader of another London group agitating for a greater war effort and attacking the corruption of many Parliamentarian leaders. Overton, operating as a free-lance propagandist, joined forces with Lilburne at this time or perhaps rather earlier – the Leveller movement was taking shape though the formation of a Leveller Party was still some way in the future. When fully developed the Levellers had all the marks of an authentic political party – a published programme, a regularly constituted leadership, a membership paying regular dues and organised in local branches or groups. Nothing like this had ever existed in England before, probably never anywhere in the world. Its democratic political thinking can be seen in Walwyn's *Englands Lamentable Slaverie* (October 1645) in which the Leveller doctrine of the sovereignty of the people is first clearly stated:

". . . a Parliamentary authority is a power intrusted by the people (that chose them) for their good saftie and freedome; and therefore a Parliament cannot justlie do anything to make the people lesse safe or lesse free then they found them."[1]

During 1646 Lilburne continued his struggle against the Lords as well as for greater democracy in the City of London. Overton, in and out of prison over his illegal printing, carried on the fight in his hard-hitting and ironical style with such pamphlets as *A Defiance against all Arbitrary Usurpations* (September) and *An Arrow Against all Tyrants . . . shot from the Prison of Newgate into the Prerogative Bowels of the Arbitrary House of Lords* (October).

In March 1647 a more systematic and sustained campaign opened with the presentation of the petition usually referred to as the *Large Petition.* [II][2]

This was the first programmatic statement and though, like all its successors, it was a collective work, it is probable that the main hand was Walwyn's. Drafted with the combination of studied reasonableness and firmness of principle of which he was a master, its very opening implies a revolutionary change, being addressed to "the right honourable and supreme Authority of this Nation, the Commons in Parliament assembled". This challenged the traditional sovereignty of the King in Parliament, which the Commons were still planning to restore, and, by implication, the very existence of Lords and Monarchy. After a number of positive achievements of Parliament had been "most thankfully acknowledged",

[1] Walwyn, *Englands Lamentable Slaverie,* p. 3.
[2] The mass petition was systematically developed by the Levellers as a political weapon. Some of their petitions received 40,000 or even more signatures. In their use of the petition the Levellers were followed by Shaftesbury's New Country Party, by John Wilkes and especially by the Chartists.

the Petition sets out a whole programme of reforms in which the main lines of Leveller policy were laid down.

Several thousand signatures having been collected, the Petition was presented to the Commons on March 19th by Major Tulidah and Nicholas Tue, accompanied by some hundreds of supporters. The Commons rejected the Petition out of hand and ordered the arrest of Tulidah and Tue. A petition of protest against these arrests was rejected, as was a third petition on May 20th, which was ordered to be burned by the common hangman. In all, six unsuccessful appeals were made to the Commons between March and June. Lilburne remained in prison, increasingly angry, and suspicious of all about him, till he was released on parole in November.

It became clear that the House, with its entrenched Presbyterian majority, was immovable and that no further progress was possible in this direction. Lilburne gave a detailed account of the struggle in *Rash Oaths Unwarrantable* (May 31st) and Walwyn described it more briefly and analytically in *The Poore Wise-mans Admonition* [V] and *Gold Tried in the Fire* [IV]. The latter is mainly a narrative of events, the former is notable for its assessment of the class forces involved. The enemies of the Petition were the secret Royalists, the rich monopolists in the City and all those who had profited by the war. Its other features were a turn to the Army, whose conduct is eulogised, and a strong appeal for soldier-citizen unity to secure a just solution of the nation's problems. The tactics which had so far been followed to make Parliament respond to the will of the people were abandoned in favour of a much bolder line in which the Army was to play a central role. Events there had indeed reached a crisis which made such an approach imperative. It would not be too much to say that at this point the Levellers moved from a struggle for the redress of grievances to a struggle for political power.

2. The Struggle in the Army

Leveller involvement with Army affairs was not, of course, new. Ever since March, when the Presbyterian majority in the Commons had set to work to destroy the Army by disbanding part and sending the rest to Ireland under uncongenial officers, they had intervened to stiffen and channel Army resistance. From the start it was noticeable that in this conflict between Army and Parliament it was the rank and file who led and the officers who followed. Fairfax maintained an attitude of scrupulous constitutional correctness throughout, Cromwell, at this time without an official commission but representing the Army unofficially from his place in Parliament, was doing his best to compromise till well into May.

Even in March there is evidence that organised groups in contact with the Levellers were at work. In April a decisive step was taken when the cavalry regiments elected "Agitators" or "Agents" to represent them and voice their demands. The nearest modern equivalent would perhaps be shop stewards: no army had ever taken such a step before. Late in the month they formed a Council representing the eight cavalry regiments, and the regiments of Foot soon followed this example. On April 28th they issued over the signatures of Edward Sexby, William Allen, Thomas Sheppard and fourteen others, letters of protest to Fairfax, Stapleton and Cromwell in which the professional grievances of the Army were coupled with Leveller political demands. Summoned before the House of Commons the three troopers defended themselves with such skill as to force Parliament to realise the Army's determination.

New Parliamentary Commissioners were sent to the Army, now quartered at Saffron Walden, with some concessions, but like all their offers these were too little and too late. It is clear that by this time the Army Levellers were determined to resist disbandment not only till their professional claims had been met – arrears of pay, indemnity, provision for the disabled and for families of those killed, but till basic political changes had been assured. Some documents have survived which show the Council of the Agitators at work. One calls for the setting up of a printing press at Oxford to make the case of the Army known to the people. This was done under the direction of John Harris. Another is reprinted in this volume [XVII].[1]

In face of the Army's evident intention to resist, the Commons continued to press on the plan for disbandment. On May 18th a decision was taken in principle: the next day the Agitators of eight regiments of Horse and four of Foot issued a letter calling on the Army to stand firmly together:

> "Fellow soldiers, the sum of all this is, if you do but stand and not accept of anything nor do anything without the consent of the whole Army, you will do good to yourselves, your officers and the whole kingdom. Stand with your officers and one with another you need not fear. If you divide you destroy all."[2]

It is evident that the communications between the Army and London were excellent.

On May 25th the Commons passed a resolution arranging in detail for the disbandment of a number of regiments, starting with Fairfax's Foot, at Chelmsford on June 1st.[3] This proposal precipitated a crisis in which events moved very fast and whose details will perhaps never be entirely clear. Fairfax felt himself obliged to call a Council of War for May 29th. Meanwhile

[1] Brailsford, op. cit., pp. 187–188. Woodhouse, pp.398–401.
[2] Brailsford, op. cit., p. 192.
[3] As General, Fairfax had titular command of one regiment each of Horse and Foot, thus supplementing his pay. The acting command of his Foot was Lt. Col. Jackson, a noted Presbyterian. The Commons must have supposed that this was the regiment least likely to give trouble.

the Agitators of sixteen regiments had presented a petition saying that they meant to resist, whatever their commanders decided, and calling for a Rendezvous of the whole Army. Fairfax's Regiment drove out Lt. Col. Jackson, refused to disband and marched out of Chelmsford for Newmarket under the command of Major White, an officer known for his Leveller views.

When the Council of War met at Bury St Edmunds it agreed by an overwhelming majority to resist disbandment and to support the Agitators' demand for a Rendezvous. This was to be held at Newmarket on June 4th. "It is incredible the unitie of Officers and Soldiers", an Agitator reported of this Council. The next day Fairfax wrote to the Earl of Manchester, Speaker of the House of Lords, "I am forc'd to yeeld something out of order, to keep the Army from disorder, or worse inconveniencies."[1]

Meanwhile the Agitators struck two other blows. As the events we have been describing had been going on, there had been long and complicated three-sided negotiations between King Charles, the Parliament and the Army. Charles was attempting to play one enemy against another while plotting a new war with the help of the Scots and his English supporters. A point had been reached at which the Presbyterians seemed likely to bring Charles to London and use him as a weapon against the Army. The Agitators, to forestall this, sent a Leveller officer, Cornet Joyce, to Holmby House in Northants, where Charles was held, to secure him, and, if necessary, to bring him to Army headquarters. Joyce reached Holmby on June 2nd and brought him away on June 4th.

Simultaneously the artillery train, which was at Oxford, and which Parliament had sent a party of dragoons to secure, was snatched from under their noses by

[1] Wolfe, pp. 29, 30.

the men of Rainborough's Regiment. Rainborough said they were acting without his orders, but it is unlikely that many people believed him, and it should be remembered that he was the Army's siege specialist – no one knew better the value of artillery or was more skilled in its use.

Much has been written about Cromwell's possible part in the seizure of the King. Joyce saw him in London on May 31st, and they may be presumed to have discussed it. It is most unlikely that Cromwell initiated the plan. It is certain that he acquiesced in it once it was done. It is possible that he gave it some kind of approval in advance. We can be fairly certain that Fairfax was kept in the dark. It is also clear that in the last days of May, after long hesitation, Cromwell swung substantially towards the Agitators, not because he believed in Leveller ideas but as the only way to restore the unity of the Army under the command of Fairfax and himself. At this point (and Cromwell was usually content to take one step at a time) he saw the Presbyterians as the greater danger. It is of interest that about this time he appears to have had a number of conversations with Walwyn, who wrote later:

> "The Lieutenant Generall also knows, upon what grounds I then perswaded him to divide from that Body [the Commons], to which he was united; that if he did not it would be his ruine, and the ruine of the Generall, and of all those Worthyes that had preserved us; that if he did do it in time, he should not only preserve himself and them, and all consciencious people, but he should do it without spilling one drop of bloud."[1]

On June 3rd Cromwell rode out of London to join the Army at Newmarket, where he resumed his old position as Lieutenant General.

[1] *Walwyns Just Defence.* H. and D., p. 358.

At the Newmarket Rendezvous the document known as *A Solemne Engagement of the Army* [III] was read to the regiments and accepted by the Army with acclamation on June 5th. It pledged itself not to divide or disband till all its demands had been met. More important, it set up a body, the Council of the Army, in which two representatives of the rank and file and two of the junior officers of each regiment were added to the senior officers who already constituted the Council of War. This was a historic and quite unprecedented step, yet not without its dangers. While it gave the soldiers a new status and influence, it also exposed them to the influence of their commanders and placed upon the Agitators responsibilities for decisions which, by themselves, they might not have taken. Still the fact that the Grandees, as the group of leading officers round Cromwell and Ireton came to be called, killed the Council at the first opportunity is an indication that its formation was forced upon them and was not a tactical move.

At this point there seemed every possibility of an armed clash. The Presbyterians in Parliament tried to mobilise the London trained bands, while making some concessions to win time. The Army began to march towards London, halting at St Albans where it was met by another Parliamentary Commission offering more concessions. There was to be no more talk of disbanding. At St Albans the Army adopted a new and more political manifesto. Where the *Solemne Engagement* had confined itself mainly to specific Army grievances, *A Declaration or Representation From his Excellency Sir Thomas Fairfax, And the Army under his Command* was openly political, demanding a speedy ending of the Long Parliament and its replacement by a more representative body. It insisted that the soldiers were also citizens with full political rights and not "a meere mercinary Army, hired to serve any Arbitrary power of a State; but called forth and conjured, by the severall Declarations of Parliament, to the defence of our owne and the peoples just rights, and liberties; and so we took up Armes, in judgement and conscience to those ends, and have so continued them, and are resolved according to your first just desires in your Declarations, and such principles as we have received from your frequent informations, and our own common sence concerning those our fundamentall Rights and Liberties, to assert and vindicate, the just power, and Rights of this Kingdome in Parliament for those common ends premised, against all arbitrary power, violence and oppression, and against all particular parties, or interests whatsoever."[1]

These words became the basis on which the Army Levellers rested their case and are constantly quoted and referred to from *The Case of the Armie* (October 1647) to *The Levellers Vindicated* (August 1649) [XV]. Yet neither the *Engagement* nor the *Declaration* are strictly Leveller documents. They are generally regarded as the work of Ireton, and his style is perhaps apparent in passages which sound very radical but when analysed can be seen to avoid any precise statement. Nevertheless, if written by Ireton, it was not by Ireton in isolation but under all sorts of pressures and with the need to satisfy men like Sexby and Rainborough, looking over his shoulder. And perhaps even Ireton was to some extent swept along by the events of those weeks of crisis. As time went on he must have grown very sick of having his own words thrown back at him.

With the Army little more than a day's march away, Parliament gave way again. Eleven M.P.s most obnoxious to the Army withdrew from the House. The

[1] H. and D., p. 55.

Army remained poised within striking distance of London but the prospect of a confrontation receded. There was never to be an opportunity for another under conditions anything like so favourable for the Leveller cause.

3. Putney and Ware

The Agitator who described the unity of officers and men as "incredible" was perhaps speaking more truly than he knew, at least so far as the Grandees were concerned. They could not afford to allow the Army, their great political weapon, to be destroyed. Once that danger had been averted their normally conservative outlook reasserted itself, and as the chastened Commons gave way over the Army's professional demands they came to meet it politically. The Presbyterians took heart again, the eleven excluded Members returned. On July 26th a riot contrived by their supporters in the City invaded Parliament and "compelled" it to invite the King to London and to mobilise the London militia against the Army. At this time of hunger and high taxes it was not difficult to organise a Church and King mob.

The Independent Members with the two Speakers took refuge with the Army which proceded to march on London. Resistance collapsed, the London Levellers reasserted themselves, the eleven Members vanished once more, the Army settled itself at Kingston – nearer to London than ever before. This easy victory only increased the complacency of the Grandees: the demand of the Agitators, endorsed by the Council of the Army, for a complete purge of the Presbyterians, was refused, negotiations continued with the King, with whom Cromwell and Ireton appeared to many of the soldiers to be on dangerously friendly terms. When on September 22nd Marten and Rainborough moved in the Commons that no further addresses be made to the King, they were defeated by 84 votes to 34 and both Cromwell and Ireton voted with the majority.

There was an immediate reaction to this news, which confirmed many of the growing doubts about the sincerity of the Grandees. Early in October five regiments of Horse, including Cromwell's and Ireton's, dismissed their Agitators as not being active enough, and appointed new ones. They met at Guilford to discuss the situation and, with the help of the civilian Levellers, produced a new manifesto, *The Case of the Armie Truly Stated*. It was signed by all the Agitators, who no doubt had a hand in drafting it, but it is generally thought that Wildman, Overton and perhaps Lilburne all had a large share in its actual composition. It drew attention to the way the pledges in the *Engagement* and the *Declaration* had been ignored or broken, and went on to outline a programme similar to that of the *Large Petition* [II]. An important feature new to the Leveller programme concerns Parliamentary elections:

"Whereas the people have been prevented of Parliaments, though many positive lawes have been made for a constant succession of Parliaments, that therefore it be positively and resolvedly insisted upon, that a law paramount be made, enacting it, to be unalterable by Parliaments that the people shall of course meet without any warrants or writs once in every two yeares upon an appointed day in their respective Countyes for the election of representatives in Parliament, and that all the freeborn at the age of 21 yeares and upwards, be the electors, excepting those that have or shall deprive themselves of that their freedome, either for some yeares, or wholly by delinquency."[1]

[1] Wolfe, p. 212. H. and D., p. 78. It was generally assumed from this and other statements that the Levellers were in principle in favour of manhood suffrage, though, as will be seen, they later agreed to exceptions in the case of servants and those receiving alms. In 1962 Prof. C. B. Macpherson argued in *The Political Theory of Possessive Individualism*, pp. 107–159, that this was mistaken and

Another new demand, which may reflect the rural origins of many of the troopers, as opposed to the London population with whom the civilian Levellers had so far been mainly concerned, is:

> "That all the antient rights and donations belonging to the poore, now imbezeled and converted to other uses, as inclosed Commons, Alms houses, etc. throughout all parts of the land, may be forthwith restored to the antient publique use and service of the poore, in whose hands soever they be detained."[1]

The Case was submitted to Fairfax on October 18th, published as a pamphlet about the same date and discussed by the Army Council ten days later. This discussion was brief, for in the interval a new programme document *An Agreement of the People* [VI] had been prepared. This was the first version of a programme around which the political campaigning of the Levellers was to centre so long as they remained an effective party.

The passage just quoted from *The Case of the Armie*, refers to the need for a "law paramount", which no Parliament could alter. The *Agreement* was to be the basis for such a law. It originates from the idea of a social contract, already widespread, which would underlie much political theorising from Hobbes to Rousseau. The Levellers argued that as a result of the war, which

that they had always tacitly made these exceptions. More will be said about this in connection with the debates of the Army Council at Putney, but it is impossible here to discuss it in detail. A case against Prof. Macpherson's theory is argued in A. L. Morton, *The World of the Ranters,* pp. 197–218. The issue, essentially, seems to be whether the Levellers believed that a voice in government is a privilege, attached to certain forms of property ownership, which it might be proper to extend to some who do not yet enjoy it, or a natural right, and so proper to all, even though it may not be possible for all to enjoy it under existing conditions.

[1] Wolfe, p. 216, H. and D., p. 82.

had destroyed the traditional sovereignty of King, Lords and Commons, the people are now "dissolved into the originall law of nature".[1] Or, as Lilburne put it more tersely in *Legall Fundamentall Liberties,* "all legal Authority in England was broke."[2] What was now needed was a new social contract, an agreement, which would provide a new legality and protect the nation's freedoms for all future ages. Such an agreement could only come from the people themselves, since they were "the origin of all just power", and could be bound only by their own act.

The idea of such an agreement was not only a commonplace of contemporary political thinking, it was familiar in life. The Scottish opposition to Charles had begun with the signing of a National Covenant, and their entry into the war in England was marked by the Solemn League and Covenant to which all were invited to subscribe. Nearer home, the idea was familiar to thousands of people, including many leading Levellers, who had been at some time involved in the formation of a "gathered church". This always involved the collective signing of a covenant or agreement setting out the rights and duties of the members. The *Agreement of the People* would, in effect, make England into a gathered nation. It would, however, be a new kind of agreement, not divisive, setting a little group of saints apart from the world, but inclusive, uniting a whole people.

An Agreement of the People, as presented to the Council of the Army at Putney church on October 29th, was not intended to be a completed constitution but rather a draft for discussion. For the Agitators the principal spokesman was Rainborough, supported by Sexby and other Agitators and some officers. In addition, two prominent civilian Levellers, John Wildman and Maxi-

[1] Lilburne, *Jonahs Cry out of the Whales belly.* Wolfe, p. 33.
[2] H. and D., p. 433.

milian Petty were there to help them present their case. On the other side the weight of the argument was carried by Ireton. Cromwell, in the chair, tried to preserve some appearance of impartiality but came to Ireton's rescue from time to time when his tactless logic threatened to antagonise the meeting.

From the start the debate turned on the question of the franchise. Ireton opened by saying that the wording of the *Agreement* made him think that "every man that is an inhabitant is to be equally considered, and to have an equal voice in the election of those representers". To this Petty replied:

"We judge that all inhabitants that have not lost their birthright should have an equal voice in elections." And Rainborough, with much greater decision:

"I desired that those that had engaged in it might be included. For really I think that the poorest he that is in England hath a life to live, as the greatest he; and therefore truly, sir, I think it's clear, that every man that is to live under a government ought first by his own consent to put himself under that government; and I do think that the poorest man in England is not bound in a strict sense to that government that he hath not had a voice to put himself under; and I am confident that, when I have heard the reasons against it, something will be said to answer those reasons, insomuch that I should doubt whether he was an Englishman or no, that should doubt of these things."[1]

From talking about the franchise, the Council soon found that it was talking about property. Ireton was quite clear about this:

"All the main thing that I speak for, is because I would have an eye to property. I hope we do not

[1] Woodhouse, pp. 52–53.

come here to contend for victory – but let every man consider to himself that he do not go to take away all property. For here is the case of the most fundamental part of the constitution of the kingdom, which if you take away, you take away all by that ... by that same right of nature (whatever it be) that you pretend, by which you can say, one man hath an equal right with another to the choosing of him that shall govern him – by the same right of nature he hath the same right in any goods he sees – meat, drink, clothes – to take and use them for his sustenance."[1]

The Grandees argued that if political power were given to the propertyless "five parts of the nation", they would inevitably use their power to destroy property. Rainborough replied that if they were excluded, "the one part shall make hewers of wood and drawers of water of the other five and so the greatest part of the nation be enslaved", and Sexby:

"There are many thousand of us soldiers that have ventured our lives; we have had little propriety in the kingdom as to our estates, yet we have had a birthright. But it seems now, except a man hath a fixed estate in this kingdom, he hath no right in this kingdom. I wonder we were so much deceived."[2]

Finally, a compromise was reached, that the franchise should be given to all except servants and those receiving alms. Today this may seem shockingly undemocratic. But in the circumstances of the seventeenth century, with no secret ballot and many small, closely knit communities where every man's doings were known to all his neighbours, it is easy to see that in practice universal suffrage might mean putting large blocks of votes in

[1] Woodhouse, p. 58.
[2] ibid., p. 67, 69.

44

the control of the richest and most reactionary elements with numbers of servants and dependents. Their agreement to these exceptions did not necessarily mean that the Levellers did not regard the franchise as a natural right to which all were entitled in principle, but perhaps rather that they realised that it was impossible and perhaps dangerous to demand more at that time. We must remember that they were not mere academic political theorists, but a practical political party, conducting a political struggle under very difficult and complex conditions. It may be, too, that there were some differences within their own ranks on these questions.[1]

No official minute of the conclusion of the Council's debate has survived, but the text of its resolution is given in *A Letter from Several Agitators to the Regiments*:

> "We sent some of them to debate in love the matter and manner of the Agreement. And the first article thereof, being long debated, it was concluded by vote in the affirmative: – *Viz.,* That all soldiers and others, if not servants or beggars, ought to have their voices in electing those which shall represent them in Parliament, although they have not forty shillings per annum in freehold land. And there were but three voices against this your native freedom."[2]

This resolution was passed on November 4th or 5th, and was followed by another, moved by Rainborough, that a general Rendezvous of the whole Army should be called. The Levellers were convinced that they had won, that at the Rendezvous the *Agreement* would be submitted to the Army for approval, and that after being approved, as it undoubtedly would be, the whole influence of the Army would be used to secure its acceptance by the nation. Perhaps they were too honest to realise

[1] Hill, op. cit., pp. 93–99.
[2] Woodhouse, p. 452.

how far the Grandees would go when they felt that the rights of property were in danger.

On November 8th or 9th the Council met again. Of this meeting only fragmentary reports have survived. Fairfax himself presided, as he had not done at previous meetings, and a series of resolutions was passed which had the effect of nullifying those of the earlier meeting. The Council was suspended and the Agitators ordered to return to their regiments. Parliament was asked for more money to pay off a month's arrears of wages, and, most important, "they declared they would divide the Army into three parts, to rendezvous severally. And all this appears to be only to draw off the Army from joining together to settle those clear foundations of freedom propounded to you."[1] The first of the three Rendezvous was to be held at Corkbush Field, Ware, on November 15th.

Instead of the *Agreement* being submitted to the soldiers a *Remonstrance* was drawn up in which Fairfax complained of divisions and indiscipline and threatened to resign. He called on all to resume their obedience and promised, if they did, to do his utmost to secure their demands over pay, indemnity and other grievances, and also promised support for a number of rather vaguely formulated democratic political reforms which certainly fell far short of what was contained in the *Agreement*. Fairfax had always held aloof from political discussions, so that the universal respect felt for his courage and military leadership provided an untapped reserve of goodwill on which the Grandees were now able to draw.

Events helped them. Just as the removal of the King from Holmby House had played an important part in the May-June crisis, so his escape from Hampton Court on November 11th dominated the Ware Rendezvous.

[1] Woodhouse, p. 453.

We shall probably never know whether, as was suspected at the time and since, this escape was contrived by the Grandees, but it could not have happened at a more convenient moment. By November 15th it is likely that the Grandees knew where Charles was; the rank and file certainly did not. They must have supposed, or at least feared, that he was about to summon his supporters and the Scots to begin a new war. At such a time they could hardly be expected to resist the appeal of their old commanders for unity and discipline.

At Ware Robert Lilburne's Regiment appeared contrary to orders, having driven away most of their officers, under the command of Captain William Bray, and wearing copies of the *Agreement* stuck in their hats. Colonel Harrison's Regiment also appeared unsummoned.

Present also were Rainborough, Eyres, Major Scott and other prominent Leveller officers. Fairfax wrote in his report of events to the House of Lords that Rainborough

> "tendered the enclosed Petition, together with the *People's Agreement* annexed thereunto. And (by what hands I yet know not fully) very many copies were dispersed among the soldiers, thereby to engage them."[1]

Eyres and the others rode among the regiments urging them to stand firm. Their task was hopeless. Even without the escape of the King the soldiers were pulled in two ways – as citizens their sympathies were with the Levellers, but as members of a victorious and well-disciplined army the sense of military obligation was always powerful. In other circumstances, off duty or in discussion, political convictions might prevail: on the

[1] Maseres, *Select Tracts*, I, p. xliii. The petition said that the Army must remain in arms in defence of the native rights for which they had fought. It asked Fairfax to lead them to these ends.

47

parade ground, under command, they were likely to act rather as soldiers. So it turned out at Ware. Fairfax and Cromwell soon brought the two rebel regiments to order and the others followed without trouble.

Three alleged ringleaders were picked out for execution and forced to draw lots. Two were pardoned, the third, Richard Arnold, was shot immediately. Eyres, Scott and Bray were placed under arrest. Rainborough's position was particularly delicate. As an experienced soldier with a magnificent military record, he was no more immune than the rest to the influences affecting the troopers. As a high-ranking officer – Colonel, Vice-Admiral and also Member of Parliament – he could hardly initiate a mutiny, though he might have taken command if one had developed. At Ware he certainly came to the very edge of mutiny but did not take the final step. As things turned out he must have seen that any hope of carrying the Army for the *Agreement* against its leaders had vanished, at least for the present. The most that could be hoped for was to divide it, and as an experienced soldier he would see that to divide the Army in existing circumstances, with a renewal of the war looming up, must be fatal. It would have led with certainty to a Royalist victory and the end of all he had been fighting for.

4. New Tactics and a New War

Looking back with the advantage of hindsight we can see that the events at Ware constituted a defeat for the Levellers from which recovery was hardly possible. Their one real hope of even temporary success was to win the support of the Army: the attempt had failed, the Council of the Army was soon to be dispersed, and no such opportunity ever presented itself again. Outside the Army they had many supporters, especially in and around London, but, like the Chartists, their "constituency" did not lie among the classes in which political power traditionally rested: they could protest, they could not make their protests effective. Only in the Army was there a possible alternative power base through which fundamental change might be effected. This is obvious now, it cannot have been so at the time. All that could be seen was that a set-back had been received which made new tactics necessary, both in the Army and outside it.

In the Army a compromise was soon reached. In spite of their victory Cromwell and Ireton must have seen the danger of their position. Discipline had been restored, but the Army had not changed its political convictions overnight. Its loyalty had still to be kept, especially as the developing alliance between Royalists and many Presbyterians, backed by the Scots, made a renewal of the war almost inevitable. They realised that they needed the support of the Levellers inside the Army, and at least the neutrality of those outside, even if this involved distasteful political concessions.

The result was another meeting of the Army Council at Windsor on December 15th, the last which the Agents of the regiments attended, at which a reconciliation was effected. Rainborough and the others apologised for acts of indiscipline and promised they would not be repeated. This is not to suggest that they repudiated any of their political aims. On the other side Eyres, Scott, Bray and others were set free and restored to their commands, and a general amnesty was agreed for all past actions. On the political side the Grandees undertook that there should be no more attempts at agreement with the King – a Leveller demand which they had strongly resisted at Putney. This proved to be a genuine change of policy when Cromwell, on January 3rd, moved and carried in the House of Commons that no more addresses should be made to Charles. The unity of the Army was restored, but at the price of an important step to the left by the Grandees.

The bitterness with which they were assailed by Wildman in his pamphlet *Putney Projects* (December 30th) suggests that the civilian Levellers were slower to accept the change of tactics than their friends in the Army. Meanwhile they were developing their own new campaign. In June they had declared that it was useless to expect anything from the existing Commons, "as there is little good to be hoped for from such Parliaments as need to be Petitioned; so there is none at all to be expected from those that burn such Petitions as these." [IV] Now that they had failed to win the support of the Army they resumed their petitioning, though it must be remembered that in the interval Parliament had been purged of its leading Presbyterians. The *Petition* of November 23rd [VII] is once more addressed to the Commons as "the Supreme Authority of England". And whereas previously the *Agreement* had been submitted direct to the people, as constituting a body of fundamental law above the power of Parliament to alter, this Petition "beseeches" it "to review and debate impartially the particulars of that Agreement of the people wherein many thousands have already concurred". It also condemns the actions of the Grandees for their double-dealing, as well as for the execution of Arnold and the imprisonment of Eyres and others.

Though the Petition was drawn up in the most respectful language, Parliament at once condemned it as "seditious and contemptuous" and imprisoned Thomas Prince and Samuel Chidley by whom it had been presented. The Levellers then reprinted it, with an indignant postscript, quite different in style and apparently written by a different author.

Alongside this petitioning the Levellers were seriously engaged in building the world's first organised radical-democratic political party. They made their headquarters at the Whalebone Tavern, "in Lothbury behind the Royal Exchange", where the leadership seems to have held almost nightly meetings at this period. A substantial membership was soon recruited, paying weekly subscriptions according to their means and organised, in London at least, on a parish and ward basis. Similar groups or branches began to be built in the towns around London. A picture of all this activity is contained in a hostile pamphlet, *A Declaration of Some Proceedings of Lt Col. John Lilburn, And his Associates* (February 1648) which includes, among other Leveller documents, the letter [XVII] in which methods of work and organisation are outlined.

There is evidence, too, that in this winter of famine prices and widespread unemployment and misery, they were trying to broaden the basis of their appeal. This can be seen in their next programme document, the *Petition* of January 1648. Here, in addition to the familiar constitutional demands, are new clauses directly affecting the poor and the wage earner:

"That the too long continued shame of the Nation, *viz.* permission of any to suffer such poverty as to beg their bread, may be forthwith effectually remedied: and to that purpose that the Poor may be enabled to choose their Trustees, to discover all Stocks, Houses, Lands, etc. which of right belong to them, and their use, that they may speedily receive the benefit thereof; and that some good improvement may be made of waste Grounds for their use; and that according to the promise of this honourable House, in your first Remonstrance, care be taken forthwith to advance the native commodities of this Nation, that the poor may have better wages for their labor; and that Manufactures may be increased, and the Herring-fishing upon our own Coasts may be improved for the best advantage of our own Mariners, and the whole Nation."[1]

[1] Wolfe, p. 270.

The *Petition* also demands the ending of Excise which "lies heavy only upon the Poorer and most ingenious industrial People, to their intolerable oppression", and its replacement by a tax upon property, "to be raised by an equal Rate, according to the Proportion of mens estates".

The other significant feature is that nothing is said of an *Agreement*, but that Parliament itself is asked:

> "That therefore, that Birth-right of all English men, be forth with restored to all which are not, or shall not be legally disfranchised for some criminal cause, or are not under 21 years of age, or servants, or beggars; and we humbly offer, that every County may have its equal proportion of representers."[1]

This is the first official Leveller endorsement of the franchise demand which was accepted at Putney. The *Petition*, indeed, goes beyond this in suggesting that not only M.P.s but also magistrates and all other officials should be elected.

A couple of days later *The Mournfull Cryes of Many Thousand Poor Tradesmen* struck, perhaps, the strongest note of class hatred to be found in any Leveller writing. It asks "Members of Parliament and rich men in the City . . . What then are your rustling Silks and Velvets, and your glittering Gold and Silver Laces? are they not the sweat of our brows and the wants of our backs and bellies?" And it concludes menacingly:

> "O Parliament men and Souldiers! Necessity dissolves all Laws and Government, and Hunger will break through stone Walls . . . carry our cries in the large Petition to the Parliament, and tell them if they be still deaf, the Teares of the oppressed will wash away the foundations of their houses."[2]

[1] Wolfe, p. 269.
[2] Wolfe, pp. 275, 278.

There seems no doubt that the campaign was making considerable headway if one may judge by the amount of hostility it provoked both from Presbyterians and Independents, when it was interrupted in May by the renewal of war. There was serious fighting in South Wales, and in Kent and Essex – former Parliamentarian areas. A considerable part of the Army was tied down for months at the siege of Colchester. In August Cromwell, having disposed of the South Wales rising, marched to meet the invading Scots, leaving behind him a London whose richer citizens were looking forward to his defeat. At this point Lilburne sent him a letter characteristic both in its generosity and its self-conceit:

"If," he wrote, "I prosecuted or desired revenge for an hard and almost sterving imprisonment, I could have had of late the choice of twenty opportunities to have payed you to the purpose: but I scorn it, especially when you are low: and this assure yourself, that if ever my hand be upon you, it shall be when you are in your full glory, if then you shall decline from the righteous wayes of Truth and Justice: which, if you will fixedly and impartially prosecute, I am
Yours, to the last drop of my heart bloud,
(for all your late severe hand towards me)
John Lilburn."[1]

This letter was sent by Sexby and, it was reported, "was not a little welcome". Sexby remained with Cromwell throughout the campaign that culminated in the victory at Preston, apparently on terms of the closest intimacy.

The relative isolation of the Army at this time made the support of the Levellers indispensable and the ending of the war brought a new stage in Leveller tactics. Before discussing this, something should be said of the

[1] H. and D., p. 414.

pamphlet which Walwyn wrote while the war was still in progress. Of all the Levellers he was the most inclined to pacifism and *The Bloody Project* [VIII] while putting forward Party policy also voices his personal horror and distress at the deliberate and unnecessary renewal of fighting. This distress forced him to consider more deeply than ever before the nature and objects of the conflict, and the betrayal by the leaders, both Presbyterian and Independent, of the promises that had been made to the people. He expresses with a new clarity the disillusion which the plebeian masses, drawn in to provide the fighting force for a bourgeois revolution, feel at seeing that the real victors turn out to be only a new set of exploiters:

> "To be short, all the quarrell we have at this day in the Kingdome, is no other then a quarrel of Interests and Partyes, a pulling down of one Tyrant, to set up another, and instead of Liberty, heaping upon yourselves a greater slavery then that we fought against."

The poor, those "that depend on Farmes, Trades and small pay", are invariably the only sufferers in war, while "The king, Parliament, great men in the City and Army, have made you but the stairs by which they have mounted to Honor, Wealth and Power."

5. The Agreement Revived

The Levellers' new campaign opened with the presentation of the *Petition* of September 11th [IX], a collective statement but probably mainly drafted by Walwyn. In it most of the familiar demands were repeated, but also, for the first time, one for the laying open of all late enclosures. The *Petition*, it was claimed, received 40,000 signatures in only a few days and was supported by a mass lobby at Westminster calling for its immediate consideration by Parliament.

It contained also a demand for the execution of

"Justice upon the Capitall Authors and Promoters of the former or late Wars". This brought the Levellers into line with the feeling of the Army, where Grandees and rank and file were united in pressing for the immediate trial of the King. Parliament, meanwhile, in spite of all the evidence of his bad faith, persisted in negotiations about terms for his restoration to the throne, terms which would have involved the abandonment of much of what had been won. Such an agreement could have been made only at the expense of the Army, so that once more the Grandees were forced to bid for Leveller support. This led to a set of complex negotiations which are known to us mostly from the account given by Lilburne in *Legall Fundamentall Liberties*. This is, of course, a partisan account, but there is no reason to doubt its substantial accuracy.

Towards the end of October he had a meeting with Cromwell, who seems to have indicated that he had now come to a position close to that of the Levellers. Lilburne was sceptical. At a later meeting he and Wildman were told that the first steps must be to execute the King and purge Parliament of its Presbyterian Members (now all back in their places). Lilburne objected that

"The Army had couzened us the last yeer, and fallen from all their Promises and Declarations, and therefore could not rationally any more be trusted by us without good cautions and security: In which regard, although we should judge the King as arrant a Tyrant as they supposed him to be; and the Parliament as bad as they could make them; yet there being no other balancing power in the Kingdome against the Army, but the King and Parliament, it was our interest to keep one Tyrant to balance another, till we certainly knew what that Tyrant that pretended fairest would give us as our Freedomes . . . and therefore I pressed very hard for an Agreement amongst the People first, utterly disclaiming the thoughts of the other, till this was done."[1]

The "Gentlemen Independents were some of them desperately cholerick", but when it was clear that Leveller support could be had on no other terms, they agreed to the setting up of a committee of eight (later reduced to six). This met at the Nag's Head in London on November 15th and decided on the formation of a larger and more representative committee of sixteen — four delegates each from the Levellers, the Grandees, the House of Commons and the Independent Churches. To this committee Lilburne, Walwyn, Wildman and Petty were chosen "by unanimous consent of the Agents from our friends in and about London, at a very large meeting". Marten, the only M.P. who actually attended, worked closely with the four Levellers throughout. After some complicated manoeuvres, in which Harrison played a leading part as mediator between the Levellers and Grandees, the committee met at Whitehall

"... and a long and tedious tug we had with Commissary Generall Ireton only, yea sometimes whole nights together, Principally about Liberty of Conscience, and the Parliaments punishing where no law provides, and very angry and Lordly in his debates many times he was; but to some kind of an expedient in the first, for peace sake we condescended to please him, and so came among the major part of the 16 Commissioners, according to our originall Agreement, to an absolute and finall conclusion; and thinking all had been done as to any more debate upon it, and that it should without any more adoe be promoted for subscriptions, first at the Councell of Warre, and so in the Regiments, and so all over the Nation; but

[1] H. and D., p. 416.

alas poor fools we were merely cheated and couzened . . . for when it came to the Councel, there came the Generall, Crumwell, and the whole gang of creature Colonels and other Officers, and spent many dayes in taking it all in pieces . . . And within a little time after I took my leave of them for a pack of dissembling juggling knaves."

After that, Lilburne wrote, "having an exact copy of what the greatest part of the foresaid sixteen had agreed upon, I only mended a clause in the first Reserve about Religion, to the sense of us all but Ireton, and put an Epistle to it, of the 15 of December 1648, and printed it of my own accord, and the next day it came abroad."[1]

This new version, *Foundations of Freedom: or an Agreement of the People,* represents the Leveller conception of what had been agreed on by the Whitehall committee, and embodied the greatest concessions which either they or their opponents were ever prepared to make. On the franchise the latter abandoned their insistence that it be confined to freeholders and freemen of boroughs. The Levellers, in addition to the earlier exception of servants and takers of alms, were now prepared to restrict it also to ratepayers and householders. This second *Agreement* differed also from the first in being a much more completely worked out draft constitution, with detailed proposals for the representation of each county and city and for the method of holding elections. It contained, of course, the former prohibition of Parliament from altering fundamental constitutional rights.

The Grandees, however, were not prepared to accept this compromise, but published their own version, considerably weakened, in the form of a Petition from the Army to Parliament, on January 20th, 1649. This was

[1] H. and D., pp. 422–423.

severely criticised by the Levellers, but in fact these criticisms were only of academic importance. Instead of joining in a united effort to secure the acceptance of the *Agreement* (in whatever version) by the nation, the Grandees merely submitted it formally to Parliament, claiming that by so doing they had kept their side of the bargain. Parliament never even troubled to debate it, and it was soon evident that the Grandees' whole purpose had been to prevent any opposition from the Levellers while preparations were made to purge the House of Commons and put the King on trial. In this they succeeded, since their version of the *Agreement* was published on the very day on which the King's trial opened.

While these negotiations were going on, the Levellers suffered a serious blow in the assassination of Rainborough. After the war ended elsewhere a Royalist group continued to hold out in the strong castle of Pontefract, and Rainborough was sent to command the siege operations. On October 29th a party broke out from the castle and made their way to Rainborough's quarters some miles away, surprised him in his bed and killed him. There is no evidence to support the suspicions, voiced at the time and since, that the crime was in some way contrived by the Grandees. It is highly probable that he was sent to Pontefract to remove him from London at a time when important political moves were taking place and it is certainly true that little effort was ever made to catch the assassins. His death was a tragedy for the Levellers, since he was the one officer whose standing and ability made him a possible rival to Cromwell. Without him the Army Levellers were left without any effective leadership. His funeral in London was the occasion for an immense political demonstration, at which, in recognition of his connection with the sea, the crowds wore green ribbons. Sea-green became the recognised colour symbolising the Leveller Party.

6. The Defeat of the Levellers

It is clear that once again the Levellers had been out-generalled. The trial of the King and the setting up of a Council of State, in which all real power was centred, was pushed ahead while they were confused and divided by the apparent partial acceptance of the *Agreement*. Lilburne was offered a seat on the Court at which Charles was tried, but refused it, not because he was opposed to the trial in principle but because he objected to the timing and method. As he wrote later in *Legall Fundamentall Liberties*:

> "I pressed again and again, seeing themselves confess'd all legal Authority in England was broke, that they would stay his tryall till a new and equal free Representative upon the Agreement of the well-affected people, that had not fought against their Liberties, Rights and Freedoms, could be chosen and sit, and then either try him thereby, or else by their Judges sitting in the Court called Kings Bench."[1]

One may doubt how far the mass of Leveller supporters, especially in the Army, were able to appreciate Lilburne's rather legalistic objections. At any rate the Party was left isolated and floundering in the wake of events at the very moment when they were the only organised force which could have opposed what was in fact a military coup by the Grandees.

Their failure was the more complete because of an extraordinary and never properly explained tactical blunder. At this most critical moment in their history they simply ceased to function. Towards the end of December Lilburne left London for Durham to settle private affairs. Walwyn temporarily ceased to be active in the Party leadership. Wildman deserted the cause. From the appearance of the second *Agreement* on

[1] H. and D., p. 433.

December 15th till the end of February no Leveller pamphlet of importance was issued. This absence of publication probably reflects a collapse, or at least a total stagnation of the movement. It is impossible now to say whether this was the result of over-optimistic conviction that the Grandees were committed to the *Agreement,* of differences within the leadership,[1] of difficulties in persuading the rank and file to accept Lilburne's policy on the King's trial, or of some other cause at which we cannot now even guess.

When the Leveller campaign was resumed, the Council of State, dominated by the Grandees, was firmly in control and could only have been dislodged by a new revolution, the conditions for which did not exist.

Englands New Chains Discovered (February 26th) appealed rather desperately to what remained of the House of Commons against the illegal and usurped authority of the Council of State. It criticised the shortcomings of the Officers' *Agreement,* though this was by now a dead issue. It accused the Grandees of planning to raise new forces for use against the Leveller soldiers in the existing regiments, an accusation that seems to some extent justified by the composition of the troops later used against the Army mutineers at Burford [XV].

Englands New Chains was aimed mainly at a civilian public. A simultaneous drive was made within the Army. On March 1st five troopers addressed a petition to Fairfax, attacking the Council of State and insisting on their right to petition, which the Grandees were now denying them, and declaring:

"We are English Souldiers, engaged for the Freedoms of England; and are not outlandish mercenaries, to butcher the people for pay, to serve the pernitious

[1] It seems possible that Walwyn was more prepared to accept the Officers' *Agreement* than were some of the others.

ends of ambition and will in any person under Heaven . . . It hath been a principle by you asserted and avowed, that our being Souldiers hath not deprived us of our Rights as Commoners, and to Petition the people in Parliament, we do account in the number of our Birthrights."[1]

For this crime the five troopers were victimised and dismissed from the Army with ignominy.

On March 21st all the documents relating to the case were published, together with a stinging attack on the Grandees, under the title *The Hunting of the Foxes from Newmarket and Triploe-Heaths to Whitehall, By five small Beagles (late of the Armie)*. The beagles were the five troopers, by whom the pamphlet was signed, but the style is unmistakably that of Overton at his brilliant best, contrasting the present actions of the Grandees with the promises they had made while trying to secure the support of the Army.

The Hunting of the Foxes, threatening them at their most vulnerable point, was followed on March 24th by *The second Part of Englands New-Chaines Discovered*, no less angry and no less damaging. Attributed merely to "severall wel-affected persons . . . presenters and approvers of the late large Petition of the Eleventh of September, 1648", the authorship of Lilburne, Overton and Prince was acknowledged in a second edition published in August. The new government acted promptly. On March 26th the House of Commons voted that "the Authors, Contrivers and Framers of the said Paper are Guilty of High Treason: and shall be proceeded against as Traitors."[2] Next morning, even before daylight, large bodies of soldiers arrested Lilburne, Overton and Prince in their homes, as well as Walwyn who had in fact no part in *Englands New-Chaines*. All

[1] Wolfe, pp. 372–373.
[2] H. and D., p. 171.

four were taken before the Council of State. The first three gave an account of the proceedings in *The Picture of the Councel of State,* published in April, and Walwyn, rather later, in *The Fountain of Slaunder.* All these narratives are highly characteristic of their authors. Lilburne's is long, legalistic and indignant, Prince's short and dignified, Walwyn's bland but firm. Overton's [X], combative and at the same time philosophical.

All four took identical stands, challenging the legality of their arrests and of the authority of the Council itself, and refusing to answer any questions which might incriminate them. After all had been questioned separately, the Council discussed their fate. Lilburne "laid his ear to the door" and heard Cromwell "very loud, thumping his fist upon the Councel Table, til it rang againe", and declaring "if you do not breake them, they will break you; yea, and bring all the guilt of the blood and treasure shed and spent in this Kingdom upon your heads and shoulders; and frustrate and make voide all that work, that with so many yeares industry, toile and paines you have done, and so render you to all rationall men in the world, as the most contemptibilist generation of silly, low spirited men in the earth."[1] Ludlow, usually sympathetic, urged that they be given bail, but by a narrow majority this was rejected and all four were sent to the Tower to await trial.

This arrest coincided with a break between the Levellers and the Anabaptist congregations whom they had formerly regarded as allies. A group of ministers took this opportunity to attack them in a pamphlet signed by at least one old personal friend of Lilburne, William Kiffin – *The Humble Petition and Representation of Several Churches of God in London.* Lilburne dismissed them as "a pack of fauning daubing knaves".

[1] H. and D., p. 204.

Overton, himself a Baptist, made their attack the occasion for a brilliant declaration of moral independence, maintaining that his personal shortcomings were irrelevant and that he should be judged by his policy alone:

"... the business is, not how great a sinner I am, but how faithfull and reall to the Common-wealth; that's the matter concerneth my neighbour, and whereof my neighbour is only in this publick Controversie to take notice; and for my personall sins that are not of Civill cognizance or wrong unto him, to leave them to God."

A turning point had been reached with a complete breach between the Levellers and the Churches. Independent ministers visited them in the Tower, urging submission. Towards the end of April Baptists and Independents cooperated to publish *Walwins Wiles,* a slanderous personal attack on Walwyn, whose sceptical and tolerant attitude had always disturbed them. He had recently added to his offences by dissecting the sects in *The Vanitie of the Present Churches* in which he wrote that

"all their preachings and prayings are only for mony, and that their greatest skill and labour, is to hold men ever in suspence; and upon pretence of truth, to give them a bastard Scholastick knowledge, which only serve to make men proud, wrangling Sophisters, and Disputers, vain boasters, talkers, busie-bodies, censurers, Pharisees, wise in their own eyes, and despising others, void of all true piety or reall Christian vertue."[1]

He replied in detail to *Walwins Wiles* in *Walwyns Just Defence,* and having disposed of the charges against him, expressed his amazement that his enemies, who called themselves Christian people

[1] H. and D., p. 263.

". . . should harbour this wretched slander six yeares amongst them, and be bringing it forth this time, and that time, but finde no time their season but when I was violently taken out of my bed, and house, and made a prisoner; if this be their way of visiting of prisoners, would not it make men think they had forgot the Scriptures; nay, might they not go to the heathens to learn some Charity."[1]

From this point the Levellers were increasingly isolated, and forced to continue their political battles without their former allies. This they did, resisting with the weapons in whose use they had become so skilled – the mass petition and the agitational pamphlet. Only four days after their arrest a petition was presented to Parliament with 10,000 signatures. A fortnight later it was followed by a second, and, perhaps still more noteworthy, a week later by a *Petition of divers wel-affected Women*. In the Tower the prisoners were preparing a new version of *An Agreement of the People*, and, to prepare the way for this, *A Manifestation* [XII]. Signed by all four, but regarded as mainly the work of Walwyn, it outlines the political thinking implicit in the *Agreement*, and rebuts many of the charges usually made against them.

Published on May 1st, the *Agreement* in its final form was the last and most carefully considered of all the Levellers' programmatic statements [XIII]. Many, though not all, of the earlier demands reappear. Some of the concessions which had been made in the *Agreement* of December are no longer felt necessary. The property qualification for voters disappears and the clause on religious toleration is considerably strengthened. It represents, as *A Manifestation* promised, "the Standard and ultimate scope of our Designes . . . to settle the Common-wealth upon the fairest probabilities of a lasting Peace, and contentfull Establishment."

[1] H. and D., p. 364.

While the prisoners in the Tower were busy drafting their appeal and their supporters in London protesting outside, events were moving quickly in the Army. The greatest single reason for the alarm felt by the Grandees over *The Hunting of the Foxes* and *Englands New Chains* was undoubtedly the knowledge that before long they had to persuade, and if persuasion failed to coerce, an unwilling Army into fighting an unwanted war in Ireland. Three sorts of objections at three political levels were to be expected. First, the natural dislike of men who had still not been paid for their service in one war to set out on one more distant, more dangerous and more full of hardships. Irish wars were notorious for their high rate of casualties, especially from disease.

Second, many soldiers still stood by the promise made in the *Engagement* of 1647 [III] that the Army would neither divide nor disband without the consent of a Council including their own elected representatives. They saw the plan for an Irish campaign, with justice, as a device of the Grandees to split the Army and destroy its political effectiveness. They were unwilling to go before the "native freedoms", so often promised but still unsecured, had been won.

Third, there were objections to the Irish war on principle. How widespread these were among the troops it is impossible to say, but the Levellers at least have the honour of being the first to protest against an aggressive colonial war. Walwyn was alleged to have said:

"That the sending over Forces to Ireland is nothing else but to make war by the blood of the Army to enlarge their territories of power and Tyranny, That it is an unlawful War, a cruel and bloody work to go to destroy the Irish Natives for their Consciences, and to drive them from their proper natural and native Rights."[1]

[1] *Walwins Wiles*. H. and D., pp. 288–289.

It is significant that in his detailed reply this is the one charge Walwyn never attempted to answer. Prince, in *The Silken Independents Snare Broken,* expressed the view that no campaign should be attempted before *An Agreement of the People* had been adopted, and that then it might not be needed as the Irish might well "be willing to change their bondage for freedom". Earlier than this, about May 5th, the Levellers had issued *The English Souldiers Standard* [XI]. H. N. Brailsford, attributing this pamphlet to Walwyn, remarks on the close resemblance of its ideas about a just war and the responsibility of all engaged in it to those of *The Bloody Project.* If this is correct it would account for the bitterness of the attack made in *Walwins Wiles.* At any rate, the *Standard* combined the second and third objections to an Irish war in a very convincing way, and must have had a considerable effect.

Four days before the Levellers were arrested a committee of officers had met to discuss an Irish campaign and a decision was taken that four regiments of Horse and four of Foot should be chosen by lot. Men who volunteered to go would have a large part of their arrears paid, those who refused would be discharged with little or nothing. The soldiers replied by demanding the re-election of Agitators and adherence to the terms of the *Engagement.* About the middle of April the names of the selected regiments were announced.

The tension that existed was shown by the mutiny on April 24th of a part of Whalley's Regiment, quartered in London. It was crushed and a young trooper, Robert Lockyer, a former Agitator with an outstanding record and character and a recognised political leader in his regiment, was shot. While these events were taking place a Leveller leaflet was circulated in London calling on soldiers to refuse to march for Ireland and to set up a Council of Agitators. A number of regiments responded, including several of those chosen for Ireland. A lead was given by Scroop's Horse, who on May 1st unanimously agreed not to go. They were supported by at least five others, who together set up a Council of Agitators.[1]

What followed is fully described in *The Levellers Vindicated* [XV], and need not be repeated here in detail. The men of Scroop's Regiment, after being subjected to every kind of pressure, mutinied at Salisbury and issued a Declaration explaining why they refused to go to Ireland. Political issues were carefully avoided, except for a general reference to the restitution of freedoms. Joined by Ireton's Regiment they moved north through Wantage to Abingdon, where they were joined by part of Harrison's Regiment coming from Buckingham. They then turned west, presumably to link with Horton's Regiment in Gloucester, who had also pledged support. Their ultimate objective may have been Bristol. When they reached Burford they were surprised on the night of May 14th by Fairfax and Cromwell. Many escaped and scattered, but some hundreds were captured and imprisoned in Burford church. Next morning three were executed in sight of their comrades lined up on the church roof.

The mutiny had put the Grandees in a most difficult situation. When Fairfax and Cromwell held a review in Hyde Park on May 9th, many paraded with sea-green ribbons in their hats. Cromwell was forced to promise that those who left the Army as well as those who stayed would receive payments of their arrears, and that the programme of the Officers' *Agreement* would be carried out. Neither promise was in fact kept. Two other points remain obscure. We shall never know whether Major White was, as the Levellers seem to have thought, a party to their deception, or whether, as seems more probable, he was tricked by the Grandees into becoming their unwitting accomplice. Similarly, it

[1] Brailsford, op. cit., p. 507.

5*

remains uncertain whether Denne was a traitor and provocateur from the start, as his fellow soldiers believed, or merely suffered a moral collapse in face of the threat of death.

A second and parallel, though unconnected, mutiny was going on at the same time. The self-styled "Captain" William Thompson, friend and protégé of Lilburne, gathered a miscellaneous force, largely drawn from dissatisfied elements in Reynolds' Regiment, at Banbury. A statement, *Englands Standard Advanced* (perhaps written by Lilburne) was of a much more political character than that of the Salisbury mutineers. Thompson's followers, however, lacked the solidarity of men who had been accustomed to act together, and, when challenged, most of them dispersed. Thompson broke away with a few followers and, near Wellingborough, was cornered and killed.

The relief felt by the rich supporters of the Grandees, whether Presbyterian or Independent, was immense. Oxford gave Fairfax and Cromwell honorary degrees and a banquet. The City another banquet and rich gifts of plate. Not even the victory at Naseby had been greeted with such unmixed enthusiasm — for them, after all, Levellers were far more dangerous enemies than Royalists.

For the Levellers Burford was a final defeat though sympathy and support remained widespread. Another attempted mutiny at Oxford in September was quickly defeated, and, generally speaking, opposition in the Army to service in Ireland came to an end. In August Cromwell was able to embark his troops. From the Tower the Levellers continued to issue a stream of appeals, but without its leaders the Party was unable to recover from the defeat. Overton, in a witty and vigorous pamphlet *Overtons Defyance of the Act of Pardon* (July 4th) attempted to rally the London Levellers to a resumption of confidence and activity. He and his fellows in the Tower were but four men and could not be expected to carry the fight alone:

"I cannot see but that a Prison, the Gallows or halter would become the best of you as well as any of us, to vindicate or assert that Agreement of the people.

"But you spit in our mouths, and clap us on the back like Dogs, and cry ha-looe a-looe, and turn us loose upon all the Bulls, Bears, Wolves, Lyons and Dragons of the time, which are thousands to one . . . while you shrink, and skulk into your holes: Come out for shame, come out, and catch me the great Bull of Bason by the NOSE, and make him roar."[1]

Few things are more difficult than to rally a revolutionary movement once it has entered a phase of retreat, and Overton's raillery had little effect. Some even found fault with what they regarded as his coarse and undignified language. It was to these he replied in *The Baiting of the Great Bull of Bashan* (July 16th) [XIV] with its splendid defence of mirth as "of divine instinct, and I think I may boldly say, more naturall then Melancholy, and less savours of the Curse". This was to be the last of Overton's writings and there is none which shows his talents to better effect.

Meanwhile the treason laws were strengthened, and, by an Act of September 14th the censorship of all printed books and papers was tightened. The last issue of the Levellers' weekly journal, *The Moderate,* appeared on September 25th. With these safeguards, and with the Irish campaign well on the way the Council of State could venture on the long-delayed trial of its Leveller prisoners.

Lilburne, as the undisputed leader, was taken first, and his trial began in the Guildhall on October 25th. Nothing could have suited him better. On a great

[1] Royalist satirists as well as Levellers at this time were fond of comparing Cromwell to a bull. They also ridiculed his large, red nose.

dramatic occasion, with his life at stake and the whole English nation as audience, he could rise to the height of his powers. For two days he browbeat and confused his judges, appealing to the jury as fellow commoners and to the packed audience in the galleries behind them. When the jury returned a verdict of "Not Guilty" there were scenes of extraordinary enthusiasm. Bonfires were lit all over London and the church bells rung. The rejoicing, we are told, "made the Judges for fear turn pale, and hang down their heads; but the Prisoner stood silent at the Barre, rather more sad in his countenance than before."

The acquittal was no doubt a victory and showed the continued popularity both of Lilburne and the Leveller cause, but it could do nothing to prevent the disappearance of the Party as an organised political force.

Its leaders went different ways and suffered different fates. Lilburne continued to fight because this was his nature, but as an individual not as a Party leader. Something of his subsequent story can be followed in his autobiographical pamphlet *The Just Defence of John Lilburn* [XVI]. Overton returned to the shadowy world of the illegal printer. From time to time he appears, like Sexby and Wildman, in obscure conspiracies, sometimes with Royalist involvements. Bray was writing pamphlets with Leveller ideas as late as 1659. Chidley campaigned for prison reform and other radical causes. Walwyn seems to have returned to private life but in 1651 he wrote a defence of trial by jury.

Leveller ideas and hopes died slowly. The very last item in this volume [XVII] gives us a moving glimpse of Leveller soldiers trying, in something like despair, to rebuild a shattered organisation. After Cromwell's death in 1658 the political confusion led to a revival of these hopes, and fears of a new Leveller Party was doubtless one of the main reasons why all the men of property resolved so quickly on a restoration of the Monarchy.

IV

The Levellers in the English Revolution

Cromwell had thus succeeded in his aim of breaking the Levellers in pieces – but it was a hollow victory. There is no need to doubt the sincerity of his conviction that their defeat was necessary for the safety of the Revolution as a whole as he understood it. He had no doubt that a temporary Leveller victory would have resulted in confusion followed by a restoration of the Monarchy. In the circumstances of the time he may well have been right in this view. Yet the conflict between them involved him in the tragic contradiction that lies at the heart of every bourgeois revolution. And in the end, in 1660, it made inevitable the very Restoration that he was so anxious to avoid.

Every bourgeois revolution is the work not of a single class but of an alliance of classes and groups. So, in England, the progressive gentry, the middle strata in town and country and the small producers, peasants and artisans, all wanted a revolution *of some kind*: all were united at the beginning against the Monarchy and the feudal order which it represented. For this reason, at its first session, the Long Parliament was almost unanimous. Thereafter the history of the Revolution is a history of the class groupings concerned in it. At each stage a section felt that its proper objectives had been won and that a halt should be called; others wanted to press further. This was the essence of the struggles between Presbyterians and Independents, Independents and Levellers.

The historical role of these last was to carry the Revolution to the highest point then possible, higher than that at which it could be maintained, though less high than they wished. In doing this they helped to safeguard the main advance. As Engels wrote:

"As a rule, after the first great success the victorious minority became divided; one half was pleased with what had been gained, the other wanted to go still further, and put forward new demands, which, to a certain extent at least, were also in the real or apparent interests of the great mass of the people. In individual cases these more radical demands were realised, but often only for the moment; the more moderate party gained the upper hand, and what had eventually been won was wholly or partly lost again; the vanquished shrieked of treachery, or ascribed their defeat to accident. But in truth the position was mainly this: the achievements of the first victory were only safeguarded by the second victory of the more radical party; this having been attained, and with it, what was necessary for the moment, the radicals and their achievements vanished from the stage."[1]

So the Levellers vanished, and the immediate cause of their departure was their inability to prevent the reconquest of Ireland. It is now possible to see that even if their "luck" had been better, if things had gone right at Ware or at Burford, if the Grandees had been sincere in the negotiations of December 1648, their victory would have been temporary and it is unlikely that the course of history would have been greatly changed.

Yet this is only part of the story. Cromwell was essentially a man of the centre and in order to carry *his* Revolution forward he had been forced to mobilise the left, the plebeian elements, to give him the support he needed against the right. Yet in the end he had to destroy the very mass basis on which his position had been built. The Presbyterians might feast the victor of Burford, but they never either accepted or trusted him. He

---

[1] Engels, Introduction to Marx' *The Class Struggles in France*. See in general Christopher Hill, "The English Civil War Interpreted by Marx and Engels". *Science and Society*, XII, 1.

would have preferred to rely on an alliance between the middle and lower strata – on the essential condition that the latter should abandon the democratic demands which threatened the whole social and economic fabric of society as he knew it. This was impossible, and after Burford his whole story is of vain attempts to find a new permanent basis for his régime. The Nominated Parliament of 1653, the Instrument of Government later in the same year and the Humble Petition and Advice of 1657 were all such attempts and all failed. The control of an increasingly professional Army gave him a certain room for manoeuvre, but he realised that nothing permanent could be built on such a basis. It was not without reason that the Levellers called him the great Juggler, but even for the most adroit juggler the point must come when it is no longer possible to keep the balls in the air.

We must conclude, I think, that the defeat of the Levellers was unavoidable, and it is easy to see why they were almost forgotten for two and a half centuries. Yet there was a sequel. It was not quite accidental that Shaftesbury's London supporters formed a Green Ribbon Club or that Monmouth's men marched behind a sea-green banner, or that Richard Rumbold, a one-time Agitator, died on the scaffold proclaiming the magnificent Leveller commonplace. "I am sure there was no man marked of God above another; for none comes into the world with a saddle on his back, neither any booted and spurred to ride him" – a real cavalryman's metaphor.

A Party that held the centre of the stage for three of the most crucial years in our nation's history, voiced the aspirations of the unprivileged masses, and was able to express with such force ideas that have been behind every great social advance since their time, cannot be regarded as wholly a failure or deserve to be wholly forgotten.

I

A Pearle in a Dounghill

[Although unsigned this pamphlet is undoubtedly the work of Walwyn. It was published towards the end of June 1646. By this time Walwyn had known Lilburne about a year and their growing cooperation marks the formation of the Leveller Party. Characteristically, Walwyn exploits the particular issue of Lilburne's imprisonment to mount a general attack on the House of Lords and to assert the supremacy of the Commons as the representative of the sovereign people.]

A
PEARLE
IN A
DOUNGHILL.
OR
Lieu. Col. JOHN LILBURNE
in New-gate:

Committed *illegally by the* House of Lords, *first for
refusing (according to his Liberty) to answer Interrogatories, but protesting against them as
not being competent Judges, and appealing
to the House of Commons. Next committed close prisoner for his just refusing to kneel at the* House of
Lords Barre.

ALTHOUGH most of States and States men be of late turned upside down like a wheele, yet this worthy valiant and publique spirited Gentleman (unto whom his Nation is as much bound to, at least as to any one, all things considered) is the very same man (both in principles and practise) whom the Bishops so long imprisoned in the Fleet by a most cruell and barbarous sentence, which they procured in the Star-chamber against him, and so was whipt, gag'd and pilloried, yea and in his close imprisonment almost famished and murthered,

And all because he would not submit to be examined against himselfe, betray his friends, accuse his brethren, nor sell the lawfull rights and just liberties of England, for a messe or morsell of base preferment, whose fidelity, constancy and integrity the Parliament justified, and condemned that sentence as illegall, bloody, and tyranicall, delivered him out of prison, adjudged him worthy of reparation, abolished Episcopacy, the Star-chamber, High Commission, Councell-table and many such arbitrary proceedings,

All which being duely and seriously considered, may it not seeme very strange, that this so famous a man still holding forth the same tenets and practise now in time of Parliament and Reformation, should be now againe in Newgate as he was once before, by an Order from the House of Commons, both in lesse then a twelve moneth? Is it not because there is a Popish and Episcopall party under other pretences as busie working in the Kingdome now as ever? And as he was a speciall instrument of the Bishops overthrow, so those their agents are the prime causers and workers both of his ruine, and all that will take his part, if posibly they could once get that Decree sealed and un-altered, so that their should not be Separate or Sectary any more mentioned.

And though his malicious adversaries will not be warned of their Downfall, and are as mad against him, because he will not bow before them, as ever Hamon was against Mordecay; yea and more shamelesse and bloody, then ever his former adversaries in sending him to Newgate, the basest of prisons, and shewing plainly they thirst much more after his pretious life, then ever Kain did after Abels, his apparently proceeding of a present discontent, and theirs of a long forged malicious intent and therefore if God permit these wicked men thus to prevaile over the Godly, it is to crowne the sufferings of the one with glory, and to reward the persecutions of the other with misery.

But to take a view of his actions, wee find by such credible proofe, that his very adversaries shall not be able to contradict (yea and themselves did never the like) passing by both what he did, and suffered under the Episcopall tyranny, because large volumnes thereof are extant, and beginning, since his deliverance out of the Fleet prison at the beginning of the Parliament:

In the first place, hath he been ingratefull to his Deliverers, or perfidious to his Country? No his ingagements was with the first in this present warre: to defend his Country, and forseeking a comfortable and profitable way of living; his actions at Westminster-hall, Keinton-field, and Brainford, his cariage at Oxford in Iron Chaines, against strong temtations, and upon tryall for his life their, will witness: his fidelity, magnanimity, and undaunted resolution to the Parliament and Commonwealth, and that in such measure that not many, if any of this age can shew the like testimony.

And for such as would recapitulate his actions and sufferings since, let them trace him in his service to the State, under the Earle of Manchester, and defending the publique freedomes since, and they will find that with the losse both of his blood, estate and many hazards of his life, he hath performed Noble services, as the taking of Tickle castle, Sir John Wortleys house and the like, in all which, malice it selfe cannot accuse him, either of Cowardice or Covetousnesse.

No nor yet of carelesnesse, not deeming it sufficient to be faithfull himselfe, but alwaies held a watchfull eye over the actions of others, and as bold in discovery of the Fraud, Treachery, Cowardice, Cruelties, plundering and Covetousnesse, of false hearted friends, as valiant in fight against the enemies:

And now if you will begin to think why a man so faithfull in all his waies should be so lyable to trouble as he hath been (for he hath been divers times in Pursevants hands and so committed by Committees) if you shall consider how this Pearle comes to be cast upon this Dounghill, you will find, the faithfulnesse of his heart towards God and all good People, and the freenesse of his tongue against all kinde of injustice or unworthinesse, in whomsoever, is the only cause and no other.

And if you seriously weigh things, you will confesse it would grieve any good mans heart, that Treachery, Cowardice, Cruelty, plundering and Covetousnesse have bin too too slenderly punished, and faithfullnesse so many waies discouraged, and that it is a very sad thing in a time so zealously pretending to reformation: That any quiet people should be punished and reproached, for worshiping and serving of God according to their conscience, and (that trouble house) Conformity as much Cried up as in the Bishops times.

That the Presse should be stopt in time of Parliament, as barring all free informations, and admitting only what appointed Lycencers shall allow; doth it not even breake the hearts of all knowing good People, to see the dores kept shut in Committees, and men examined against themselves, and for refusing to accuse themselves, sent to Prison; and that free Commoners, who by the Lawes of the Land, are not to be adjudged of life, limb, liberty or estate, but by Commoners: should at the pleasure of the Lords, be lyable to their summons, and attachment by Pursevants, to their Oath *ex officio*, to their examination in criminall causes, to selfe-accuseing, and to imprisonment during their pleasures, the chosen Commons of England, the SUPREAME POWER, standing by like a cypher, as unconcerned, meer lookers on; this is that which puts wise men past all patience, asking, for what it is that this Nation hath ingaged in such, in so deadly a war? For what it is so much precious blood hath been spilt, so many Families wasted, so much treasure consumed, so many Widowes and fatherlesse children made miserable? Is all this to take down the High Commission, Starchamber, and Councell-Board: and to set up the Lords with the like power, to oppresse the Commons? It had been well say they, this had been declared, when our Money, Plate, Horse, and voluntary Contributions, were first desired, But then other things were mentioned, though now neglected.

We had (say they) as many Lords before the Parliament as since, and it was often boasted they should remove our grievances, as well as a Parliament, but it was done by addition, and increase of more, not by Substraction; God forbid a Parliament should doe so. But why then (say they) are we now subjected to the Lords? Is it not sufficient that they are Lords over their Tennants, but they must be Lords over the People; that every one must be at their summons, at their command, at their imprisonment, yea to Newgate; why not whipping, gagging, hanging? Oh, they are but green in their power, and do not know what the People will beare, nor what the Peoples friend (that should be) the HOUSE OF COMMONS will suffer; hereafter may be time enough, they are yet the Peoples most gracious Lords, intending to the most knowing, faithfull and religious, no worse then Newgate for the present.

And why presume ye thus Oh ye Lords? Set forth your merit before the People, and say, for this good it is, that we will raign over yee. Remember your selves, or shall wee remember yee? Which of ye before this Parliament, minded anything so much as your pleasures? Playes, Masques, Feastings, Huntings, Gamings, Dauncings, with the appurtenances. If you owed any man money, or abused any man, what law was to be had against you? What Pattents and Projects did you suppresse, or so much as move against; (nay had not a hand in?) What fearfull enemies you were to Shipmoney, and to the proceedings of the High Commission, Star-chamber, and Councell board, indeed your goodnes was inexpressible, and undiscernable, before this Parliament.

But though you cannot excuse all, you will say, you that are the good Lords were then over topt with the evill, will you then be tryed by what good you have done since this Parliament, and since the expulsion of the Popish Lords and Bishops, where will you begin? What thinke you of the stay at Worcester, till the Enemy was provided at Shrewsbury, a shrewd begining for poor England? Or what thinke you of the Earle of Bedfords busines at Sherburn Castle, or of the enemies escape at Brainford, or at Oxford or at Dennington, and to close all with that memorable but shamefull defeat in the West; It must needs be remembred how the warre thrived, whilest any Lord was imployed: and how powerfull the enemy is grown, since the New Modell, wherein there is not one Lord.

It was wont to be said when a thing was spoil'd, that the Bishops Foot had been in it, and if the LORDS

MEND NOT, it will be said so of them, and justly too.

For what other have they been, but a meer Clog to the HOUSE OF COMMONS in all their proceedings? How many necessary things have they obstructed? How many evill things promoted? What devices have they had of prudentials and expedients, to delay and pervert what is good: and subtill policies to introduce things evill.

It is easie to discerne who are their Creatures in the House of Commons, and how they were made theirs, constantly manifesting themselves, by their evill and pernitious partakings against the Freedome of the People, by whose united endeavours, Monopolies in Trades of Merchandize, Oppressions in Committees, Corruptions in Courts of Justice, grosse abuses in our Lawes and Lawyers are maintained, and the Reformation intended in all things, performed by halves, nay, quite perverted, and a meer shadow given for a substance, to the astonishment of all knowing free born Englishmen, and to their perpetuall vexation and danger; Because to know, or find fault, or discover these things, to preserve just freedome, and to withstand their exorbitances: is the most hatefull thing to these Lords, of any thing in the world, Newgate (in their esteem) is too good for all such.

And this is the only crime for which this worthy man is made the subject of their malice, a man that hath discovered more of the liberties of England, then any one man alive; a man that hath resisted all kinds of Oppressions, with the perpetuall hazard of his life, liberty and estate.

And must no place but Newgate be his habitation? Is this the reparation for his damages, and recompence for his faithfull service? Must he be here reserved a sacrifice to appease the displeasure of the late reconciled enemies of the Common-wealth.

Thou do'st well O England, to give up this thy first-born LILBURNE, the SON of thy STRENGTH, and high RESOLUTION, for FREEDOME; If thou intendest to become a Bond slave again, to either King, Lords, or any others: for he will never submit either body or mind to any kind of slavery.

But certainly those Worthyes in the House of Commons, that consider what the People have done and suffered for their libertyes will never suffer so foule a deed, it cannot be but they intend the uttermost of just freedome to the People, and love those best, that most know and affect true liberty, and are greatest opposers of exorbitant power in whomsoever; and consequently cannot but instantly deliver this just man, and in him all Englishmen, from the like oppression; and henceforth reduce the Lords to a condicion suteable to the freedome of the People, and consistent with the freedome of Parliaments.

The People are become a Knowing and Judicious People, Affliction hath made them wise, now Opression maketh wise men mad, ther's no deluding wise men, it is all one to them, who oppresseth them, oppression they cannot but hate, and if Parliaments do in deed and in truth really deliver them, they will love Parliaments, as performing the trust reposed in them, and the end for which Parliaments were ordained, otherwise they will abominate them, because, for a people to be made slaves, by, or in time of Parliament, is like as for a man to be betrayed or murthered by his own father; which God of his mercy preserve both People and Parliaments from, and that for ever.

London June, 1646.

II

The Petition of March 1647

[This, usually known as the *Large Petition,* was printed and circulated for signatures in the first half of March. On March 15th it came into the hands of the House of Commons and was at once voted seditious. This, the first programmatic statement of the Levellers, was a collective work, though Walwyn probably had a major hand in it. Its history and that of its successors is outlined in *Gold Tried in the Fire* [IV].
Wolfe, pp. 135–141. Haller, III, pp. 399–405.]

To the
RIGHT
HONOURABLE
and
SUPREME
AUTHORITY
of this Nation,

the Commons in
PARLIAMENT
assembled.

The humble Petition of many thousands,
earnestly desiring the glory of God,
the freedome of the Common-wealth,
and the peace of
all men.

Sheweth,

THAT as no Civill Government is more just in the constitution, then that of Parliaments, having its foundation in the free choice of the people; and as the end of all Government is the safetie and freedome of the governed, even so the people of this Nation in all times have manifested most heartie affections unto Parliaments as the most proper remedie of their grievances; yet such hath been the wicked policies of those who from time to time have endeavoured to bring this Nation into bondage; that they have in all times either by the disuse or abuse of *Parliaments* deprived the people of their hopes: For testimony whereof the late times foregoing this *Parliament* will sadly witnesse, when it was not onely made a crime to mention a *Parliament,* but either the pretended negative voice, (the most destructive to freedome) or a speedie dissolution, blasted the fruit and benefit thereof, whilst the whole Land was overspread with all kinds of oppressions and tyranny, extending both to soule and body, and that in so rooted and setled a way, that the complaints of the people in generall witnessed, that they would have given any thing in the world for one six moneths freedome of *Parliament.* Which hath been since evidenced in their instant & constant readinesse of assistance to this present *Parliament,* exceeding the Records of former ages, and wherein God hath blessed them with their first desires, making this *Parliament* the most absolute and free of any *Parliament* that ever was, and enabling it with power sufficient to deliver the whole Nation from all kinds of oppressions and grievances, though of very long continuance, and to make it the most absolute and free Nation in the world.

And it is most thankfully acknowledged that ye have in order to the freedome of the people suppressed the high Commission, Star-Chamber, and Councell-Table, called home the banished, delivered such as were imprisoned for matters of conscience, and brought some Delinquents to deserved punishment. That ye have suppressed the *Bishops* and Popish *Lords,* abolished *Episcopacy,* and that kind of Prelatick persecuting government. That ye have taken away Ship-money and all the new illegall Patents, whereby the hearts of all the well-affected were enlarged and filled with a confident hope, that they should have seen long ere this a compleat removall of all grievances, and the whole people delivered from all oppressions over soule or body: But such is our miserie that after the expence of so much precious time, of blood and treasure, and the ruine of so many thousands of honest families in recovering our Liberties, we still find this Nation oppressed with grievances of the same destructive nature as formerly, though under other notions; and which are so much the more grievous unto us, because they are inflicted in the very time of this present *Parliament,* under God the hope of the oppressed. For, as then all the men and women in *England* were made liable to the summons, attachments, sentences, and imprisonments of the Lords of the Councell-boord, so we find by wofull experience and sufferings of many particular persons, that the present Lords doe assume and exercise the same power, then which nothing is, or can be more repugnant and destructive to the Commons just liberties.

As then the unjust power of *Star-Chamber* was exercised in compelling of men and women to answer to Interrogatories tending to accuse themselves and others; so is the same now frequently practiced upon divers persons, even your cordiall friends that have been, and still are punished for refusing to answer to questions against themselves, and nearest relations. As then the great oppression of the high Commission was most evident in molesting of godly peaceable people, for non-conformity, or different opinion and practice in Religion, judging all who were contrary-minded to themselves, to bee Hereticks, Sectaries, Schismaticks, seditious, factious, enemies to the State, and the like; and under great penalties forbidding all persons, not licenced by them, to preach or publish the Gospel: Even so now at this day, the very same, if not greater molestations, are set on foot, and violently prosecuted by the instigation of a Clergy no more infallible then the former, to the extreame discouragement and affliction of many thousands of your faithfull adherents, who are not satisfied that controversies in Religion, can be trusted to the compulsive regulation of any: And after the Bishops were suppressed, did hope never to have seen such a power assumed by any in this Nation any more.

And although all new illegall Patents are by you abolished, yet the oppressive Monopoly of Merchant-adventurers, and others, do still remain to the great abridgement of the liberties of the people, and to the extreme prejudice of all such industrious people as depend on cloathing, or other woollen manufacture, (it being the Staple commodity of this Nation,) and to the great discouragement and disadvantage of all sorts of Tradesmen, Sea-faring-men, and hindrance of Shipping and Navigation. Also the old tedious and chargable way of deciding controversies, or suits in Law, is continued to this day, to the extreame vexation and utter undoing of multiudes of Families; a grievance as great and as palpable as any in the world. Likewise, that old, but most unequall punishment of malefactors, is still continued, whereby mens lives and liberties are as liable to the law, and corporall pains as much inflicted for small as for great offences, and that most unjustly upon the testimony of one witnesse, contrary both to the law of God, and common equity, a grievance very great, but litle regarded. Also tythes, and other enforced maintenance are still continued, though there be no ground for either under the Gospel; and though the same have occasioned multitudes of suites, quarrels and debates, both in former and latter times. In like maner, multitudes of poore distressed prisoners for debt, ly still unregarded, in a most miserable and wofull condition throughout the Land, to the great reproach of this Nation. Likewise Prison-Keepers, or Goalers, are as presumptuous as ever they were, both in receiving and detaining of Prisoners illegally committed, as cruell and inhumane to all, especially to such as are well-affected, as oppressive and extorting in their Fees, and are attended with under-officers, of such vile and unchristian demeanour, as is most abominable. Also thousands of men and women are still (as formerly) permitted to live in beggery and wickednesse all their life long, and to breed their children to the same idle and vitious course of life, and no effectual meanes used to reclaim either, or to reduce them to any vertue or industry.

And last, as those who found themselves aggrieved formerly at the burdens & oppressions of those times, that did not conform to the Church-government then established, refused to pay Ship-money, or yeeld obedience to unjust Patents, were reviled and reproached with nicknames of Puritans, Hereticks, Schismaticks, Sectaries, or were tearmed factious or seditious, men of turbulent spirits, despisers of government, and disturbers of the publike peace; even so is it at this day in all respects, with those who shew any sensibility of the fore-recited grievances, or move in any manner or measure for remedy thereof, all the reproaches, evills, and mischiefs that can be devised, are thought too few or too little to bee laid upon them, as Roundheads, Sectaries, Independents, Hereticks, Schismaticks, factious, seditious, rebellious disturbers of the publike peace, destroyers of all civill relation, and subordinations; yea, and beyond what was formerly, nonconformity is now judged a sufficient cause to disable any person though of known fidelity, from bearing any Office of trust in the Common-wealth, whilest Neuters, Malignants, and disaffected are admitted and continued. And though it be not now made a crime to mention a *Parliament*, yet is it little lesse to mention the supreme power of this honourable House. So that in all these respects, this Nation remaineth in a very sad and disconsolate condition; and the more, because it is thus with us after so long a session of so powerfull and so free a *Parliament*, and which hath been so made and maintained, by the aboundant love and liberall effusion of the blood of the people. And therefore knowing no danger nor thraldome like unto our being left in this most sad condition by this *Parliament*, and observing that ye are now drawing the great and weighty affaires of this Nation to some kind of conclusion, and fearing that ye may ere long bee obstructed by somthing equally evill to a negative voice, and that ye may be induced to lay by that strength, which (under God) hath hitherto made you powerfull to all good workes: whilest we have yet time to hope, and yee power to help, and least by our silence we might be guilty of that ruine and slavery, which without your speedy help is like to fall upon us, your selves and the whole Nation; we have presumed to spread our cause thus plainely and largely before you: And do most earnestly entreat, that ye will stir up your affections to a zealous love and tender regard of the people, who have chosen and trusted you, and that ye will seriously consider, that the end of their trust, was freedome and deliverance from all kind of temporall grievances and oppressions.

1. And that therefore in the first place, ye will bee

exceeding carefull to preserve your just authority from all prejudices of a negative voice in any person or persons whomsoever, which may disable you from making that happy return unto the people which they justly expect, and that ye will not be induced to lay by your strength, untill ye have satisfied your understandings in the undoubted security of your selves, and of those who have voluntarily and faithfully adhered unto you in all your extremities; and untill yee have secured and setled the Common-wealth in solid peace and true freedome, which is the end of the primitive institution of all governments.

2. That ye will take off all Sentences, Fines and Imprisonments imposed on Commoners, by any whomsoever, without due course of Law, or judgement of their equalls: and to give due reparations to all those who have been so injuriously dealt withall, and for preventing the like for the time to come, that yee will enact all such Arbitrary proceedings to bee capitall crimes.

3. That ye will permit no authority whatsoever, to compell any person or persons to answer to questions against themselves, or nearest relations, except in cases of private interest between party and party in a legall way, and to release all such as suffer by imprisonment, or otherwise for refusing to answer to such Interrogatories.

4. That all Statutes, Oathes and Covenants may be repealed so farre as they tend, or may be construed to the molestation and ensnaring of religious, peaceable, well-affected people, for non-conformity, or different opinion or practice in Religion.

5. That no man for preaching or publishing his opinion in Religion in a peaceable way, may be punished or persecuted as hereticall, by Judges that are not infallible, but may be mistaken (as well as other men) in their judgements, least upon pretence of suppressing Errors, Sects or Schisms, the most necessary truths, and

sincere professors thereof may be suppressed, as upon the like pretence it hath been in all ages.

6. That ye will, for the encouragement of industrious people, dissolve that old oppressive Company of Merchant-Adventurers, and the like, and prevent all such others by great penalties for ever.

7. That yee will settle a just, speedy, plaine and unburthensome way, for deciding of controversies and suits in Law, and reduce all Lawes to the nearest agreement with Christianity, and publish them in the *English* Tongue, and that all processes and proceedings therein may be true and also in *English,* and in the most usuall Character of writing, without any abreviations, that each one who can read, may the better understand their owne affaires; and that the duty of all Judges, Officers, and practicers in the Law, and of all Magistrates and Officers in the Common-wealth may be prescribed, and their fees limited under strict penalties, and published in print to the view and knowledge of all men: by which just and equitable meanes, this Nation shall be for ever freed of an oppression more burthensome and troublesome then all the oppressions hitherto by this *Parliament* removed.

8. That the life of no person may be taken away, under the testimony of two witnesses at least, of honest conversation; and that in an equitable way ye will proportion punishments to offences, that so no mans life may be taken, his body punished, nor his estate forfeited, but upon such weighty and considerable causes as justly deserve such punishments; and that all prisoners may have a speedy tryall, that they be neither starved, nor their families ruined, by long and lingring imprisonment; and that imprisonment may be used onely for safe custody untill time of triall, and not as a punishment for offences.

9. That tythes and all other enforced maintenance, may be for ever abolished, and nothing in place thereof

imposed; but that all Ministers may be paid onely by those who voluntarily contribute to them, or chuse them, and contract with them for their labours.

10. That ye will take some speedy and effectuall course to relieve all such prisoners for debt, as are altogether unable to pay, that they may not perish in prison through the hard-heartednesse of their Creditors; and that all such as have any estates, may bee inforced to make paiment accordingly, and not to shelter themselves in prison to defraud their Creditors.

11. That none may be Prison-keepers, but such as are of approved honestie, and that they may be prohibited under great penalties to receive or detaine any person or persons without lawfull warrant: That their usage of prisoners may be with gentlenesse and civility, their fees moderate and certain, and that they may give security for the good behaviour of their under-Officers.

12. That ye will provide some powerfull meanes to keep men, women, and children from begging and wickednesse, that this Nation may be no longer a shame to Christianity therein.

13. That ye will restraine and discountenance the malice and impudency of impious persons, in their reviling and reproaching the well-affected, with the ignominious titles of Round-heads, factious, seditious and the like, whereby your reall friends have been a long time, and still are exceedingly wronged, discouraged, and made obnoxious to rude and prophane people, and that ye wil not exclude any of approved fidelity from bearing office of trust in the Common-wealth for nonconformity; but rather Neuters and such as manifest dis-affection or opposition to common freedome, the admission and continuation of such being the chief cause of all these our grievances.

These remedies, or what other shall seem more effectuall to your grave wisdomes, we humbly pray may be speedily applied, and that in doing thereof, ye will be confident of the assistance of your Petitioners, and of all considerate well-minded people, to the uttermost of their best abilities, against all opposition whatsoever, looking upon our selves as more concerned now at last to make a good end, then at the first to have made a good beginnning: For what shall it profit us, or what remedy can we expect, if now after so great troubles and miseries this Nation should be left by this Parliament in so great a thraldome, both of body, mind, and estate?

We beseech you therefore, that with all your might whilest he have time, freedome and power, so effectually to fulfill the true end of Parliaments in delivering this Nation from these and all other grievances, that none may presume or dare to introduce the like for ever.

And we trust, the God of your good successe, will manifest the integrity of our intentions herein, and that our humble desires are such, as tend not onely to our owne particular, but to the generall good of the Common-wealth, and proper for this Honourable House to grant, without which this Nation cannot be safe, or happy: And that he will blesse you with true Christian fortitude, suitable to the trust and greatnesse of the worke yee have undertaken, and make the memory of this Parliament blessed to all succeeding Generations.

Shall ever be the fervent desire of your humble Petitioners.

III

A Solemne Engagement
of the Army

[This *Engagement,* the manifesto adopted on Newmarket Heath on June 5th, 1647 pledging the Army not to
disband and setting up the Council of the Army, was
included in *A Copie of a Letter,* dated from St Albans
on June 21st and published in London a few days later.
It is a letter sent by the Agitators of nine regiments to
"all the honest Sea-men of England", setting out their
case and appealing for support. Generally speaking, the
Navy was far less politically advanced than the Army
and gave it little or no support.
Wolfe, pp. 146–151.]

A
SOLEMNE
ENGAGEMENT
OF THE ARMY,

under the Command of his Excellency Sir

Thomas Fairfax,

read, assented unto, and subscribed
by all Officers, and Souldiers
of the severall Regiments,
at the

generall
Rendezvouz

neare Newmarket,
on the fift of June,
1647.

WHEREAS upon the Petition intended and agreed upon in the Army, in *March* last, to have been presented to the Generall, for the obtaining of our due and necessary concernments as Souldiers; the Honorable House of *Commons* being unseasonably prepossessed with a Copie thereof, and (as by the sequell we suppose) with some strange misrepresentations of the carriage and intentions of the same, was induced to send downe an Order for surpressing the Petition, and within two or three dayes after, upon further misinformation, and scandalous suggestions, of the like or worse nature, and by the indirect practice of some malitious and mischievous persons (as we suppose) surprizing or other wise abusing the *Parliament*. A Declaration was published in the name of both Houses, highly censuring the said Petition, and declaring the Petitioners, if they should proceed thereupon, no lesse then enemies to the State, and disturbers of the publick peace. And whereas at the same time and since, divers eminent Officers of the Army have been brought into question and trouble about the said Petition, whereby both they and the rest of the Officers were disabled, or discouraged for the time, from further acting or appearing therein on the souldiers behalfe, And wheras by the aforesaid proceedings and the effects thereof, the souldiers of this Army (finding themselves so stopt in their due, and regular way of making knowne their just grievances, and desires to, and by their Officers) were enforced to an unusuall (but in that case necessary) way of correspondence and agreement amongst themselves, to chuse out of the severall Troops and Companies severall men, and those out of their whole number, to chuse two or more for each Regiment, to act in the name and behalfe of the whole souldiery of the respective Regiments Troops and Companies, in the prosecution of their rights and desires in the said Petition, as also of their just vindication and writing in reference to the aforesaid proceedings upon and against the same, who have accordingly acted and done many things, to those ends, all which the souldiers did then approve as their owne acts.

And whereas afterwards (upon the sudden sending down of Field-Marshall *Skippon,* and those other Officers of the Army that were Members of the House of Commons, to quiet distempers in the Army, fresh hopes being conceived of having our desires again admitted to be made known, and considered in a regular way, and without such misrepresentations as formerly, the Officers and Souldiers of the Army (except some few dissenting Officers) did againe joyne in a representation of their common grievances, and the Officers (except as before) did agree upon a narrative Accompt of the grounds, rise and growth of the discontents in the Army, and their proceedings in relation thereunto, with an overture of the best expedients, to remove or satisfie the same; both which were presented to the same Members of the House, and by them reported to the House. And wheras the Parliament having thereupon voted, and ordered some particulars, onely towards satisfaction of our grievances, hath since proceeded to certain resolutions of sudden disbanding the Army by peeces; which resolution being taken, and to be executed, before full or equall satisfaction given to the whole Army in any of the grievances, before effectuall performance of that satisfaction in part, which the preceding Votes seem'd to promise, as to some of the grievances, and before any consideration at all of some others most materiall, (as by the result of a generall Councell of Warre on Saturday *May* 29. was in generall declared, and is now more fully demonstrated in particular by a representation thereupon, agreed unto by us: we all cannot but look upon the same resolutions of disbanding us in such manner, as proceeding from the same malicious and mischievous principles and intentions, and from the like indirect practises of the same persons abusing the Parliament, and is as the former proceedings against us before mentioned did, and not without carnall and bloody purposes (for some of them have not stuck to declare or intimate) after the body of the Army should be disbanded, or the Souldiers divided from their Officers, then to question, proceed against, and execute their malicious intentions upon all such particular Officers and Souldiers in the Army, as had appeared to act in the Premises in the behalfe of the Army: And whereas upon a late Petition to the Generall from the Agitants, in behalfe of the Souldiers grounded upon the preceding considerations, relating to the same resolutions of disbanding, the same generall Councell of Warre to prevent the danger and inconveniences of those disturbings, or tumultuous actings or confluences which the dis-satisfaction and jealousie thereupon also grounded, were like suddenly to have produced in the Army, to advise the Generall first to contract the Quarters of the Army, and then to draw the same to an orderly *Rendezvouz* for the satisfaction of all, and that his Excellency would immediately send up to move and desire the Parliament to suspend any present proceeding upon the said resolution of disbanding, to resume the consideration of the grievances, and desire, sent up from the Army, and not to disband it in pieces before just and equall satisfaction given to the whole; And whereas some of the Regiments appointed for disbanding, upon notice thereof withdrawing themselves from the Quarters adjacent to the appointed Rendezvouz, and drawing towards the Head-Quarters; and the contracting their Quarters, according to the said advice of the Councel of War.

We the Officers and Souldiers of severall Regiments here after named, are now met at a generall Rendezvouz, and the Regiments appointed as afore-said to be disbanded, have not appeared, nor can appeare; but are resolved not to appeare at the severall and respective Rendezvouz, appointed as aforesaid for their disbanding; and divers other things have been done by severall other parties or members of the Army, necessarily relating to the good and concernment of the whole in those affaires. Now for as much as wee know not how far the malice, Injustice, and Tiranicall Principles of our enemies, that have already prevailed so far to abuse the Parliament and the Army (as is afore mentioned) in the past proceedings against the Army may further prevaile to the danger and prejudice of our selves, or any Officers, or Souldiers of the Army, or other persons that have appeared to act any thing in behalfe of the Army, or how far the same may further prevaile to the danger or prejudice of the Kingdome in raising a new warre, or otherwise: Therefore for the better prevention of all such dangers, prejudices, or other inconveniences that may ensue; and withall for better satisfaction to the Parliament and Kingdome, concerning our desires of conforming to the authority of the one, and providing the good and quiet of the other, in the present affaires of disbanding, and for a more assured way whereby, that affaires may come to a certaine issue, (to which purpose we herein humbly implore the present and continued assistance of God, the Righteous Iudge of all) wee the Officers and Souldiers of the Army subscribing hereunto; doe hereby declare, agree, and promise, to and with each other, and to, and with the Parliament and Kingdome as followeth.

1. That wee shall chearfully and readily disband when thereunto required by the Parliament, or else shall many of us be willing (if desired) to ingage in further

Services either in *England* or *Ireland*, having first such satisfaction to the Army in relation to our grievances and desires heretofore presented, and such security, That we of our selves, when disbanded, and in the condition of private men, or other the free-borne people of *England,* to whom the consequence of our case doth equally extend, shall not remain subject to the like oppression, injury, or abuse, as in the premisses hath been attempted and put upon us, while an Army by the same mens continuance, in the same credit and power, especially if as our Judges, who have in these past proceedings against the Army so farre prevailed to abuse the Parliament and us, and to endanger the Kingdome; and also such security that we our selves, or any member of this Army or others, who have appeared to act any thing in behalf of the Army, in relation to the premises before recited, shall not after disbanding be any way questioned, prosecuted, troubled, or prejudiced for any thing so acted, or for the entring into, or necessary prosecution of this necessary agreement: (we say) having first such satisfaction and security in these things as shall be agreed unto by a Councell to consist of those generall Officers of the Army (who have concurred with the Army in the premisses) with two Commission Officers and two Souldiers to be chosen for each Regiment, who have concurred and shall concur with us in the premisses and in this agreement. And by the major part of such of them who shal meet in Councel for that purpose when they shal be thereunto called by the General.

2. That without such satisfaction and security, as aforesaid, we shal not willingly disband, nor divide, nor suffer our selves to be disbanded or divided.

And whereas we find many strange things suggested or suspected to our great prejudice concerning dangerous principles, interests and designs in this Army (as to the overthrow of Magistracy, the suppression or hindering of Presbytery, the establishment of Independent government, or upholding of a general licentiousness in Religion under pretence of Liberty of Conscience, and many such things; we shal very shortly tender to the Parliament a Vindication of the Army from all such scandals to clear our Principles in relation thereunto, and in the mean time we do disavow and disclaim all purposes or designs in our late or present proceedings to advance or insist upon any such interest, neither would we (if we might and could) advance or set up any other particular party or interest in the Kingdom (though imagined never so much our own) but shal much rather (as far as may be within our sphear or power) study to promote such an establishment of common and equal right and freedom to the whole, as all might equally partake of but those that do by denying the same to others, or otherwise render themselves incapable thereof.

FINIS

IV
Gold Tried in the Fire

[This was evidently intended to serve as a general preface to the *Large Petition* [II] and the related petitions which followed it. However, that collection was never made and the pamphlet was published separately on June 14th, 1647. It gives an account of their rejection by Parliament and reflects the growing disillusion of the Levellers with the existing House of Commons. There is little doubt that its author was Walwyn, who had been the chief organiser of this petitioning.]

GOLD
TRIED IN THE
FIRE,
OR
The burnt
Petitions revived.

A Preface.

COURTEOUS Reader, I shall give thee a short Narative of some passages upon the following Petitions, first concerning the large Petition: Divers printed coppies thereof being sent abroad to gain subscriptions, one whereof was intercepted by an Informer, and so brought to the hands of Mr. Glyn Recorder of London, and a member of the Commons House: who was pleased to call it a scandalous, and seditious paper: Whereupon it was referred to Colonell Leighes Commitee (it being that Commitee appoynted to receive informations against those men who preached without licence from the Ordainers) to find out the Authours of the said Petition; upon this a certificate being drawn up, and intended by the Petitioners, to have been delivered to the said Commitee, for vindication of the said Petition, as will appeare by the certificate herewith printed; and notice being taken of one of the petitioners named Nicholas Tue, who red the said certificate in the Court of Request; for the Concurrence of friends who had not formerly seen nor subscribed the certificate: and for his so doing he was sent for presently before the said Commitee, and for refusing to answer to Interrogatories, was presently by them Committed, and still remaineth in prison, it being at the least three Moneths since his first commitment.

Likewise Major Tuledah, was upon complaint of that Commitee, the next day committed by the House; but since discharged upon baile, without any just cause shewn for either of their Commitments: and others of the Petitioners abused, and vilified by that Committee;

some of them offering to draw their swords upon the Petitioners. All which, with more was ready to be proved to the whole House, but could by no meanes be obtained, though earnestly desired, by a Petition, presently delivered into the House, humbly desiring the examination of these miscarriages; but after eight weekes attendance, with much importunity; after many promises and dayes appointed to take their Petition into consideration, they obtained a very slight answer: which was that they could not like of their Petition.

Occasion being taken sodainely after to commit one of the Petitioners named Mr. Browne to the prison of Newgate; for his importunity in desiring an answer to that Petition, after many promises and delayes. Shortly after the slight answer obtained to the said Petition, the Petitioners thought good to deliver a second Petition to the House, to see if it were possible to obtain a better answer to their just desires; hoping that they would better consider of things, but after attendance and importunity, they obtained an answer in these words. That the Parliament had Voted it a breach of priviledge, scandalous, and seditious, and that Petition, and the large Petition, to be burned by the hand of the Hangman; which was accordingly done by Order of the House, in these words.

Die Iovis 20 May, 1647,

Resolved &c. That the Sheriffes of London and Middlesex be required, to take care that the Petition and paper be burnt, which accordingly was done, before the Exchange, two dayes after the said Vote and Order of the House.

And shortly after this the Petitioners prepared a third Petition, which is the last Petition herewith printed: and after much importunity with the Members of the House; after almost two dayes attendance, obtained so much favour from one of the Members, as to present that Petition to the House, and after all this could obtaine no other answer to that Petition; but the House after long dispute thereupon passed this Vote.

Upon the 2d. of June, 1647. That no answer shall be given to the Petition at the present: and two dayes after the Petitioners attended the House, for a further answer delivering copies of their Petition to the severall Members of the House, but could obtaine no further answer thereunto; but received many vilifying, and disgracefull speeches, from severall Members of the House: and so after a whole dayes attendance, departed without any hope, to receive any answer to their just desires in the said Petition.

And thus I have faithfully, and truly (though briefly) given ye an account of the proceedings upon the ensuing Petitions. Now let the judicious and considerate Reader judge whether the Petitioners have received equall and even dealing herein from this present Parliament: the Petitioners being such who have laid out themselves, both in their persons and purses, far above their abilities; who have not valued their lives, their childrens lives, nor their servants lives, nor estates, to deare for the service of the Parliament, and Common-wealth.

And is this the reward they shall receive, after they have thus laid out them selves? Nay, they have just cause to feare that they and their friends are men appointed to utter ruine, and destruction; otherwise what meaneth all the rayling, reviling, and reproachfull speeches of their Ministers, and Agents, out of the pulpit and presse, to stirre up the rude multitude to fall upon them and destroy them; is not this ingratitude in the highest degree, shall not the very Heathen rise up in judgement against such a generation, of degenerate men as these? Who could say, *Si ingratum dixeris, omnia dixeris.*

You cannot chuse but take notice of severall Remonstrances, and Petitions presented to the House from these men, who call themselves Lord Mayor, Aldermen and Commons, of the City of London in Common-councell assembled, what high affronts they have offered to the Parliament; yet they have in some measure by steps, and degrees, answered the Remonstrances, and granted their Petitions, and you may observe what answer they have given to their last Petition, for raising of Horse, &c. (The tendencie whereof may be of very dangerous consequence if well weighed) which is thus. Mr. Speaker by command of the House, expresse unto them the true sense the House hath of their constant good affections to this Parliament; and that no alterations whatsoever can work any change in their duty, and love; for which he is to give them the hartiest thanks of this House.

I could enlarge my selfe, but I affect brevitie, and the judicious and considerate Reader, may enlarge himselfe in his own thoughts: well weighing the matter in the said Remonstrances, and Petitions; and upon due consideration may judge whether their Petitions, or the Petitions burnt, vilified, and disgraced, deserve most thanks, or tend most to the safetie of the Parliament, and Common-wealth.

And will henceforth conclude, that as there is little good to be hoped for from such Parliaments, as need to be Petitioned; so there is none at all to be expected from those that burn such Petitions as these.

If the endeavours of good Common-wealths-men in the House could have prevailed, these Petitions had not been burnt, nor the Petitioners abused; but the sons of Zerviah were to strong for them, that is to say, the Malignants, and Delinquents, the Lawyers (some few excepted) the Monopolising merchants, the sons and servants of the Lords; all these joyning together, over Voted them about 16 Voyces; but God in time, will we trust, deliver the people of this Nation, from their deceipt, and malice; and therefore let us not sorrow as men without hope, nor be discouraged, but goe on and persist, for the just liberties of England, a word to the wise is sufficient. Farewell.

By a well-wisher to truth and peace.

Printed in the yeere 1647.

V

The Poore Wise-mans Admonition

[Another of Walwyn's contributions to the campaign around the *Large Petition*. Its importance lies in its praise of the Army and its call for solidarity between soldiers and citizens. It marks the turn of the Levellers from Parliament to concentration upon the struggle in the Army. Published June 10th, 1647.]

The poore Wise-mans
ADMONITION

UNTO
All the plaine People
of *London,* and
the Neighbour-Places.

To strengthen
them in the houre of temptation,
that they may be happy and exemplary
instruments to all other People,
in preserving the City, Parliament,
and whole Nation,
from imminent and sudden
destruction.

[Quotations from *Eccles.* 37.16., *Prov.* 16.20.,
Eccles. 7.21., *Prov.* 1.32,33.]

Printed in the Yeere 1647.

Deare Friends;

ALTHOUGH ye and your families, are they who in all publike calamities do suffer most, yet seem ye altogether insensible of your owne danger untill it be directly upon you, yee looke not into publike affaires your selves, but trust wholly unto others; and if they either through weaknesse, wilfulnesse, corruption or treacherie faile in their trust or turne oppressors and tyrants, ye remaine liable to be deluded and betrayed by them into tumults, wars, miseries and bondage.

But believe it, yee have need to look about you, and that verie quickly, to see into affaires your selves, and understand how things go, for ye are likely very speedily to be put upon the greatest triall of your wisdom and faithfulnesse that ever men were put upon; which if ye withstand or get cleare through with an upright mind, your peace, freedome, and happinesse will certainly be continued, but if ye yeeld yee will involve yourselves, your wives, children and servants into far greater miseries and extremities then those ye have already past through.

The case is briefly and truly thus, ye remember in what a languishing distracted condition ye were in, before the warre was betrusted to the present Army, then called, The new Modell, and with what faithfulnesse, diligence, expedition and courage thay have vanquish'd the enemy, restored you to your trades and livelihoods, which ye cannot with any conscience, but thankfully acknowledge and remember.

But what they by their fidelity and activity gained abroad, is through want of care utterly destroyed at home; for whilst they supplant the enemy in strength, he is supplyed with authority, and so in effect made Master of that strength by which he hath been vanquished.

Ye will wonder how it should be so, and yet if yee shall judge the tree by the fruits, which is so infallible a rule that it cannot deceive you, ye shall find nothing more evident.

For, what Authority now extant can ye name, that affords this Army any countenance or encouragement? nay, that hath not manifested a jealousie and hatred of them, and that most unjustly, seeing the Army is still the same it was, minding the safety, peace, freedome and happinesse of all peaceable people without any difference at all.

But herein it consisteth, Authority is changed and hath proposed other ends to it selfe now at last, then when this Army was first raised; those men that saw a necessity of their raising, which appeared from the languishing condition of the Kingdome under the former Forces, had then the major Vote and the opposite party were esteemed dis-affected favourers of the enemy, Remora's to the honest proceedings of the House at that time, but are now become by the addition of divers ill affected men of knowne malignity out of the quarters redeemed from the enemy, the swaying party weigh down the ballance, and decree all.

From hence proceeds this different aspect upon the Army; the late bitter Declaration against them for endeavouring to petition their owne Generall in an orderly and peaceable way, for that which many by their losse of health, and all of them by induring the hardships and extremities of war, and hazarding their lives, have dearly earned; these are now judged enemies to the State, disturbers of the peace, even of purpose to turn the faces of honest men against them, and all to maintaine the unjust cause, and work out the wicked designes of tyrants and oppressors.

Divers men by corruptions are growne rich, from small estates or nothing to be very wealthy; and finding that this Army and such as love them, because they love their Country, are inquisitive and unwilling to see the State abused, and the people defrauded, fearing that the mountaines of wealth they have raised, may yet be returned to their right owners, or the common stock, and that their unjust actions may undergo scrutiny and tryall, have for prevention thereof, desperately resolved to embroyle us in a new warre, and bring all to the former confusion, if not utter desolation; finding by experience, that they can fish best in troubled waters, and escape best in the presse; that corruption and injustice is no otherwise mantainable, but by might and force, and for that very end and purpose have contrived to engage you against the Army, and those that wish them well, by which policie they suppose all your thoughts wil be diverted from thinking upon them and their corruptions.

In order to this, the Army and their friends are made odious to you, as Secretaries, even as heretofore the wel-affected party were rendered hateful to you as Puritans; they provoke the Army what they can, by declaring them disturbers of the peace, molesting divers of their Officers and Souldiers, sleighting petitions of many thousands of good and godly people, and burning some of them by the common Hang-man, and by many other signes giving them to see what they and their friends are like to suffer after disbanding, hoping hereby to put them upon extremitie, and enforce them to stand upon their guard, and capitulate for their safety, which they will interpret rebellion, and hold forth to you as a true ground of destroying them, inciting you from thence to take up Armes, and engage in their unjust quarrell, even for the maintenance of their exorbitant wills, and ambitious ends, yea and defence of their lives and ill-gotten estates.

The heads of this designe are the corrupt men in the House of Commons, even such as have been formerly of the enemies party abroad, and done him services here at home, by discovering our counsels (as appeareth by interception of some of their letters,) partaking with the conspirators in the City (as in Wallers plot) opposing the raising of this Army, (by which the worke hath been so speedily ended) appearing crosse in all debates of the House for redresse of grievances, or relief of the oppressed and much abused people, constantly manifesting, That they have proposed other ends to themselves, then the common good of the Nation.

Assistant to these is the Mayor of London, hitherto past over, (when the well-affected party had most sway in the City) as a man favouring the enemy, and never manifesting any affection to the Parliament, in their undertaking to make us a free people; also many of the Aldermen and great men of the Citie whose interest depends upon Prerogative, and is supported by the subjection of the plaine people.

The City Militia likewise in reference to this project was altered, because the former men who had shewed themselves faithfull to the Common-wealth and City, were not (it seems) judged fit instruments for this secret work; and yee the Commoners of London likewise, they hope, will by some deceitfull trick or other follow, though to the destruction of your selves, your wives and families.

This makes them so confidently give out, that if the Army will not disband, that ye the plaine men of this City, your sons and servants shall make a new Army to compell them; they verily thinke yee are not so well principled as to collect your thoughts (on such a sudden as they intend to surprize you) and consider what a dangerous businesse to the whole Kingdome ye go about, but that ye will doe it for no other reason, but because they bid you: that ye will forget the good services that the Army have done, the speedie overthrow of a power-full enemy, the so sudden recovery of trading by the ending of a long and languishing warre, which if continued, had in probability utterly wasted your Traine-Bands, and hazzarded the ruine both of City and King-dome.

These benefits (they think) they can easily make you forget, with old tales of private mens preaching, Conventicles, rebaptizing; and now by clamours of rebellion, and contempt of authority, which both the present necessity, and the common safety of the People requireth as a duty, and is purposely procured by themselves, for the maintenance of their tyranny and corruptions.

But look back into what is past, and survey the actions of these men, their weekly donations of great summes amongst themselves, their pride and Lordlinesse: Compare them with the Army; see if the Army have not made themselves poor, to make the Common-wealth rich, whilest these men have made themselves rich and us poore.

Consider whether these men, and their Agents, who shall be most forward to egg you on, and cry an Alarme, have not made advantages of your troubles, swolne great by the losse of your Friends and Neighbours bloods, whilest they that ingaged most heartily, are disrespected, the poor Souldiers unpaid, the widdow and fatherlesse by warre little regarded, so small recompence made, as there is scarce a livelihood afforded to them that have lost their limbs out of affection to their Countrey, whilest those that shall appeare most earnest for a new warre, are such as know the way very well how to thrive by it, have gained thousands by the former, found the sweetnesse of having the Common-wealths money at their dispose: And as they have been liberall every week, in converting the Common-wealths Treasury to their owne particular coffers, so hope they (with all possible speed, and by all indirect means) to be yet more bountifull, and for every hundred, give one another a thousand.

Consider, that warres are easily and suddenly, and out of a heat begun, but very hardly and slowly ended: Let late experience make us wise, so to foresee evills, as we may prevent them. The Scots will be ingaged againe, and forraigne Forces called in, which is already attempted by private Agents, from the aforesaid corrupt and ill-affected party in the Parliament.

This Citie may avoid all their malice, and crush all their wicked designes in the birth, before they come forth, if they will but abate their unjust and causelesse eagernesse against men of different opinions, and equally consider the just cause, desires and intentions of the Armie, and the peaceablenesse of those people in the Citie and Countrey, who did lately petition for libertie, and that their ends herein are evidently the good and peace of all men.

Take it to heart also, that we are in as much bondage as before this Parliament; all sorts of men are insensible of it, and full of complaints; the very oppressions cried out upon at the beginning of this Parliament, and removed, are not onely now again practised, but many new ones brought upon us; besides that which alone amounts to all the rest, the EXCISE, which (upon pretence of paying publike debts, and supplying other to-be-invented necessities) is like to be a lasting burden upon us.

Customes are still as much inhanced as ever, without any convoy and protection of Merchants, which is the end of paying them, and the poore Seamen and Marriners wrack'd to the utmost point of extreamity: infinite sums have been dispended, and yet debts both unpaid, and the publike Treasury emptied.

Consider the grievances complained of in the late Petition which was burned, and collect from thence what usage ye are like to finde, unlesse ye resolve to sit downe under oppression, and expect no redresse of grievances, which those honest men petitioning for in a discreet, peaceable, and humble manner, were abused, reproached, some of them imprisoned, the rest threatned, all termed seditious, and what not, even as men formerly were for moving against Ship-money, and the oppressions of those times.

In this lamentable condition, the honest and plaine people being still now, as they were then, in greatest danger, and wicked men most secure, and not only most countenanced by Authority, but endeavoured to be brought into all places thereof; judge, ye citizens of London, and other neighbour-places, whether the Army have not just cause, to stand upon their guard, and whether it be not high time for them again to appear for the defence and protection of the distressed people of this land; judge likewise what kind of enemies to the common wealth, peace, freedom, and safety of this Nation they are that shal oppose them herein, how inexcusable and evidently guilty of procuring their owne bondage, and maintaining abused authority, to their owne misery, if not destruction: yet this is the strong temptation wherewith ye are likely very suddenly to be assaulted.

The bait they will use will be the suppressing of Hereticks and Schismaticks, which henceforth ye shall find to be but nick-names for any that oppose Tyrants and Oppressors, by which they have ever endeavoured to make those odious to the rude multitude, whose honestie and conscience could not otherwise be blemished.

Looke therefore with a cleare eye upon the Army and those that love and affect them, whether in Parliament or elsewhere, and see if they be not the truest promoters of just freedome, least advancers of themselves; and when ye are tried, may ye prove like gold seven times fined in the fire; so shall your wisdome, faithfulnesse, thankfulnesse and integrity appeare in this sad day of Englands greatest extremity, when a major vote of Parliament must of necessity be disobeyed.

But this is an age of wonders: what greater wonder I pray, is there in this Nation, then a continuall Parliament, already drawing to the end of the seventh yeare; or that this Parliament should begin in suppressing the High-commission, Star-chamber, Bishops, Popish Lords and all oppressors, make a most bloody war against them, subdue them by a faithfull Army, and now act, tolerate, and justifie the same oppressions, under other notions, hate none so much as those that abhor oppression, and likewise vex, molest, and suffer to be hanged those very Souldiers that preserved their own lives, even in their greatest extremities, and that for actions necessarily and warrantably performed in prosecution of their own services.

And because all admonitions are most acceptable when the causes thereof are cleared, and proved to be good and just, by true examples, and forcible reasons, I will give an instance for your better satisfaction, in the things whereof I forewarne you, and so fore-arme you, Yee cannot but remember, that as those peaceable people who were at the beginning of this Parliament, called Round-heads, and afterwards Independents, and by such other Titles as best please the Clergy to devise, and the rude multitude to expresse, did adventure their lives voluntarily day and night, in guarding and defending the Parliament against all their enemies, who were like to swallow them up, before they had either guard or Army to take their part; and did not this worthy Army the like unto them, when no other Army could doe the businesse?

Did not yee your selves, and many thousands of others, bestow a great part of your estates freely and voluntarily to help, further, and assist the Parliament in all their publick affaires for the Common-weale, and safety of the people: and yet now, who are more despised, hated and persecuted by means or conivance of the Parliament, then both yee, they, and the Army, who have been their truest and best friends? And likewise, who have been more assessed and extorted in advancing more and more summes to fill their Coffers, then those who gave them most freely and liberally at the first; yea, and too many of them more then they could well spare.

Therefore, deare friends, remember this seasonable and loving premonition, while it is yet time, that when yee have done all yee can, and perhaps past the bounds of your abilities, yee may easily perceive both by former experience your selves, and infinite discontents, murmurings and out-cries of others, that if yee doe not persist both in fulfilling their wils in what they wil command concerning your bodies, and in yeelding what they will demand of your Estates, yea, or refuse them in any jot, or trifle they require, though never so unjust, ye will be subject to loose all ye have done, and their favour too.

These are wonders indeed, besides hundreds of others which might be expressed; but these if well weighed, will put you upon examination how it is possible such things as these should be.

The Army doubtlesse doth highly esteme the authority of Parliament, being rightly constituted, and intending the well-fare and safety of the people, and such a Parliament both the Army and the well-affected of the Kingdome thought this would have proved; for which they have fought, as for their own and the peoples liberties.

But when through the policies, feastings, private letters, making use of interests and relations, with many other indirect practices, elections shall be corrupted, and not freely made by the people, but in effect the one part of the Parliament procure the election of the other, when by meanes hereof the ill affected party is growne most potent, and the peoples faithfull friends are overpowred, when their courses shall tend evidently to make themselves great, upon the peoples ruins, even to prevent the end for which a Parliament is called, is there any just cause to the contrary, but the same necessity and publike safety that justifieth the Parliament against the King, will also justifie the Army against them, by the same rule of right reason, and law of equity, as the souldiers of an Army may oppose the Generall, when he turneth the mouth of his Cannon upon them.

And all this the Army do not against, but for Parliaments, as the onely orderly meanes for the peoples safety, and freedome now in such a high time of extreame danger, after the tryall of all other lawfull and possible faire and submissive meanes.

It is not to be imagined, that the Army meaneth in any wise to usurpe the government, or give lawes to their brethren; nothing can be more odious to their spirits, or further from their thoughts: their ayme is only to rescue and succour the people that are oppressed, and defend themselves from the malicious plots and practices of wicked men, untill such time as the right constitution of Parliaments be recovered, the Accompt of the Kingdomes Treasury required, and the Authors of our miseries according to justice punished.

The obstruction whereunto is a great number of tyrannicall and oppressive men in the House, against whom just exceptions will be evidently made appeare to all the world; if upon offer of proofe, all these enormities should be set into a way of tryall, this great and much threatning designe, may be prevented, without trouble, warre or bloodshed, wherein it rests in you at this time to do very much.

If ye forbeare to engage against the Army, whom God hath made his instruments to deliver you, and withall, second their just desires for purging out the corrupt Members of the Parliament, ye will not onely herein be an example of wisdome, fidelity and integrity to the whole Nation, but prevent a world of mischiefe and inconvenience, which otherwise might come to passe by your negligence, or rather slavish obedience.

Ye cannot but perceive, that in the great alteration which is made of the Committee of the Militia and the removall of your knowne Commanders in the forces of London, that they intend to engage you against the Army. Is not this evident to all judicious men? For what neede is there of any such change now at this time, and that onely of such persons as are affected to the Army?

Let not faire shewes or pretences of zeale, religion, or reformation of whatsoever kinde any longer delude you, but observe him for a traitor to his Countrey, that would now entangle you in any unjust warre against a most worthy Army, whom God hath so exceedingly blessed, yea and you also and all of us, by their faithfull meanes and effectuall endeavours.

Looke wisely and narrowly to your Officers of trust in all places, and see that they bring forth fruits suitable to your peace, preservation, and freedome, or else shun them as serpents, whose property is to destroy you.

Be not deluded into a groundlesse beliefe, that the Army do intend any kinde of prejudice to any just interest, or propriety in the Common wealth, seeing they have manifested both by word and deed to the world, in despite of the mallice of all their treacherous enemies (though pretended friends) that the outmost extent of their desires, is onely to see equity and justice florish in all Estates, so that no man may be punished under the colour of law or otherwise, without a just cause.

Allow the Army to be as free Englishmen as any whosoever, and your worthy and beloved brethren; have not many of you fought, shed your blood, and adventured your lives in the very same just cause for which they most couragiously do yet (through Gods goodnesse) stand. And would yee now unjustly resigne both that good cause, and so renowned an Army, into the treacherous and bloody hands of such as maliciously hate

133

both them and you, howsoever, they may flatter you at this time for their own base ends, but neither for your own nor the Kingdomes good.

God forbid that so just a cause which hitherto hath been so valiantly prosecuted, should escape so many and violent stormes, and cruell tempests in the main Ocean, and yet perish in the Harber, and that only for want of prudence and timely care.

But our hope is, that the same just and good God, who hath hitherto preserved you, the Army, Citie, Parliament, and just cause, will also in his due and appointed time, to his own everlasting praise, and the comfort of all that trust in him, perfect his great worke in justice and righteousness, if in the mean time yee will be so truly wise, as to be thankfull for mercies received, and not forgetfull of the worthy instruments he hath employed for your preservation, but doe them good to your utmost abilitiese in the day of their visitation.

So shall God crown all your labours of love with peace, and both your selves, the whole Nation and posterity with freedome.

Amen.

The Printer to the Reader.

I Desire thee to amend with thy pen, one fault escaped in the printing, by negligence, and the Authors absence, which is in the 3. page and 10. line, namely secretaries for sectaries: And if there be any more faults (as none liveth without some) I also desire that thou wilt shew thy patience by thy silence, and that thou may rather make a profitable use of the sence, then anywise strive about words; even as thou wouldest except the like favour of me or any other in thy absence, if thou be one that shewest thy selfe thus carefull and zealous for the publike: especially now in such extreeme need. Farewell.

FINIS.

VI

An Agreement of the People

[*The Case of the Armie Truly Stated* (October 15th, 1647) had demanded "a law paramount to be made ... unalterable by Parliaments". This involved, for the first time in England, a written constitution, and the first draft of such a constitution was this version of the *Agreement*. It was probably written during the week before it was debated by the Council of the Army at Putney on October 29th. It appeared in London as a printed pamphlet on November 3rd. Its authorship is uncertain: it is impossible to determine how far it was actually drafted by the Agitators who signed it and how far by the Leveller leaders in London. We may assume that the part of the latter was considerable.
Wolfe, pp. 225–234.]

AN
AGREEMENT
OF THE
PEOPLE
FOR

A firme and present Peace, upon
grounds of common-right and freedome;

As it was proposed by the Agents of the five
Regiments of Horse; and since by the generall approbation of the Army, offered to the joynt concurrence of all the free COMMONS of
ENGLAND.

The Names of the Regiments which have already
appeared for the Case,
of *The Case of the Army truly stated,*
and for this present Agreement, *V I Z.*

1. Gen. Regiment.		1. Gen. Regiment.	
2. Life-Guard.		2. Col. Sir Hardresse	
3. Lieut. Gen. Regiment.		Wallers Reg.	
4. Com. Gen. Regiment.	Of	3. Col. Lamberts Reg.	Of
5. Col. Whaleyes Reg.	Horse	4. Col. Rainsboroughs	Foot.
6. Col. Riches Reg.		Regiment.	
7. Col. Fleetwoods Reg.		5. Col. Overtons Reg.	
8. Col. Harrisons Reg.		6. Col. Lilburns Reg.	
9. Col. Twisldens Reg.		7. Col. Backsters Reg.	

Printed *Anno. Dom.* 1647.

HAVING by our late labours and hazards made it appeare to the world at how high a rate wee value our just freedome, and God having so far owned our cause, as to deliver the Enemies thereof into our hands: We do now hold our selves bound in mutual duty to each other, to take the best care we can for the future, to avoid both the danger of returning into a slavish condition, and the chargable remedy of another war: for as it cannot be imagined that so many of our Country-men would have opposed us in this quarrel, if they had understood their owne good; so may we safely promise to our selves, that when our Common Rights and liberties shall be cleared, their endeavours will be disappointed, that seek to make themselves our Masters: since therefore our former oppressions, and scarce yet ended troubles have beene occasioned, either by want of frequent Nationall meetings in Councell, or by rendring those meetings ineffectuall; We are fully agreed and resolved, to provide that hereafter our Representatives be neither left to an uncertainty for the time, nor made uselesse to the ends for which they are intended: In order whereunto we declare.

I.

That the People of England being at this day very unequally distributed by Counties, Cities, & Burroughs, for the election of their Deputies in Parliament, ought to be more indifferently proportioned, according to the number of the Inhabitants: the circumstances whereof, for number, place, and manner, are to be set down before the end of this present Parliament.

II.

That to prevent the many inconveniences apparently arising from the long continuance of the same persons in authority, this present Parliament be dissolved upon the last day of September, which shall be in the year of our Lord, 1648.

III.

That the People do of course chuse themselves a Parliament once in two yeares, *viz.* upon the first Thursday in every 2d. March, after the manner as shall be prescribed before the end of this Parliament, to begin to sit upon the first Thursday in Aprill following at Westminster, or such other place as shall bee appointed from time to time by the preceding Representatives; and to continue till the last day of September, then next ensuing, and no longer.

IV.

That the power of this, and all future Representatives of this Nation, is inferiour only to theirs who chuse them, and doth extend, without the consent or concurrence of any other person or persons; to the enacting, altering, and repealing of Lawes; to the erecting and abolishing of Offices and Courts; to the appointing, removing, and calling to account Magistrates, and Officers of all degrees; to the making War and peace, to the treating with forraign States: And generally, to whatsoever is not expresly, or implyedly reserved by the represented to themselves.

Which are as followeth,

1. That matters of Religion, and the wayes of Gods Worship, are not at all intrusted by us to any humane power, because therein wee cannot remit or exceed a tittle of what our Consciences dictate to be the mind of God, without wilfull sinne: neverthelesse the publike

way of instructing the Nation (so it be not compulsive) is referred to their discretion.

2. That the matter of impresting and constraining any of us to serve in the warres, is against our freedome; and therefore we do not allow it in our Representatives; the rather, because money (the sinews of war) being alwayes at their disposall, they can never want numbers of men, apt enough to engage in any just cause.

3. That after the dissolution of this present Parliament, no person be at any time questioned for anything said or done, in reference to the late publike differences, otherwise then in execution of the Judgments of the present Representatives, or House of Commons.

4. That in all Laws made, or to be made, every person may be bound alike, and that no Tenure, Estate, Charter, Degree, Birth, or place, do confer any exemption from the ordinary Course of Legall proceedings, whereunto others are subjected.

5. That as the Laws ought to be equall, so they must be good, and not evidently destructive to the safety and well-being of the people.

These things we declare to be our native Rights, *and therefore are agreed and resolved to maintain them with our utmost possibilities, against all opposition whatsoever, being compelled thereunto, not only by the examples of our Ancestors, whose bloud was often spent in vain for the recovery of their Freedomes, suffering themselves,* through fradulent accommodations, *to be still deluded of the fruit of their Victories, but also by our own wofull experience, who having long expected, & dearly earned the establishment of these certain rules of Government are yet made to depend for the settlement of our Peace and Freedome, upon him that intended our bondage, and brought a cruell Warre upon us.*

For the noble and highly honoured the Free-born People of ENGLAND, in their respective Counties and Divisions, these.

Deare Country-men, and fellow-Commoners,
For your sakes, our friends, estates and lives, have not been deare to us; for your safety and freedom we have cheerfully indured hard Labours and run most desperate hazards, and in comparison to your peace and freedome we neither doe nor ever shall value our dearest bloud and wee. professe, our bowells are and have been troubled, and our hearts pained within us, in seeing & considering that you have been so long bereaved of these fruites and ends of all our labours and hazards, wee cannot but sympathize with you in your miseries and oppressions. It's greife and vexation of heart to us; to receive your meate or moneyes, whilest you have no advantage, nor yet the foundations of your peace and freedom surely layed: and therefore upon most serious considerations, that your principall right most essentiall to your well-being is the clearnes, certaintie, sufficiencie and freedom of your power in your representatives in Parliament, and considering that the original of most of your oppressions & miseries hath been either from the obscuritie and doubtfulnes of the power you have committed to your representatives in your elections, or from the want of courage in those whom you have betrusted to claime and exercise their power, which might probably proceed from their uncertaintie of your assistance and maintenance of their power, and minding that for this right of yours and ours wee engaged our lives; for the King raised the warre against you and your Parliament, upon this ground, that hee would not suffer your representatives to provide for your peace safetie and freedom that were then in danger, by disposing of the *Militia* and otherwise, according to their trust; and for the maintenance and defense of that pow-

er and right of yours, wee hazarded all that was deare
to us, and God hath borne witnesse to the justice of our
Cause. And further minding that the only effectual
meanes to settle a just and lasting peace, to obtaine remedie for all your greivances, & to prevent future oppressions, is the making clear & secure the power that
you betrust to your representatives in Parliament, that
they may know their trust, in the faithfull execution
whereof you wil assist them. Vpon all these grounds, we
propound your joyning with us in the agreement herewith sent unto you; that by vertue thereof, we may have
Parliaments certainly cal'd and have the time of their
sitting & ending certain & their power or trust cleare
and unquestionable, that hereafter they may remove
your burdens, & secure your rights, without oppositions
or obstructions, & that the foundations of your peace
may be so free from uncertainty, that there may be no
grounds for future quarrels, or contentions to occasion
warre and bloud-shed; & wee desire you would consider,
that as these things wherein we offer to agree with you,
are the fruites & ends of the Victories which God hath
given us: so the settlement of these are the most absolute meanes to preserve you & your Posterity, from slavery, oppression, distraction, & trouble; by this, those
whom your selves shall chuse, shall have power to restore you to, and secur you in, all your rights; & they
shall be in a capacity to tast of subjection, as well as
rule, & so shall be equally concerned with your selves,
in all they do. For they must equally suffer with you
under any common burdens, & partake with you in any
freedoms; & by this they shal be disinabled to defraud
or wrong you, when the lawes shall bind all alike, without priviledge or exemption; & by this your Consciences shall be free from tyrannie & oppression, &
those occasions of endlesse strifes, & bloudy warres, shall
be perfectly removed: without controversie by your joyning with us in this Agreement, all your particular &

common grievances will be redressed forthwith without delay; the Parliament must then make your reliefe and common good their only study.

Now because we are earnestly desirous of the peace and good of all our Country-men, even of those that have opposed us, and would to our utmost possibility provide for perfect peace and freedome, & prevent all suites, debates, & contentions that may happen amongst you, in relation to the late war: we have therefore inserted it into this Agreement, that no person shall be questionable for any thing done, in relation to the late publike differences, after the dissolution of this present Parliament, further then in execution of their judgment; that thereby all may be secure from all sufferings for what they have done, & not liable hereafter to be troubled or punished by the judgment of another Parliament, which may be to their ruine, unlesse this Agreement be joyned in, whereby any acts of indempnity or oblivion shalbe made unalterable, and you and your posterities be secure.

But if any shall enquire why we should desire to joyn in an Agreement with the people, to declare these to be our native Rights, & not rather petition to the Parliament for them; the reason is evident: No Act of Parliament is or can be unalterable, and so cannot be sufficient security to save you or us harmlesse, from what another Parliament may determine, if it should be corrupted; and besides Parliaments are to receive the extent of their power, and trust from those that betrust them; and therefore the people are to declare what their power and trust is, which is the intent of this Agreement; and its to be observed, that though there hath formerly been many Acts of Parliament, for the calling of Parliaments every yeare, yet you have been deprived of them, and inslaved through want of them, and therefore both neccessity for your security in these freedomes, that are essentiall to your well-being, and wofull experience of the manifold miseries and distractions that have been lengthened out since the war ended, through want of such a settlement, requires this Agreement and when you and we shall be joyned together therein, we shall readily joyn with you, to petition the Parliament, as they are our fellow Commoners equally concerned, to joyn with us.

And if any shall inquire, Why we undertake to offer this Agreement, we must professe, we are sensible that you have been so often deceived with Declarations and Remonstrances, and fed with vain hopes that you have sufficient reason to abandon all confidence in any persons whatsoever, from whom you have no other security of their intending your freedome, then bare Declaration: And therefore, as our consciences witnesse, that in simplicity and integrity of heart, we have proposed lately in the Case of the Army stated, your freedome and deliverance from slavery, oppression, and all burdens: so we desire to give you satisfying assurance thereof by this Agreement wherby the foundations of your freedomes provided in the Case, &c. shall be setled unalterably, & we shall as faithfully proceed to, and all other most vigorus actings for your good that God shall direct and enable us unto; And though the malice of our enemies, and such as they delude, would blast us by scandalls, aspersing us with designes of Anarchy, and community; yet we hope the righteous God will not onely by this our present desire of setling an equall just Government, but also by directing us unto all righteous undertakings, simply for publike good, make our uprightnesse and faithfulnesse to the interest of all our Countreymen, shine forth so clearly, that malice it selfe shall be silenced, and confounded. We question not, but the longing expectation of a firme peace, will incite you to the most speedy joyning in this Agreement: in the prosecution whereof, or of any thing that you shall desire for publike good; you may be confident, you shall never want the assistance of

Your most faithfull fellow-Commoners, now in Armes for your service.

Edmond Bear	⎱ Lieut. Gen. Regiment.
Robert Everard	⎰
George Garret	⎱ Com. Gen. Regiment.
Thomas beverley	⎰
William Pryor	⎱ Col. Fleetwoods Regiment.
William Bryan	⎰
Matthew Weale	⎱ Col. Whalies Regiment.
William Russell	⎰
John Dover	⎱ Col. Riches Regiment.
William Hudson.	⎰

Agents coming from other Regiments unto us, have subscribed the Agreement to be proposed to their respective Regiments, and you.

For Our much honoured, and truly worthy Fellow-Commoners, and Souldiers, the Officers and Souldiers under Command of His Excellencie Sir T H O M A S F A I R F A X.

Gentlemen and Fellow Souldiers;
The deepe sense of many dangers and mischiefes that may befall you in relation to the late War, whensoever this Parliament shall end, unlesse sufficient prevention be now provided, hath constrained Us to study the most absolute & certain means for your security; and upon most serious considerations, we judge that no Act of Indempnity can sufficiently provide for your quiet, ease, and safety; because, as it hath formerly been, a corrupt Party (chosen into the next Parliament by your Enemies meanes) may possibly surprize the house, and make any Act of Indemnity null, seeing they cannot faile of the Kings Assistance and concurrence, in any such actings against you, that conquered him.

And by the same meanes, your freedome from impressing also, may in a short time be taken from you, though for the present, it should be granted; wee apprehend no other security, by which you shall be saved harmlesse, for what you have done in the late warre, then a mutuall Agreement between the people & you, that no person shall be questioned by any Authority whatsoever, for any thing done in relation to the late publike differences, after the dissolution of the present house of Commons, further then in execution of their judgment; and that your native freedome from constraint to serve in warre, whether domestick or forraign, shall never be subject to the power of *Parliaments,* or any other; and for this end, we propound the Agreement that we herewith send to you, to be forthwith subscribed.

And because we are confident, that in judgment and Conscience, ye hazarded your lives for the settlement of such a just and equall Government, that you and your posterities, and all the free borne people of this Nation might enjoy justice & freedome, and that you are really sensible that the distractions, oppressions, and miseries of the Nation, and your want of your Arreares, do proceed from the want of the establishment, both of such certain rules of just Government, and foundations of peace, as are the price of bloud, and the expected fruites of all the peoples cost: Therefore in this Agreement wee have inserted the certaine Rules of equall Government, under which the Nation may enjoy all its Rights and Freedomes securely; And as we doubt not but your love to the freedome and lasting peace of the yet distracted Country will cause you to joyn together in this Agreement.

So we question not: but every true English man that loves the peace and freedome of England will concurre with us; and then your Arrears and constant pay (while you continue in Armes) will certainly be brought in out of the abundant love of the people to you. and then shall the mouthes of those be stopped, that scandalize you and us, as endeavouring Anarchy, or to rule by the sword; & then will so firm an union be made between the people and you, that neither any homebred or forraigne Enemies will dare to disturbe our happy peace. We shall adde no more but this; that the knowledge of your union in laying this foundation of peace, this Agreement, is much longed for, by

Yours, and the Peoples most faithfull Servants.

Postscript.

GENTLEMEN.

We desire you may understand the reason of our extracting some principles of common freedome out of those many things proposed to you in the Case truly stated, and drawing them up into the forme of an Agreement. Its chiefly because for these things wee first ingaged gainst the King, He would not permit the peoples Representatives to provide for the Nations safety, by disposing of the Militia, and otherwayes, according to their Trust, but raised a Warre against them, and we ingaged for the defence of that power, and right of the people, in their Representatives. Therefore these things in the Agreement, the people are to claime as their native right, and price of their bloud, which you are obliged absolutely to procure for them.

And these being the foundations of freedom, its necessary, that they should be setled unalterably, which can be by no meanes, but this Agreement with the people.

And we cannot but mind you, that the ease of the people in all their Grievances, depends upon the setling those principles or rules of equal Government for a free people, & were but this Agreement established, doubtlesse all the Grievances of the Army and people would be redressed immediately, and all things propounded in your Case truly stated to be insisted on, would be forthwith granted.

Then should the House of Commons have power to helpe the oppressed people, which they are now bereaved of by the chiefe Oppressors, and then they shall be equally concerned with you and all the people, in the settlement of the most perfect freedome: for they shall equally suffer with you under any Burdens, or partake in any Freedome. We shall onely adde, that the summe of all the Agreement which we herewith offer to you, is but in order to the fulfilling of our Declaration of Iune the 14. wherein we promised to the people, that we would with our lives vindicate and cleare their right and power in their Parliaments.

Edmond Bear	} Lieut. Gen. Reg.
Robert Everard	
George Garret	} Com. Gen. Reg.
Thomas Beverley	
William Pryor	} Col. Fleetwood Reg.
William Bryan	
Matthew Wealey	} Col. Whaley Reg.
William Russell	
Iohn Dober	} Col. Rich Reg.
William Hudson	

Agents coming from other Regiments unto us, have subscribed the Agreement, to be proposed to their respective Regiments and you.

VII

The Petition of November 23rd, 1647

[After the set-back at the Ware Rendezvous the Levellers reverted to their earlier tactic of petitioning Parliament. This Petition is directed primarily against the Grandees and their rule by arbitrary military force. It appeared in two forms. The original Petition must have been printed and circulated for signatures some days before its presentation to Parliament on November 23rd. After its rejection it was reprinted on November 25th with the indignant comments given here. These are different in style from the original Petition and very probably the work of another author.
Wolfe, pp. 237–241.]

TO THE
SUPREAM
Authority
OF ENGLAND,

the COMMONS in
PARLIAMENT
assembled.

The humble Petition of many free-born people.
Together with a Copy of the Order of the
Commitment of five of the Petitioners,
viz. Mr. Thomas Prince, and
Mr. Samuel Chidley in the Gate-House.
Capt. Taylor, Mr. William Larner,
and Mr. Ives in Newgate.
As also some Observations
upon the said
Order.

Sheweth,

THAT as the ground of the late war between the King and you, was a contention whether he or you should exercise the supreame power over us, so its vain to expect a settlement, of peace amongst us, untill that point be clearly and justly determined, that there can be no liberty in any Nation where the Law giving power is not solely in the people or their Representatives.

That upon your Invitation, the people have hazarded their lives, consumed their estates, lost their trades, and weltered in blood to preserve that your just authority, and therein their own freedoms.

That notwithstanding, for attributing the supream authority of this Nation to this Honourable House, which alone represents the people, we have been accounted the off-scouring of the land, we have had our Petitions burned, our persons imprisoned, and many other wayes abused.

That when the ears of the chosen deliverers were stopped, the Law of Nature enjoyned us to addresse our selves to the Army, from whom we had reason to expect relief, according to their many promises and engagements.

That those promises seeming to be wholly forgotten by the ruling part of the Army; it pleased God to raise up the spirits of some Agents therein, to consider of an agreement of the people upon grounds of common right; & to offer it to the Generall Councell of the army for their concurrence; the matter wereof (seriously debate being had thereupon) was so far from being disallowed, that a necessity of ending this Parliament at the day prefixed therein, was concluded; the providing for a constant succession of Parliaments thought necessary, that the people should be more equally represented was confessed; and a certain rule to be set between the people and their representative was judged fit, and the supream authority of this nation acknowledged by that Councell to be where the Agreement placeth it: And particularly Lievtenant General *Cromwell,* and Commissary General *Ireton* declared, that in case they did not Act for the settlement of those freedoms, yet they would never oppose.

That those Agents in further discharge of their duty to their Country; did not long since present unto this Honourable House the said Agreement, with a petition relating thereunto.

That the same Agreement, with another Petition, was lately offered to the Generall, by a worthy Commander, and divers Officers of the Army, at the first generall Rendezvouz neare Ware: and all that was done in a further prosecution, was a peaceable proposing of the same Petition, to the Souldiery, for their concurrence: and we wonder that we should now be reputed mutinous, to offer a Petition to the Souldiery when it was esteemed formerly good service to draw them to an ingagement.

That notwithstanding all this clear open and legal dealing, in those our friends, for the performance of their solemne engagements, both they and we, who adhered to them, are reproached and slandered with imputations of plottings and designing not only the Kings death, in a base murderous way; and of imbrueing the nation in blood, but of strange endeavours to levell all mens estates, and subvert all Government and although the scandals are but the same which the open enemies formerly cast upon your selves, yet our just endeavours for freedom, are so ill resented by this meanes, that some of us are imprisoned, and others threatned to be proceeded against as persons disaffected to this Honourable House, whereas the true object of our enemies mallice is, that authoritie of yours, which we labour to preserve. Yet such is our sad condition, as our actions and intentions are in like manner mis-apprehended by you, though we doubt not but the Agreement duly weighed, will demonstrate all such reproaches to be only the invention of wicked men to exasperate you against us.

And therefore we beseech you in your bowells of compassion to an oppressed people, to review and debate impartially the particulars of that Agreement of the people, wherein many thousands have already concurred: And to suffer us by your countenance, to use our Native Liberty, in moving the people for an happie union amongst themselves, in setling those foundations of Common freedom; that thereby this honourable house, may with more assurance of the peoples alliance, proceed forthwith (without attending for the assent and concurrence of any other) to deliver them from all kind of tyranny and oppression.

And that you would be pleased to account of the sufferings of our dear fellow Commoners Co. *Ayers,* Ca. *Bray,* and others at the severall Rendezvouz of the Army, only for their just and peaceable persuance of Freedome.

And especially that you will make inquisition for the blood of that Soldier, *viz. Richard Arnall* of Col. *Lilburns* Regiment, which was shot to death neere Ware.

And we further desire, that without prejudice against our persons, it might be laid to heart, that the large effusion of blood, and the many spoyles made in the late War, cannot be justified upon any other ground, then the settlement of those freedoms contained in the Agreement, and in your just indeavours to clear and secure those you may expect the blessing of peace and prosperity,   *And your petitioners shall pray.*

Die Martis. November, 1647.

Resolved, that Thomas Prince, *Cheesemonger, and* Samuel Chidley *be forthwith committed prisoners to the prison of the Gate-house, there to remain prisoners during the pleasure of this House, for seditious and contemptuous avowing and prosecuting of a former Petition and paper annexed, stiled an agreement of the people, formerly adiudged by this house, to be destructive to the being of Parliaments, and fundamentall government of this kingdom.*

Hen. El. Cl. Par. Dom. Com.

By vertue of an Order of the House of Commons, these are to require you to receive from the Sergeant at armes his deputie or deputies, the bodies of Thomas Prince, *Cheese monger, and* Samuel Chidley *into the prison of the Gate-house Westminster, and them safely to detain as your prisoners, untill the pleasure of the house be signified to you to the contrary, and for so doing this shall be your Warrant.*
Dated 23. Novemb. 1647.

William Lenthall, Speaker.
To the Keeper of the prison of
the Gate-house of Westminster.

O men of England that love your freedom I beseech you observe the injustice, arbitrarynesse, and tyranny of this your Parliament, who have invited you, and caused your deare friends to expend their blood upon pretences to deliver you from injustice and arbitrary powers. *See their Rmon. of May 26. 1642.*

1. Observe their palpable iniustice in stiling an humble, rationall and iust petition (presented in a peaceble manner) a seditous and contemptuous, avowing a former petition, these men declared formerly, that they ought to receive petitions, though against things established by law, and now when a petition striks at their

corrupt interest, its seditious because its against a vote of theirs, and what damnable endeavours here are to deceive you Commons, they represent these mens petition as a contempt of them when they rendred them the highest honour in their petition.

2. Observe their iniustice in committing these your brethren without laying any crime to their charge, by the law, sedition nor faction is no crime, for no man knows what is sedition or faction, but they put unknown reproachfull tearms upon their just petition to deceive you, and let me informe you, that these treacherous dissemblers that put these infamous tearms upon the petition, durst not suffer this petition to be printed with their votes concerning it, for when they ordered the votes should be printed, an honest member moved that the petition it selfe might be printed with them, that the people might see the reason of such votes, and these Hypocrites opposed it with rage and fury, will ye be alwayes thus abused O yee Commons.

3. Observe the falshood and lyes in their vote. First, these petitioners did not avow any former petition or paper annexed, as this vote say they did. 2ly. The House did never adiudge the Agreement to be distructive to the being of Parliaments, &c. but only the petition of the Agents of the Army, they never durst debate the Agreement, lest they should be forced by the strength of reason to consent to it, they shut their eyes and will not see, for many of the greatest opposers have confessed its iust, *but they love not the light because their deeds are evill*. But seeing it was never debated in one particular, could a iudgement be passed upon it, and have you not a wise, faithfull Parliament, that would not debate the particulars of such great concernment to settle a peace.

4. Observe how these men exercise an absolute tyranny over you, ruling by their crooked wills, and damnable lusts, they commit your fellow Commoners to pris-

ons amongst Theeves and Murtherers, only for begging for their freedoms, and this during their pleasure, that is, till their base malicious humors be satisfied. According to law and iustice, imprisonment is only for safe custody of persons, untill the appointed day of tryall in the ordinary Courts of iustice, and it was the Councell table and High Commission that ruled by their lusts, which imprisoned men during their pleasure, and yet these Apostates dare in the face of the sun proclaime their wickednesse and arbitrarinesse, by committing men during their lust. Certainly their consciences tell them that these faithfull, honest petitioners did not offend, for if they had known any offence, they would have been ready to have proceeded against them, or reserved them for tryall which they intend not. O yee Commons of England! can you still beare it? to see your freedomes undermined, and your brethren abused, and presidents made daily for inslaving you to the wills and lusts of tyrants, when will you shew your selves English men? O now! now is the opportunity. O! that you might see even in this your dayes the things that belong to your peace and freedom, before they be hid from your eyes. *Vale.*

VIII

The Bloody Project

[This unsigned pamphlet is undoubtedly the work of
Walwyn and shows him at his most characteristic. Its
publication is dated by Thomason as August 21st, 1648.
Colchester fell on August 27th and the news of Cromwell's victory at Preston (August 17th) could hardly
have reached London before its completion. It therefore reflects Walwyn's reactions to a war still in progress.
H. and D., pp. 135–146.]

THE
Bloody
PROIECT,

Or a discovery of the
New Designe, in the present War.
BEING
A perfect Narrative of the present
proceedings of the severall Grandee Factions,
for the prevention of a Just Peace, and promoting
of a causelesse Warre, to the destruction of

THE
KING, PARLIAMENT & PEOPLE.

Whereunto is annexed
Several Expedients for an happy Accommodation
tending to the satisfaction of all Parties, without
the further effusion of blood.
By W. P. Gent.

Printed in this Yeare of dissembling, 1648.

IN ALL undertakings, which may occasion war or bloodshed, men have great need to be sure that their cause be right, both in respect of themselves and others: for if they kill men themselves, or cause others to kill, without a just cause, and upon the extreamest necessity, they not only disturbe the peace of men, and familyes, and bring misery and poverty upon a Nation, but are indeed absolute murtherers.

Nor will it in any measure satisfy the Conscience, or Gods justice, to go on in uncertainties, for in doubtfull cases men ought to stand still, and consider, untill certainty do appear, especially when killing and sleying of men (the most horrid worke to Nature and Scripture) is in question.

Far be it from any man hastily to engage in any undertaking, which may occasion a War, before the cause he is to fight for, be rightly, and plainly stated, well considered, and throughly understood to be just, and of absolute necessity to be maintained; nothing being more abominable in the sight of God or good men, then such persons who runne but to shed blood for money, or to support this or the other Interest, but neither consider the cause for which they engage, nor ought else, but pay, interest, honour, &c. such are they who so eagerly endeavour to support the interest of a King, by the destruction of the Peoples Interest, the Interest of the Scots against the Interest of the English, the Interest of the Independents, by the ruine of the Presbyterians: and because it best consists with their present honour, profit or humours, make it their busines to pick quarrels, and encrease divisions, and jealousies, that so they may fish in the waters which they themselves have troubled.

But let such know, who ever they be, that though they may and do for a while brave it out, and flourish, yet a time is comming, and draweth on apace, when for all the murthers they have caused, and mischiefs they have committed, they shall come to judgement, and then their Consciences will be as a thousand witnesses against them.

But especially let men pretending conscience take heed how they either engage themselves, or perswade others to engage to fight and kill men, for a cause not rightly stated, or not throughly understood to be just, and of necessity to be maintained; for it is one of the most unreasonable, unchristian, and unnaturall things that can enter into the mind of man, though it be to be feared that more then a few that have of late both in the Citie and Country [been], (and at present are) active to engage in killing and sleying of men cannot acquit themselves of this abomination.

I beseech you, (you that are so forward and active to engage in the defence of the Kings, Presbyterian, or Independent interest, and yet know no just cause for either) consider, was it sufficient that the King at first invited you in generall termes to joyn with him, for the defence of the true Protestant Religion, his own just Prerogatives, the Priviledges of Parliament, and the Liberty of the Subject; but never declared in particular what that Protestant Religion was he would have defended, or what Prerogative would please him, what priviledges he would allow the Parliament, or what Freedoms the People?

Or was it sufficient thinke you now, that the Parliament invited you at first upon generall termes, to fight for the maintenance of the true Protestant Religion, the Libertyes of the People, and Priviledges of Parliament; when neither themselves knew, for ought is yet seen, nor you, nor any body else, what they meant by the true Protestant Religion, or what the Liberties of the People were, or what those Priviledges of Parliament were, for which yet neverthelesse thousands of men have been slain, and thousands of Familyes destroyed?

It is very like that some of you that joyned with the King upon his invitation, thought, that though the King had formerly countenanced Popery, and Superstition, had stretcht his Prerogative to the oppression and destruction of his People, by Pattents, Projects, &c. yet for the future he would have been more zealous for the truth, and more tender of his People, and not have persisted (notwithstanding his new Protestations) to maintain his old Principles.

And so likewise many of you that joyned with the Parliament, who had formerly seen, felt, or considered the persecution of godly conscientious people by the Bishops and their Cleargy, with the reproaches cast upon them, and their grievous and destructive imprisonment, did beleeve the Parliament under the notion of Religion, intended to free the Nation from all compulsion in matters of Religion, and from molestation, or persecution for opinions, or non-conformity; and that all Lawes or Statutes tending thereunto should have been repealed: But since you find (by killing and destroying their opposers) you have enabled them to performe all things that might concern your freedome, or be conducible to the peace of the Kingdome. But do you now find that they do mean that, or the contrary? And will your consciences give you leave any longer to fight or engage in the cause of Religion, when already you see what fruits you and your friends reap thereby.

And no doubt many of you understood by the Liberties of the People, that they intended to free the Commons in Parliament the peoples Representative, from a Negative voyce, in King, or Lords, and would have declared themselves the highest Authority, and so would

167

have proceeded to have removed the grievances of the Common-wealth: And when you had seen Pattents, Projects, and Shipmoney taken away, the High Commission, and Starchamber abolished, did you ever imagine to have seen men and women examined upon Interrogatories, and questions against themselves, and imprisoned for refusing to answer? Or to have seen Commoners frequently sentenced and imprisoned by the Lords? Did you ever dream that the oppressions of Committees would have exceeded those of the Councel-table; or that in the place of Pattents and Projects, you should have seen an Excise established, ten fold surpassing all those, and Shipmoney together? You thought rather that Tythes would have been esteem'd an oppression, and that Trade would have been made perfectly free, and that Customs if continued, would have been abated, and not raysed, for the support of domineering factions, and enrichment of foure or five great men, as they have been of late times, to the sorrow and astonishment of all honest men, and the great prejudice of the Trade of the Nation.

Doubtlesse you hoped that both Lawes and Lawyers, and the proceeding in all Courts should have been abreviated, and corrected, and that you should never more have seen a Begger in England.

You have seen the Common-wealth enslaved for want of Parliaments, and also by their sudden dissolution, and you rejoyced that this Parliament was not to be dissolved by the King; but did you conceive it would have sat seavn yeares to so little purpose, or that it should ever have come to passe, to be esteemed a crime to move for the ending thereof? Was the perpetuating of this Parliament, and the oppressions they have brought upon you and yours, a part of that Liberty of the People you fought for? Or was it for such a Priviledge of Parliament, that they only might have liberty to oppresse at their pleasure, without any hope of remedy? If all these put together make not up the cause for which you fought, what was the Cause? What have ye obtained to the People, but these Libertyes, for they must not be called oppressions? These are the fruits of all those vast disbursements, and those thousands of lives that have been spent and destroyed in the late War.

And though the Army seemed to be sensible of these grosse juglings, and declared, and engaged against them, and professed that they tooke not paines as a mercenary Army, hired to fight for the Arbitrary ends of a State, but in judgement and conscience, for the preservation of their own, and the Peoples just Rights and Libertyes: Yet when they had prevailed against those their particular opposers, and accomplished the ends by them aymed at, all these things were forgotten, and those persons that appeared for the Peoples Freedoms, by them esteemed and proceeded against as Mutineers, or Incendiaries.

In like manner, the present Ruling Party of Presbyterians make a great shew of their apprehensions of the great slavery and servitude brought upon the People, by the exercise of an Arbitrary power in the Parliament, and by the jurisdiction of the Sword in the hands of the Army: They tell us that by this meanes the Trade of the Nation is destroyed, and that without the removall of these things, the peace of the Nation cannot be secured: And it is exceeding true: But I beseech you consider, whether they do not revive the same Play, and drive the same Designe, which was acted by the Parliament at first, and by the Army the last Summer.

First, they cry out against the exercise of an arbitrary power in the Parliament, and yet labour to invest it in the King, nay challenge the exercise of it by themselves: for what greater arbitrary power can there be in the world, then that a Priest or two, and a few Lay Elders, under the name of a Presbytery, should have power to bind or loose, bring in, or cast out, save or destroy at their pleasure, and enforce all persons within the limits of their jurisdiction, to beleeve as they beleeve, and submit to whatever they command, or else to be by them delivered over to Sathan.

Nay if you looke into those of that party of the Magistracy of this City, that are the great promoters of the present worke: do there any men in the world exercise a more arbitrary power? Do not many of them act only by the Rule of will and pleasure, and have they not openly professed themselves to be obliged to observe no other Rule then Discretion.

And though they decry against the power of the Sword in the hands of the Independents, yet do they not with all their might, labour to get it into the hands of the Presbyterians? and being there, will they not do that themselves, which they complain of in others? will they not say that there are gain-sayers whose mouthes must be stopt, and with the Sword rather then faile, and though Royalists or Independents may not use the Sword to enforce their Principles, yet Presbyterians may, as if all knowledge of the truth were centred in a Presbytery, consisting of halfe Scotch, halfe English, part Puritan, part Cavalier, luke-warm christianity, neither hot nor cold, zealous for the truth which they know not, only by heare-say, and only because they love not Independency, that being to pure, nor Episcopacy, that being too prophane, they will be between both, (but not in a golden Meane, for that were well) but more zealous then either in outward performances, but for the power of godlines. – I cease to judge, but we say we may know the tree by the fruit, and certain I am that Thistles never bore Figgs.

But if you shall examine what grounds of freedome they propose in all their Papers; what equall Rules of justice they offer to be insisted on as a sure foundation for a lasting peace? Surely if you looke but seriously into the bottom of their design, you will find that the peace they aime at is only their own; not the Nations, and that their own ease, honour and dominion, is the only thing they pursue, and so they could enjoy ease and plenty, and stretch themselves upon Beds of Down, they would never care what the poor Country should suffer.

To be short, all the quarrel we have at this day in the Kingdome, is no other then a quarrel of Interests, and Partyes, a pulling down of one Tyrant, to set up another, and instead of Liberty, heaping upon our selves a greater slavery then that we fought against: certainly this is the Liberty that is so much strove for, and for which there are such fresh endeavours to engage men; but if you have not killed and destroyed men enough for this, go on and destroy, kill and sley, till your consciences are swoln so full with the blood of the People, that they burst agen, and upon your death-beds may you see your selves the most horrid Murtherers that ever lived, since the time that Cain kild his brother without a just Cause; for where, or what is your cause? Beleeve it yee have a heavy reeckoning to make, and must undergo a sad repentance, or it will go ill with you at the great day, when all the sophistry of your great Reformers will serve you to little purpose, every man for himselfe being to give an account for the things which he hath done in the body, whether they be good or evill: Then it will serve you to little purpose to say, the King, Parliament, Army, Independents, Presbyterians, such an Officer, Magistrate, or Minister deluded me; no more then it did Adam, to say the woman whom thou gavest, &c. It being thus decreed in heaven, the soule which sinneth shall surely dye.

And though what is past cannot be recalled, yet it must be repented of, and speciall care taken for the future, that you sin no more in this kind, and either stand still or go right for the Future, to which end, let these following directions be your guide.

1. You are to know, that a People living under a Government, as this Nation hath done, and doth, cannot lawfully put themselves into Arms, or engage in War, to kill and sley men, but upon a lawfull call and invitation from the Supream Authority, or Law-making power.

Now if the Supream Authority of this Nation were never yet so plainly declared, as that you understand certainly where it is, and who are invested therewith, you have then had no Warrant for what you have done, nor have any Plea in Law for your Indempnity, as some of all Parties have lately found to their costs.

And that this point of Supream Authority was ever certainly stated, is absolutely denyed; for according to the common supposition, it is 3. Estates, which till within these few yeares were ever taken to be 1. Lords Spirituall. 2. Lords Temporall. 3. The Commons in Parliament assembled.

Now if these three were essentiall and equall, as all former Times seem to allow; How could the Lords Temporall and the Commons, cast out the Lords Spirituall? For by the same rule, the Lords Spirituall, and Lords Temporall, might have cast out the Commons, but the casting out the Bishops hath both answered the question, and ended the controversie.

Since when the supream Authority is pretended to rest in the King, Lords and Commons; and if so, when did the King assent to your Proceedings in this War, which all the art in the world will not perswade him to be for him, but against him, and to ruine him and his? Or when did the Parliament assent to the proceedings of you that joyned with the King in the late war pretendedly raised for the defence of Religion, the priviledges of Parliament, and Liberty of the Subject; and if the supream power reside in all three, King, Lords and Commons, how can the King justly do any thing without the consent of the Lords and Commons, or the

Lords and Commons without the King? May not the King and Lords as justly proceed to make Laws, War or Peace, without the Commons as they without the King? If they are not equal, which of them are supream, and declared and proved by convincing reason so to be? If any, that you are to observe? If none, what have you done? what can you lawfully do?

That there should be either three or two distinct Estates equally supream is an absurd nullity in government, for admit two of them agree, and not the third, then there can be no proceedings or determination, and if there be but two, as is now pretended, in Lords and Commons, whose Ordinances have served (how justly judge you) to make War and confiscate mens estates: admit they agree not, then also nothing can be done, which in Government is ridiculous to imagine, besides it is now a known case that their Ordinances are not pleadable against the Laws, and give no Indempnity, which were they the known supream Authority, could not but be effectual. That the King single and alone is the supream Authority himself never pretended to it, claiming only a negative voyce in the Law-making Power, by which rule nothing can be done without him, then which nothing is more unreasonable: The Lords also never pretended to more then an equal share with the Commons, which in effect is a negative voyce and as unreasonable as in the King: And when the Commons have been by Petitioners stiled the supream authority, they have punished the Petitioners, and disclaimed the supream Authority: and as two years since, so very lately they have voted that the Kingdom shall be governed by King, Lords and Commons; which is a riddle that no man understands; for who knoweth what appertains to the King, what to the Lords, or what to the House of Commons? It is all out as uncertain as at first; and if the trumpet give an uncertain sound, who shall prepare himself for the battel? If by all your endeavors you cannot prevail to have the supream Authority declared and proved, how can you lawfully fight, or upon what grounds with a good conscience can you engage your selves, or perswade others to engage in killing and slaying of men?

And if you should have the supream Authority rationally proved and declared to be in the Commons distinct from any other, as being the sole Representative of the people; you must note that you are a free people, and are not to be pressed or enforced to serve in Wars like horses and bruit beasts, but are to use the understanding God hath given you, in judging of the Cause, for defence whereof they desire you to fight, for it is not sufficient to fight by lawful authority, but you must be sure to fight for what is just: Lawful authority being sometimes mistaken, and many times so perverted and corrupted, as to command the killing and imprisoning men for doing that which is just and commendable, and for opposing what is unjust and destructive. Therefore as you are to forbear till you see the supream Authority distinctly and rationally stated; so also you are not to engage till the Cause be expresly declared, lest after your next engagement you are as far to seek of a just cause as now you are; and after you have prevailed, in stead of finding your selves and your associates freemen, you find your selves more enslaved then you were formerly. For by experience you now find you may be made slaves as effectually by a Parliament, as by any other kind of Government; why then persist you to divide and fall into Factions? to kill and slay men for you know not what, to advance the honor and interest of you know not whom; the King, Parliament, great men in the City and Army can do nothing without you, to disturb the Peace of the Nation; upon you therefore both Soldiers and People, who fight, pay and disburse your estates, is to be charged all the evil that hath been done; if you on all hands had not been and were not so hasty to engage for the advancement of Interests to the prejudice of the Nation, it is very likely we had not only escaped those late bloody turmoils that have happened among us, but also might prevent greater threatned dangers, which like an inundation begin to break in upon us: And if you now stop not, your Consciences will be loaded with all that is to come, which threatneth far worse then what is past; Therefore, if ye are either men or Christians, hold your hands till you know what you fight for, and be sure that you have the truth of Freedom in it, or never medle, but desist, and let who will both fight and pay.

Certainly there is none so vile, considering what hath been said, that will again incur the guilt of murtherers, and fight before the Cause be plainly stated and published, and if that were done as it ought to be, possibly it may be attained without fighting, and might have been all this while, the difference not being so great as was imagined; Besides, where is the man that would fight against the supream Authority, and a just Cause? and certainly there is none of you (whether Royalists, Presbyterians or Independents) so wicked as to desire to kill men without exceeding just grounds and upon the greatest necessity, it being the saddest work in the world.

For the preventing whereof, let us, I beseech you, examine what good things there are wanting, that are essential to the Peace, Freedom, and happiness of the Nation, that may not be obtained without fighting.

1. Is there wanting the certain knowledg where the supream Authority is, and of right ought to be; It is confest no one thing is more wanting, nor can the Nation ever be quiet, or happy without it.

But can it be any where justly and safely but in the House of Commons, who are chosen and trusted by the People? Certainly did men consider that in opposing thereof, they renounce and destroy their own freedoms, they would not do it for any thing in the world.

If the consideration of the manifold evils brought upon us by this House of Commons, deter them, the next thing that is wanting is, That a set time be appointed for the ending of this Parliament, and a certainty for future Parliaments, both for their due elections, meeting, and dissolving: And who will be so unreasonable as to oppose any of these? certainly the number cannot be considerable.

Is it also necessary That Parliaments be abridged the power of impressing men, to serve as bruit beasts in the Wars, who will be against their being bounded therein? a good Cause never wanted men, nor an authority that had money to pay them.

Hath it proved destructive in Parliaments to meddle in Religion, and to compel and restrain in matters of Gods worship? Are they evidently such things as cannot be submitted to Judgment? Doth every man find it so that hath a living Conscience? Who then will be against their binding herein, though they be entrusted to establish an uncompulsive publike way of worship for the Nation?

Is it unreasonable that any person should be exempt from those proceedings of Law, unto which the generality of the People are to be subject? Who is there then that will not willingly have all from the highest to the lowest bound alike?

That Parliaments should have no power to punish any person for doing that which is not against a known declared Law, or to take away general property, or to force men to answer to questions against themselves, or to order tryals, or proceed by any other ways then by twelve sworn men, who would not rejoyce to have such boundaries?

Then, that the proceedings in Law might be rectified, and all Laws and the duty of Magistrates written and published in English: That the Excise might have a speedy end, and no Taxes but by way of subsidies: That

Trade might be free, and a less burthensom way for the maintenance of Ministers be established, then that of Tythes; and that work and neccessaries be provided for all kind of poor people. Certainly for the obtaining of these things a man may justly adventure his life; all these being for a common good, and tend not to the setting up of any one party or faction of men.

These then are the Causes to be insisted on, or nothing: And if the supream Authority adhere to this Cause, they need neither fear Scotch, French, nor English Enemies; but if they decline this Cause, they are to be declined; the just freedom and happiness of a Nation, being above all Constitutions, whether of Kings, Parliaments, or any other.

For shame therefore (Royalists, Presbyterians, Independents,) before you murther another man hold forth your Cause plainly and expresly; and if any Adversaries appear either within or without the Land, reason it out with them if it be possible, deal as becometh Christians, argue, perswade, and use all possible means to prevent another War, and greater blood-shed: your great ones, whether the King, Lords, Parliament men, rich Citizens, &c. feel not the miserable effects thereof, and so cannot be sensible; but you and your poor friends that depend on Farmes, Trades, and small pay, have many an aking heart when these live in all pleasure and deliciousness: The accursed thing is accepted by them, wealth and honor, and both comes by the bleeding miserable distractions of the Common-wealth, and they fear an end of trouble would put an end to their glory and greatness.

Oh therefore all you Soldiers and People, that have your Consciences alive about you, put to your strength of Judgment, and all the might you have to prevent a further effusion of blood; let not the covetous, the proud, the blood-thirsty man bear sway amongst you; fear not their high looks, give no ear to their charms, their promises or tears; they have no strength without you, forsake them and ye will be strong for good, adhere to them, and they will be strong to evil; for which you must answer, and give an account at the last day.

The King, Parliament, great men in the City and Army, have made you but the stairs by which they have mounted to Honor, Wealth and Power. The only Quarrel that hath been, and at present is but this, namely, whose slaves the people shall be: All the power that any hath, was but a trust conveyed from you to them, to be employed by them for your good; they have mis-imployed their power, and instead of preserving you, have destroyed you: all Power and Authority is perverted from the King to the Constable, and it is no other but the policy of Statesmen to keep you divided by creating jealousies and fears among you, to the end that their Tyranny and Injustice may pass undiscovered and unpunished; but the peoples safety is the supream Law; and if a people must not be left without a means to preserve it self against the King, by the same rule they may preserve themselves against the Parliament and' Army too; if they pervert the end for which they received their power, to wit the Nations safety; therefore speedily unite your selves together, and as one man stand up for the defence of your Freedom, and for the establishment of such equal rules of Government for the future, as shall lay a firm foundation of peace and happiness to all the people without partiallity: Let Justice be your breastplate, and you shall need to fear no enemies, for you shall strike a terrour to your now insulting oppressors, and force all the Nations Peace to fly before you. Prosecute and prosper.

Vale.

Postscript.

Can there be a more bloody Project then to engage men to kill one another, and yet no just cause declared?

178

Therefore I advise all men that would be esteemed Religious or Rational, really to consider what may be done for the future that is conducible to the Peace of the Nation; If the Peace of the Nation cannot be secured without the Restauration of the King, let it be done speedily and honorably, and provide against his misgovernment for the future; let his power be declared and limited by Law.

If the Peace of the Nation cannot be secured by the continuance of this Parliament, let a Period be set for the dissolution thereof, but first make certain provision for the successive calling, electing and sitting of Parliaments for the future; let their Priviledges be declared and power limitted, as to what they are empowred and what not; for doubtless in Parliaments rightly constituted consists the Freedom of a Nation: And in all things do as you would be done unto, seek peace with all men.

But above all things, abandon your former actings for a King against a Parliament, or an Army against both; for the Presbyterians against the Independents, &c. for in so doing you do but put a Sword into your enemies hands to destroy you, for hitherto, which of them soever were in power, they plaid the Tyrants and oppressed, and so it will ever be, when Parties are supported: Therefore if you engage at all, do it by Lawfull Authority, let your Cause be declared, and just also, and let it be for the good of the whole Nation, without which you will not only hazard being Slaves, but also contract upon your selves, and Posterities the guilt of Murtherers. *vale.*

FINIS.

IX

The Petition
of September 11th, 1648

[The outbreak of the second Civil War had temporarily halted Leveller activities. Its end saw them resumed with this *Petition*. A new emphasis can be noted. Lilburne's overtures to Cromwell had been well received and the Army leaders had declared against any further negotiations with the King and for his trial. There seemed some prospect that they might be moving towards other Leveller policies. This *Petition,* therefore, is noticeably friendly towards the Army (see clause 26 in the list of demands) and its edge is turned against the Presbyterian majority in the House of Commons. A collective work, like their other Petitions, this was perhaps mainly written by Walwyn with Lilburne's help. It was frequently referred to in later Leveller publications as an authoritative statement of their policy. Presented to the Commons on September 11th, 1648 it must have been printed some days earlier as it was claimed by then to have 40,000 signatures. It was also printed in *The Moderate* of September 5th–12th.

Wolfe, pp. 283–290. H. and D., pp. 148–155.]

TO THE
RIGHT
HONORABLE,
THE
Commons of England
In Parliament Assembled.

The humble Petition
of divers wel affected Persons
inhabiting the City of London,
Westminster,
the Borough of Southwark,
Hamblets,
and places adjacent.

SHEWETH,

THAT although we are as earnestly desirous of a safe and wel-grounded Peace, and that a finall end were put to all the troubles and miseries of the Common-wealth, as any sort of men whatsoever: Yet considering upon what grounds we engaged on your part in the late and present Wars, and how far (by our so doing) we apprehend ourselves concerned, Give us leave (before you conclude as by the Treaty in hand) to acquaint you first with the ground and reason which induced us to aid you against the King and his Adherents. Secondly, What our Apprehensions are of this Treaty. Thirdly, What we expected from you, and do still most earnestly desire.

Be pleased therefore to understand, that we had not engaged on your part, but that we judged this honourable House to be the supream Authority of *England,* as chosen by, and representing the People; and entrusted with absolute power for redresse of Grievances, and provision for Safety: and that the King was but at the most the chief publike Officer of this Kingdom, and accomptable to this House (the Representative of the People, from whom all just Authority is, or ought to be derived) for discharge of his Office: And if we had not bin confident hereof, we had bin desperately mad to have taken up Armes or to have bin aiding and assisting in maintaining a *War against Him;* The Lawes of the Land making it expresly a crime no lesse than Treason for any to raise War against the King.

But when we considered the manifold oppressions brought upon the Nation, by the King, His Lords, and

Bishops; and that this Honourable House declared their deep sence thereof; and that (for continuance of that power which had so opprest us) it was evident the King intended to raise Forces, and to make War; and that if he did set up his Standard, it tended to the dissolution of the Government: upon this, knowing the safety of the People to be above Law, and that to judge thereof appertained to the Supream Authority, and not to the Supream Magistrate, and being satisfyed in our Consciences, that the publike safety and freedom was in imminent danger, we concluded we had not only a just cause to maintain; but the supream Authority of the Nation, to justifie, defend, and indempnifie us in time to come, in what we should perform by direction thereof; though against the known Law of the Land, or any inferiour Authority, though the highest.

And as this our understanding was begotten in us by principles of right reason, so were we confirmed therein by your own proceedings, as by your condemning those Judges who in the case of Ship-money had declared the King to be Judge of safety; and by your denying Him to have a Negative voice in the making of Laws; where you wholly exclude the King from having any share in the supream Authority: Then by your casting the Bishops out of the House of Lords, who by tradition also, had bin accounted an essential part of the supream Authority; And by your declaring to the Lords, That if they would not joyn with you in setling the Militia, (which they long refused) you would settle it without them, which you could not justly have done, and they had any real share in the supream *Authority*.

These things we took for real Demonstrations, that you undoubtedly knew your selves to be the supream Authority; ever weighing down in us all other your indulgent *expressions concerning the King or Lords*. It being indeed impossible for us to believe that it can consist either with the safety or freedom of the Nation, to be governed either by 3. or 2. Supreams, especially where experience hath proved them so apt to differ in their Judgements concerning Freedom or Safety, that the one hath been known to punish what the other hath judged worthy of reward; when not only the freedom of the people is directly opposite to the Prerogatives of the King and Lords, but the open enemies of the one, have been declared friends by the other, as the Scots were by the House of Lords.

And when as most of the oppressions of the Common-wealth have in all times bin brought upon the people by the King and Lords, who nevertheless would be so equal in the supream Authority, as that there should be no redress of Grievances, no provision for safety, but at their pleasure. For our parts, we profess our selves so far from judging this to be consistent with Freedom or Safety, that we know no great cause Wherefore we assisted you in the late Wars, but in hope to be delivered by you from so intollerable, so destructive a bondage, so soon as you should (through Gods blessing upon the Armies raised by you) be enabled.

But to our exceeding grief, we have observed that no sooner God vouchsafeth you victory, and blesseth you with success, and thereby enablet you to put us and the whole Nation, into an absolute condition of freedom and safety: but according as ye have bin accustomed, passing by the ruine of a Nation, and all the bloud that hath bin spilt by the King and his Party, ye betake your selvs to a Treaty with him, thereby puting him that is but one single person, and a publike Officer of the Common-wealth, in competition with the whole body of the people, whom ye represent; not considering that it is impossible for you to erect any authority equall to your selves; and declared to all the world that you will not alter the ancient Government, from that of King, Lords, and Commons: not once mentioning (in case of difference) which of them is supream, but leaving that point (which was the chiefest cause of all our publike differences, disturbances Wars and miseries) as uncertain as ever.

In so much as we who upon these grounds have laid out our selves every way to the uttermost of our abilities: and all others throughout the land, Souldiers and others who have done the like in defence of our supream authority, and in opposition to the King, cannot but deem our selves in the most dangerous condition of all others, left without all plea of indemnity, for what we have done; as already many have found by losse of their lives & liberties, either for things done or said against the King; the law of the land frequently taking place, and precedency against and before your authority, which we esteemed supreame, and against which no law ought to be pleaded. Nor can we possibly conceive how any that have any waies assisted you, can be exempt from the guilt of murders and robbers, by the present laws in force, if you persist to disclaime the Supreame Authority, though their owne conscience do acquit them, as having opposed none but manifest Tyrants, Oppressors and their adherents.

And whereas a Personall Treaty, or any Treaty with the King, hath been long time held forth as the only means of a safe & wel-grounded peace; it is well known to have been cryed up principally by such as have been dis-affected unto you; and though you have contradicted it: yet it is believed that you much fear the issue; as you have cause sufficient, except you see greater alteration in the King and his party then is generally observed, there having never yet been any Treaty with him, but was accompanied with some underhand dealing; and whilst the present force upon him (though seeming liberty) will in time to come be certainly pleaded, against all that shall or can be agreed upon: nay, what can you confide in if you consider how he hath been provoked; and what former Kings upon lesse provocations have done, after Oaths, Laws, Charters, Bonds, Excommunications, and all ties of Reconsilliations, to the destruction of all those that had provoked and opposed them: yea, when your selves so soone as he had signed those bils in the beginning of this Parliament, saw cause to tell him, *That even about the time of passing those bils, some design or other was one fact which if it had taken effect would not only have rendred those bills fruitlesse, but have reduced you a worse condition of confusion than that wherein the Parliament found you.*

And if you consider what new wars, risings, revolting invasions, and plottings have been since this last cry for a Personall Treaty, you will not blame us if we wonder at your hasty proceedings thereunto: especially considering the wonderfull victories which God hath blessed the Army withall.

We professe we cannot chuse but stand amazed to consider the inevitable danger we shall be in, though all things in the Propositions were agreed unto, the Resolutions of the King and his party have been perpetually violently and implacably prosecuted & manifested against us; and that with such scorn and indignation, that it must be more than such ordinary bonds that must hold them.

And it is no lesse a wonder to us, that you can place your own security therein, or that you can ever imagine to see a free Parliament any more in England.

The truth is (and we see we must either now speak it or for ever be silent,) We have long expected things of an other nature from you, and such as we are confident would have given satisfaction to all serious people of all Parties.

1. That you would have made good the supreme of the people, in this Honourable House, from all pretences of Negative Voices, either in King or Lords.

2. That you would have made laws for election of representatives yearly and of course without writ or summons.

3. That you would have set expresse times for their meeting Continuance and Dissolution: as not to exceed 40 or 50 daies at the most, and to have fixed an expressed time for the ending of this present Parl.

4. That you would have exempted matters of Religion and God, from the compulsive or restrictive power of any Authoritie upon earth, and reserved to the supreme authoritie an uncompulsive power only of appointing a way for the publick worship, whereby abundance of misery, prosecution, and hart-burning would for ever be avoyded.

5. That you would have disclaimed in your selvs and all future Representatives, a power of Pressing and forcing any sort of men to serve in warrs, there being nothing more opposite to freedom, nor more unreasonable in an authoritie impowered for raising monies in all occasions, for which, and a just cause, assistants need not be doubted: the other way serving rather to maintain in justice and corrupt parties.

6. That you would have made both Kings, Queens, Princes, Dukes, Earls, Lords, and all Persons, alike liable to every Law of the Land, made or to be made; that so all persons even the Highest might fear & stand in aw and neither violate the publick peace, nor private right of person or estate, (as hath been frequent) without being lyable to accompt as other men.

7. That you would have freed all Commoners from the jurisdiction of the Lords in all cases: and to have taken care that all tryalls should be only of twelve sworn men, and no conviction but upon two or more sufficient known witnesses.

8. That you would have freed all men from being examined against themselves, and from being questioned or punished for doing of that against which no Law hath bin provided.

9. That you would have abbreviated the proceedings in Law, mitigated and made certain the charge thereof in all particulars.

10. That you would have freed all Trade and Marchandising from all Monopolizing and Engrossing, by Companies or otherwise.

11. That you would have abolished Excise, and all kind of taxes, except subsidies, the old and onely just way of England.

12. That you would have laid open all late Inclosures of Fens, and other Commons, or have enclosed them onely or chiefly to the benefit of the poor.

13. That you would have considered the many thousands that are ruined by perpetual imprisonment for debt, and provided to their enlargement.

14. That you would have ordered some effectual course to keep people from begging and beggery, in so fruitful a Nation as through Gods blessing this is.

15. That you would have proportioned Punishments more equal to offences; that so mens Lives and Estates might not be forfeited upon trivial and slight occasions.

16. That you would have removed the tedious burthen of Tythes, satisfaying all Impropriators, and providing a more equal way of maintenance for the publike Ministers.

17. That you would have raised a stock of Money of those many confiscated Estates you have had, for payment of those who contributed voluntarily above their abilities, before you had provided for those that disbursed out of their superfluities.

18. That you would have bound your selves and all future Parliaments from abolishing propriety, levelling mens Estats, or making all things common.

19. That you would have declared what the duty or busines of the Kingly office is, and what not, and ascertained the Revenue, past increase or diminution, that so there might never be more quarrels about the same.

20. That you would have rectified the election of publike Officers for the Citie of London, of every particular Company therin, restoring the Comunalty thereof to their just Rights, most unjustly withheld from them, to the producing and maintaining of corrupt interest, opposite to common Freedom, and exceedingly prejudecal to the trade and manufactures of this Nation.

21. That you would have made full and ample reparations to all persons that had bin oppressed by sentences in high Commission, Star-Chamber, and Council Board, or by any kind of Monopolizers, or projectors, and that out of the estates of those that were authors, actors or promoters of so intollerable mischiefs, and that without much attendance.

22. That you would have abolished all Committees, and have conveyed all businesses into the true method of the usuall Tryalls of the Commonwealth.

23. That you would not have followed the example of former tyrannous and superstitious Parliaments, in making Orders, Ordinances or lawes, or in appointing punishments concerning opinions or things super-naturall stiling some blasphemies others heresies; when as you know your selves easily mistaken and that divine truths need no human helps to support them: such proceedings having bin generally invented to divide the people amongst themselves, and to affright men from that liberty of discourse by which Corruption & tyranny would be soon discovered.

24. That you would have declared what the businesse of the Lords is, and ascertain their condition, not derogating them the Liberties of other men, that so there might be an end of striving about the same.

25. That you would have done Justice upon the Capitall Authors and Promoters of the former or late Wars, many of them being under your power: Considering that mercy to the wicked, is cruelty to the in-

nocent: and that all your lenity doth but make them the more insolent and presumptuous.

26. That you would have provided constant pay for the Army, now under the Command of the Lord Gen. *Fairfax,* and given rules to all Judges, and all other publike Officers throughout the Land for their indempnity, and for the saving harmlesse all that have any wayes assisted you, or that have said or done any thing against the King, Queen, or any of his party since the begining of this Parl. without which any of his party are in a better condition then those who have served you; nothing being more frequent with them, then their reviling of you and your friends.

The things and worthy Acts which have bin done and atchived by this Army and their Adherents (how ever ingratefully suffered to be scandalized as Sectaries and men of corrupt Judgements) in defence of the just authority of this honourable House, and of the common liberties of the Nation, and in opposition to all kind of Tyranny and oppression, being so far from meriting an odious Act of Oblivion, that they rather deserve a most honourable Act of perpetual remembrance, to be as a patern of publike vertue, fidelity, and resolution to all posterity.

27. That you would have laid to heart all the abundance of innocent bloud that hath bin spilt, and the infinite spoil and havock that hath been made of peaceable harmlesse people, by express Commissions from the King; and seriously to have considered whether the justice of God be likely to be satisfyed, or his yet continuing wrath appeased, by an Act of Oblivion.

These and the like we have long time hoped you would have minded, and have made such an establishment for the Generall peace and contentfull satisfaction of all sorts of people, as should have bin to the happines of all future generations, and which we most earnestly desire you would set your selves speedily to effect;

whereby the almost dying honour of this most honourable House, would be again revived, and the hearts of your Petitioners and all other well affected people, be a fresh renewed unto you, the Freedom of the Nation (now in perpetuall hazard) would be firmly established, for which you would once more be so strengthened with the love of the people, that you should not need to cast your eyes any other wayes (under God) for your security: but if all this availeth noteing, God be our Guide, for men sheweth us not a way for our preservation.

FINIS.

X

The Picture of the Councel of State: Overton's Narrative

[Overton's account of his arrest and examination follows that of Lilburne and occupies pp. 25–47 of *The Picture*. Colonel Axtel, a Baptist like Overton, was not of quite such humble origins as is here suggested. He was in charge of the arrangements for the King's execution and was one of the regicides executed after the Restoration. In Ireland he was noted for his severities towards the native population. Overton's narrative is dated April 4th, 1649; *The Picture* was published sometime between that date and April 11th.
H. and D., pp. 214–233.]

THE
Proceedings
OF THE
Councel of State
AGAINST
Richard Overton,

now prisoner
in the Tower of
London.

UPON the twenty eighth of March 1649, a partie of Horse and Foot commanded by Lieut. Colonel Axtel (a man highly pretending to religion,) came betwixt five and six of the morning to the house where I then lodged, in that hostile manner to apprehend me, as by the sequel appeared.

But now, to give an account of the particular circumstances attending that action, may seem frivolous, as to the Publick; but in regard the Lieutenant Colonel was pleased so far to out-strip the capacity of a Saint, as to betake himself to the venomed Arrows of lying calumnies and reproaches, to wound (through my sides) the too much forsaken cause of the poor oppressed people of this long wasted Common-wealth: like as it hath been the practice of all perfidious Tyrants in all ages. I shall therefore trouble the Reader with the rehearsall of all the occurrant circumstances which attended his apprehension of me, that the world may cleerly judge betwixt us. And what I here deliver from my pen as touching this matter, I do deliver it to be set upon the Record of my account, as I will answer it at the dreadfull day of judgment, when the secrets of all hearts shall be opened, and every one receive according to his deeds done in the flesh: and God so deal with me at that day, as in this thing I speak the truth: And if the rankorous spirits of men will not be satisfied therewith, I have no more to say but this, to commit my self to God in the joyful rest of a good conscience, and not value what insatiable envie can suggest against me. Thus then to the businesse it self.

In the House where I then lodged that night there lived three families, one of the Gentlemen being my very good friend, with whom all that night hee and I onely lay in bed together, and his Wife and childe lay in another bed by themselves: and when they knock'd at the door, the Gentleman was up and ready, and his Wife also, for she rose before him, and was suckling her childe: and I was also up, but was not completely drest; And of this the Gentleman himself (her Husband) hath taken his oath before one of the Masters of the Chancery. And we three were together in a Chamber discoursing, he and I intending about our businesse immediately to go abroad, and hearing them knock, I said, Yonder they are come for me. Whereupon, some books that lay upon the table in the room, were thrown into the beds betwixt the sheets (and the books were all the persons he found there in the beds, except he took us for printed papers, and then there were many;) and the Gentleman went down to go to the door; and as soon as the books were cast a toside, I went to put on my boots; and before the Gentleman could get down the stairs, a girl of the house had opened the door, and let them in, and so meeting the Gentleman upon the stairs, Axtel commanded some of the souldiers to seize upon him, and take him into custodie, and not suffer him to come up: And I hearing a voice from below, that one would speak with me, I went to the chamber door (it being open) and immediatly appeared a Musketier (Corporal Neaves, as I take it) and he asked me if my name were not Mr. Overton: I answered, it was Overton; and so I sat me down upon the bed side to pull on my other boot, as if I had but new risen, the better to shelter the books; and that Corporal was the first man that entered into the chamber, and after him one or two more, and then followed the Lieutenant Colonel; and the Corporal told me, I was the man they were come for, and bade me make me ready: and the

Lieutenant Colonel when he came in, asked me how I did, and told me, they would use me civilly, and bid me put on my boots, and I should have time enough to make me ready: And immediately upon this the Lieutenant Colonel began to abuse me with scandalous language, and asked me, if the Gentlewoman who then sate suckling her childe, were not one of my wives, and averred that she and I lay together that night. Then the Gentleman hearing his Wife call'd Whore, and abused so shamefully, got from the souldiers, and ran up stairs; and coming into the room where we were, he taxed the Lieutenant Colonel for abusing of his Wife and me, and told him, that he and I lay together that night: But the Lieutenant Colonel, out of that little discretion he had about him, took the Gentleman by the hand, saying, How dost thou, brother Cuckcold? using other shamefull ignorant and abusive language, not worthy repeating. Well, upon this his attempt thus to make me his prisoner, I demanded his Warrant; and he shewed me a Warrant from the Councell of State, with Mr. Bradshaw's hand to it, and with the Broad Seal of England to it, (as he call'd it) to apprehend Lieutenant Colonel Lilburn, Mr. Walwine, Mr. Prince, and my self, where-ever they could finde us. And as soon as I was drest, he commanded the Musketiers to take me away; and as soon as I was down stairs, he remanded me back again into the chamber where he took me, and then told me, he must search the house, and commanded the trunks to be opened, or they should be broken open: and commanded one of the souldiers to search my pockets. I demanded his Warrant for that: He told me, he had a Warrant, I had seen it. I answered, That was for the apprehension of my person; and bid him shew his Warrant for searching my pockets, and the house: and according to my best remembrance, he replyed, He should have a Warrant. So little respect had he to Law, Justice, and Reason; and *vi & armis,* right or wrong, they fell to work, (inconsiderately devolving all law, right, and freedom betwixt man and man into their Sword; for the consequence of it extends from one to all) and his party of armed Horse and Foot (joyned to his over-hasty exorbitant will) was his irresistible Warrant: And so they searched my pockets, and took all they found in them, my mony excepted, and searched the trunks, chests, beds, &c. And the Lieutenant Colonel went into the next chamber, where lived an honest Souldier (one of the Lieutenant Generals Regiment) and his wife, and took away his sword, and vilified the Gentleman and his wife, as if she had been his whore, and took him prisoner for lying with a woman, as he said. He also went up to the Gentleman who lets out the rooms, and cast the like imputations upon his wife, as also upon a Maid that lives in the house, and gave it out in the Court and Street, amongst the souldiers and neighbours that it was a Bawdy-house, and that all the women that lived in it were whores, and that he had taken me in bed with another mans Wife. Well, he having ransack'd the house, found many books in the beds, and taken away all such writings, papers, and books, of what sort or kind soever, that he could finde, and given them to the souldiers, (amongst which he took away certain papers which were my former Meditations upon the works of the Creation, intituled, *Gods Word confirmed by his Works;* wherein I endeavoured the probation of a God, a Creation, a State of Innocencie, a Fall, a Resurrection, a Restorer, a Day of Judgment, &c. barely from the consideration of things visible and created: and these papers I reserved to perfect and publish as soon as I could have any rest from the turmoils of this troubled Common-wealth: and for the loss of those papers I am only troubled: all that I desire of my enemies hands, is but the restitution of those papers, that what-ever becomes of me, they may not be buried in oblivion, for they may prove usefull to many.) Well, when the Lieutenant Colonel had thus far mistaken himself, his Religion and Reason thus unworthily to abuse me and the houshold in that scandalous nature, unbeseeming the part of a Gentleman, a Souldier, or a Christian (all which titles he claimeth) and had transgressed the limits of his Authority, by searching, ransacking, plundering, and taking away what he pleased, he march'd me in the head of his party to Pauls Church-yard, and by the way commanded the souldiers to lead me by the arm; and from thence, with a guard of three Companies of Foot, and a party of Horse, they forced me to Whitehall; and the souldiers carried the books some upon their Muskets, some under their arms: but by the way (upon our march) the Corporall that first entred the room (whose word in that respect is more valuable then Axtels) confess'd unto me (in the audience of the Souldier they took also with them from the place of my lodging) that the Lieutenant Colonel had dealt uncivilly and unworthily with me, and that there was no such matter of taking me in bed with an other woman, &c. And this the said souldier will depose upon his oath.

When I came to White-hall, I was delivered into the hands of Adjutant General Stubber, where I found my worthy friends Lieutenant Collonel John Lilburn, Mr. Wallwin, and Mr. Prince in the same captivity under the Martiall usurpation: and after I had been there a while, upon the motion of Leiutenant Collonell Lilburne, that Leiutenant Collonell Axstell, and I might be brought face to face about the matter of scandall that was raised, he coming there unto us, and questioned about the report he had given out, there averd, that he took me a bed with an other mans wife; and being asked if he saw us actually in bed together, he answered, we were both in the Chamber together, and the woman had scarce got on her coates, (which was a notorious untruth) and she sate suckling of her child, and from these circumstances he did believe we did lie together, and that he spake according to his conscience what he beleeved: These were his words, or to the like effect, to which I replied, as afore-mentioned. But how short this was of a man pretending so much conscience and sanctity as he doth I leave to all unprejudiced people to judge: it is no point of Christian faith (to which [he] is so great a pretender) to foment a lye for a wicked end, and then to plead it his beleif and conscience, for the easier credence of his malitious aspertion: but though the words belief and Conscience be too specious Evangelicall tearms, no truely consciencious person will say they are to be used, or rather abused to such evill ends. Well in that company I having taxed him for searching my pockets, and without warrant, he answered; that because I was so base a fellow, he did what he could to destroy me. And then the better to make up the measure of the reproach he had raised, he told us, it was now an opinion amongst us to have community of women; I desired him to name one of that opinion, he answered me, It may be I was of that opinion, and I told him, it may be he was of that opinion, and that my may be was as good as his May be: whereupon he replyed, that I was a sawsy fellow. Surely the Lieuten-ant Collonel at that instant had forgot the Bugget from whence he dropt, I presume when he was a pedler in Harford-shire he had not so lofty an esteem of himself, but now the case is altered, the Gentleman is become one of the Grandees of the Royall palace: one of the (mock-) Saints in season, now judgeing the Earth, in-spired with providence and oppertunities at pleasure of their own invention as quick and as nimble as an Hocas Spocas, or a Fiend in a Juglers Box, they are not flesh and bloud, as are the wicked, they are all spirituall, all heavenly, the pure Camelions of the time, they are this or that or what you please, in a trice, in a twinkling of an eye; there is no form, no shape that you can fancy among men, into which their Spirituallities are not changeable at pleasure; but for the most part, these holy men present themselves in the perfect figure of Angels of light, of so artificiall resemblance, enough to deceive the very Elect if possible, that when they are entered their Sanctum Sanctorum, their holy convocation at White-hall, they then seem no other than a quire of Arch-Angels, of Cherubins and Seraphims, chanting their fals-holy Halelujaes of victory over the people, having put all principalities and powers under their feet, and the Kingdom and dominion and the greatness of the Kingdom is theirs, and all Dominions, even all the people shall serve and obey them, [excuse me, it is but their own Counterfeit Dialect, under which their pernitious hipocrisy is vailed that I retort into their bosoms, that you may know them within and without, not that I have any intention of reflection upon holy writ] and now these men of Jerusalem (as I may terme them) those painted Sepulchers of Sion after their long conjuring together of providences, opportunities and seasons one after another, drest out to the people in the sacred shape of Gods Time, (as after the language of their new fangled Saint-ships I may speak it) they have brought their seasons to perfection, even to the Season of Seasons, now to rest themselves in the large and full enjoyment of the creature for a time, two times and half a time, resolving now to ware out the true asserters of the peoples freedom, and to change the time and laws to their exorbitant ambition and will; while all their promises, declarations and engagements to the people must be null'd and made Cyphers, and cast aside as wast paper, as unworthy the fulfilment, or once the remembrance of those Gentlemen, those magnificent stems of our new upstart Nobillity, for now it is not with them as in the dayes of their engagement at Newmarket and Triploe heath, but as it was in the days of old with corrupt persons, so is it in ours, *Tempora mutantur* −.

But to proceed to the story: the Lieutenant Collonel did not only shew his weakness, (or rather his iniquity) in his dealing with me, but he convents the aforesaid Souldier of Leiutenant Generalls Regiment before divers of the Officers at White-hall, and there he renders the reason wherefore he made him a prisoner, because said he, he takes Overtons part, for he came and asked him how he did, and bid him be of good comfort, and he lay last night with a woman: To which he answered It is true, but the woman was my wife. Then they proceeded to ask, when they were married, and how they should know shee was his wife, and he told them where and when, but that was not enough, they told him, he must get a Certificate from his Captain that he was married to her and then he should have his liberty.

Friends and Country-men, where are you now? what shall you do that have no Captains to give you Certificates? sure you must have the banes of Matrimony re-asked at the Conventicle of Gallants at White-hall, or at least you must thence have a Congregationall Licence, (without offence be it spoken to true Churches) to lye with your wives, else how shall your wives be chast or the children Legitimate? they have now taken Cognizance over your wives and beds, whether will they next? Judgement is now come into the hand of the armed-fury Saints. My Masters have a care what you do, or how you look upon your wives, for the new-Saints Millitant are paramount [to] all Laws, King, Parliament, husbands, wives, beds, &c. But to let that passe.

Towards the evening we were sent for, to go before the Counsell of State at Darby-house, and after Lieutenant Collonel John Lilburne, and Mr. Wallwine had been before them, then I was called in, and Mr. Bradshaw spake to me, to this effect.

Master Overton, the Parliament hath seen a Book, Intituled, *The Second Part of Englands New-Chains*

Discovered, and hath past several Votes thereupon, and hath given Order to this Councel to make inquiry after the Authors and Publishers thereof, and proceed upon them as they see Cause, and to make a return thereof unto the House: And thereupon he Commanded Mr. Frost their Secretary to read over the said Votes unto me, which were to this purpose, as hath since been publickly proclaimed:

Die Martis, 27 Martii, 1649.

The House being informed of a Scandalous and Seditius Book Printed, entituled, *The Second Part of Englands New-Chains Discovered.*

The said Book was this day read.

Resolved upon the Question by the Commons assembled in Parliament, That this printed Paper, entituled, *The Second Part of Englands New-Chains Discovered* &c. doth contain most false, scandalous, and reproachful matter, and is highly Seditious and Destructive to the present Government, as it is now Declared and setled by Parliament, tends to Division and Mutiny in the Army, and the raising of a New War in the Commonwealth, and to hinder the present Relief of Ireland, and to the continuing of Free-Quarter: And this House doth further Declare, That the Authors, Contrivers, and Framers of the said Papers, are guilty of High Treason, and shall be proceeded against as Traytors; And that all Persons whatsoever, that shall joyn with, or adhere unto, and hereafter voluntarily Ayd or Assist the Authors, Framers, and Contrivers of the aforesaid Paper, in the prosecution thereof, shall be esteemed as Traytors to the Common-wealth, and be proceeded against accordingly.

Then Mr. Bradshaw spake to me much after this effect;

Master Overton, this Councel having received Information, That you had a hand in the Contriving and Publishing of this Book, sent for you by their Warrant to come before them; Besides, they are informed of other Circumstances at your Apprehension against you, That there were divers of the Books found about you. Now Mr. Overton, if you will make any Answer thereunto, you have your Liberty.

To which I answered in these words, or to the like effect:

Sir, what Title to give you, or distinguish you by, I know not; Indeed, I confesse I have heard by common report, that you go under the name of a Councel of State; but for my part, what you are I cannot well tell; but this I know, that had you (as you pretend) a just authority from the Parliament, yet were not your Authority valuable or binding, till solemnly proclaimed to the people: so that for my part, in regard you were pleased thus violently to bring me before you, I shall humbly crave at your hands, the production of your Authority, that I may know what it is, for my better information how to demean my self.

Presid.] Mr. Overton, We are satisfied in our Authority.

Ric. Overt.] Sir, if I may not know it, however I humbly desire, that I may be delivered from under the force of the Military power; for having a naturall and legall title to the Rights of an Englishman, I shall desire that I may have the benefit of the Law of England, (which Law taketh no cognizance of the Sword). And in case you or any man pretend matter of crime against me, in order to a tryall, I desire I may be resigned up to the Civil Magistrate, and receive a free and legall tryall in some ordinary Court of Justice, according to the known Law of the Land; that if I be found a transgressor of any established declared Law of England, on Gods name let me suffer the penalty of that Law.

Further, Sir, In case I must still be detained a prisoner, it is my earnest desire, that I may be disposed to some prison under the jurisdiction and custody of the

Civill Authority: For, as for my own part, I cannot in conscience (to the common right of the people) submit my self in any wise to the tryall or custody of the Sword; for I am no Souldier, neither hath the Army any Authoritie over me, I owe them neither dutie nor obedience, they are no Sheriffs, Justices, Bailiffs, Constables, or other Civil Magistrates: So that I cannot, neither will I submit unto their power, but must take the boldnesse to protest against it.

Presid. Mr. Overton, If this be your Answer, you may withdraw.

R. Overt. Sir, I humbly desire a word or two more.

Lieut. Gen. Let him have liberty.

Presid. Mr. Overton, You may speak on.

R. Over. Gentlemen, for future peace and securitie sake, I shall humbly desire to offer this unto your consideration; namely, that if you think it meet: That you would chuse any four men in England, pick and chuse where you please; and we (for my part, I speak it freely in my own behalf, and I think I may say as much in theirs) shall endeavour to the utmost of our power by a fair and moderate Discourse, to give the best account and satisfaction concerning the matter of difference betwixt us, that we can, that if possible, peace and agreement may be made: And this, after the weaknesse of my small understanding, I judge to be a fair and reasonable way: if you shall be pleased to accept of it, you may; if not, you may use your pleasure; I am in your hand, do with me as you think good, I am not able to hinder you.

Presid. Mr. Overton, If this be all you have to say, withdraw.

R. Overt. Sir, I have said.

So I was commanded into a little withdrawing room close by the Councel; and I supposed they would have taken my motion into consideration: But after I had been there a while, I was ordered to the Room again, where Lieut. Col. Lilburn, Mr. Walwine, &c. were.

And now that it may be clear unto the whole world, that we heartily desire the prevention and cessation of all differences and divisions that may be bred and break forth in the Land, to the hazard, if not actuall imbroilment thereof in a new exundation of blood in the prosecution of this controversie, wee do freely from the heart (that heaven and earth may bear witnesse betwixt our integrity to the peace of the Common-wealth, and their dealings with us) make this proffer as to be known to the whole world; that wee (in the first place I may best speak for my self; and I so far know the minds of Lieutenant Col. John Lilburn, Mr. Walwine, and Mr. Prince, that I may as freely speak it in their behalfs) wil, by the Assistance of God, give any four men in England that they shall chuse (although the Lieutenant General, and the Commissarie Generall be two of them) a free and moderate debate (if they shall think it no scorn) touching all matters of difference betwixt us, as to the businesse of the Common-wealth (for therein doth consist the controversie betwixt us) that if possibly, new flames and combustions may be quenched, and a thorow and an hearty composure be made betwixt us, upon the grounds of an equall and just Government. And that the businesse may be brought to a certain issue betwixt us, let them, if they please, chuse two Umpires out of the House, or else-where, and we will chuse two; and for our parts, we shall stand to the free determination or sentence, that these four, or any three of them shall passe betwixt us. Or else, if they please but to center upon *The Agreement of the People,* with amendments according to our late sad Apprehensions, presented to the House upon the 26 of February 1648,[1] for our parts, we shall seal a Contract of Oblivion for all by-past matters, relating either to good name, life,

[1] i. e. 1649, modern style.

libertie or estate; saving, of making Accompt for the publick Monies of the Common-wealth: And in such an Agreement we will center, to live and die with them in the prosecution thereof. And if this be not a fair and peaceable motion, let all well-minded people judge.

But if nothing will satisfie them but our bloud, we shall not (through the might of God) be sparing of that, to give witnesse to the Right and Freedom of this Common wealth against their Usurpation and Tyranny; but let them know this, That Building hath a bad Foundation that is laid in the bloud of honest men, such as their own knowledge and consciences bear them record, are faithfull to the common interest and safety of the People: out of our ashes may possibly arise their destruction. This I know, God is just, and he will repay the bloud of the innocent upon the head of the Tyrant. But to return to the Narrative.

After some small space that we had all been before them, we were called in again; first, Lieut. Col. John Lilburn, then Mr. Walwine, and then my self: And coming before them the second time, Mr. Bradshaw, spake to this effect:

Presid. Mr. Overton, The Councel hath taken your Answer into consideration, and they are to discharge their dutie to the Parliament, who hath ordered them to make enquiry after the Book, intituled, *The second part of England's new Chains,* &c. and thereof they are to give an account to the House: And the Councel hath ordered me to put this question unto you, Whether you had an hand in the contriving or publishing this Book, or no?

R. Overt. Sir, I well remember, that since you cut off the King's head, you declared (or at least the Parliament, from whence you pretend the derivation of your Authoritie) that you would maintain the known fundamentall Laws of the Land, and preserve them inviolable, that the meanest member of this Common-wealth, with the greatest, might freely and fully enjoy the absolute benefit thereof. Now Gentlemen, it is well known, and that unto your selves, that in cases criminall, as now you pretend against me, it is against the fundamentall Laws of this Common-wealth to proceed against any man by way of Interrogatories against himself, as you do against me: and I beleeve (Gentlemen) were you in our cases, you would not be willing to be so served your selves; (what you would have other men do unto you, that do you unto them.) So that for my part, Gentlemen, I do utterly refuse to make answer unto any thing in relation to my own person, or any man or men under heaven; but do humbly desire, that if you intend by way of Charge to proceed to any Triall of me, that it may be (as before I desired at your hands) by the known established Law of England, in some ordinary Court of Justice appointed for such cases (extraordinary waies being never to be used, but abominated, where ordinarie waies may be had) and I shall freely submit to what can be legally made good against me.

But I desire that in the mean time you would be pleased to take notice, that though in your eye I seem so highly criminal, as by those Votes you pretend; yet am I guiltie of nothing, not of this paper, intituled, *The second part of England's new Chains,* in case I had never so much an hand in it, till it be legally proved: for the Law looketh upon no man to be guiltie of any crime, till by law he be convicted; so that, I cannot esteem my self guiltie of any thing, till by the Law you have made the same good against me.

And further Sir, I desire you to take notice, that I cannot be guiltie of the transgression of any Law, before that Law be in being: it is impossible to offend that which is not; Where there is no Law there is no Transgression: Now, those Votes on which you proceed against me are but of yesterdaies being; so that, had I an hand in that Book whereof you accuse me, provided it were before those Votes, you cannot render me guiltie by those Votes: If I had done any thing in it, since the Votes (provided you had solemnly proclaimed the same) then you might have had some colour to have proceeded against me: but I have but newly heard the Votes, and since that you know I could do nothing.

Presid. Mr. Overton, I would correct your judgment in one thing: We are not upon any Triall of you; we are onely upon the discharge of our dutie, and that trust committed unto us by the Parliament, to make enquiry after the authors, contrivers and framers of the Book; and having information against your self and your Comrades, we sent for you, and are to return your Answer to the House, howsoever you dispute their Authority.

R. Overt. Dispute their Authoritie, Sir! That's but your supposition, and supposition is no proof. And Sir, as you say you are to discharge your dutie, so must I discharge mine. And as for matter of triall, I am sure you taxe me in a criminall way, and proceed to question me thereupon. But Sir, I conceive it my dutie to answer to none of your Questions in that nature, and therefore shall utterly refuse.

Now Gentlemen, I desire you to take notice, that I do not oppose you as you are members of the Commonwealth; for it is well known, and I think to some here, that I have ever been an opposer of oppression and tyrannie, even from the daies of the Bishops to this present time; and the Books* that I have writ and published do in some measure bear witness thereof, and it is well known, that my practice hath ever been answerable thereunto. I suppose no man can accuse me, but that I have opposed Tyrannie where-ever I found it: It is all one to me under what name or title soever oppression be exercised, whether under the name of King,

* *viz. Arraignment of Persecution. Ordinance of Tythes Dismounted. The Game at Scotch and English, &c.*

Parliament, Councel of State, under the name of this, or that, or any thing else; For tyrannie and oppression is tyrannie and oppression to me where-ever I finde it, and where-ever I finde it I shall oppose it, without respect of persons.

I know I am mortall and finite, and by the course of nature my daies must have a period, how soon I know not; and the most you can do, it is but to proceed to life; and for my part, I had rather die in the just vindication of the cause of the poor oppressed people of this Common-wealth, then to die in my bed; and the sooner it is, the welcomer, I care not if it were at this instant, for I value not what you can doe unto me.

But Gentlemen, I humbly desire yet a word or two. I confesse, I did not expect so much civilitie at your hands as I have found, and for the same I return you hearty thanks.

Now whereas you commonly say, That we will have no Bottom, center no where, and do taxe us by the Votes you read unto me, of destruction to the present Government, division and mutinie in the Armie, &c. But here I do professe unto you, as in the presence of the all-seeing God, before whom one day I must give an account of all my actions, That in case you will but conclude upon an equall and just Government by way of an Agreement of the People, as was honourably begun by the Generall Officers of the Army; and but free that Article in it which concerns the liberty of Gods Worship from the vexatious entanglements and contradictions that are in it, that so consciencious people might freely (without any fear of an insulting Clergie) live quietly and peaceably in the enjoyment of their consciences; As also to add unto it a Barr against Regalitie, and the House of Lords; As also to make provision in it against the most weighty oppressions of the Land; that thereby they may be utterly removed, and for the future prevented, and the people setled in freedom and safetie: And then, for my part, neither hand, foot, pen, tongue, mouth or breath of mine shall move against you; but I shall with my utmost power, with hand, heart, life and bloud, assist you in the prosecution thereof, and therein center. Try me, and if I fail of my word, then let me suffer.

Presid. Mr. Overton, If you have no more to say, you may withdraw.

R. Overt. Sir, I humbly crave the further addition of a word or two. Gentlemen, I desire (as I did before) that I may (according to the common right of the people of England) be forthwith freed from under the power of the Sword, and be delivered into the hands of the Civil Magistrate, in case I shall be still detained a prisoner; for I am so much against the intrusion of the Military power into the seat of the Magistrate, that I had rather you would fetter me legs and hands, and tie me neck and heels together, and throw me into a Dungeon, and not allow me so much as the benefit of bread and water till I be starved to death, then I would accept of the best Down-bed in England, with sutable accommodation, under the custody of the Sword.

President. Mr. Overton, I would correct your Judgment a litle, you are not under the Military power, but under the Civil authority; for by the Authority of Parliament this Counsel by their Warrant hath sent for you.

R. Overton. Sir, it is confest, that *pro forma tantum,* for matter of Forme, inke or paper, I am under the Civil Authoritie, but essentiallie and reallie, I am under the Martial power; for that Warrant by which I was taken, was executed upon me by the Military power, by a Partie of Horse, and divers Companies of Foot in Arms, and in that Hostile manner (like a prisoner of War) I was led Captive to White-hal, and there ever since, till commanded hither, I was kept amongst the Souldiers, and I am still under the same force: Besides,

Sir, these men are meer Souldiers, no Officers of the Magistracie of England, they brought no Warrant to me from anie Justice of Peace, neither did carrie me before anie Justice of Peace, but seised on me, and kept me by their own force: Therefore it is evident and cleer to me, That I am not under the Civil, but the Martial power.

President. Master Overton, If this be your Answer, you may withdraw.

R. Overton. Sir, I have said.

And so I was conducted to the Room where they had disposed Lieutenant Col. Lilburne and Mr. Walwine: And the next news we heard from them, was, of our Commitment to the Tower, and Master Prince and I were joyned as yoak-fellows in one Warrant; a Copie whereof is as followeth;

These are to will and require you, to receive herewith into your Custody the Persons of Master Richard Overton, and Master Thomas Prince, and them safely to keep in your prison of the Tower of London, until you receive further Order: They being Committed to you upon suspition of High Treason; of which you are not to fail; and for which this shall be your Warrant: Given at the Councel of State at Darby-House this Twentie eighth day of March, 1649.

> Signed in the Name, and by the Order of the Councel of State, appointed by Authority of Parliament.

To the Lieutenant of
the Tower.

> Jo. Bradshaw, President.

Thus all un-interested, unprejudiced persons, (who measure things as they are in themselves, having nothing in admiration with respect of persons, who simply and sincerely mind the freedom and prosperity of the Common-wealth) may clearly see, as in a Glass, by this tast of Aristocraticall Tyranny towards us, a perfect and lively resemblance of the Councell of State; *Ex pede Leonem,* you may know a Lion by his foot, or a Bear by his paw: by this you may see their nature and kind, what and from whence they are, and whether they tend, by this line you may measure the height depth and breadth of their new Architecture of State, and by making our case but yours, you will find your selves new fettered in chaines, such as never England knew or tasted before; that you may (truly if you will but measure it in the consequence thereof,) break forth and cry out, Their little finger is thicker then our Fathers loines; our Fathers made our yoke heavie, but these adde unto our yoake; our Fathers chastised us with whips, but these chastise us with Scorpions. Who would have thought in the daies of their glorious pretences for Freedom, in the daies of their Engagements, Declarations and Remonstrances, while they were the hope of the oppressed, the joy of the righteous, and had the mighty confluence of all the afflicted and well-minded people of the Land about them, (I principally reflect upon the Victors of the times) I say, who would have thought to have heard, seen, or felt such things from their hands as we have done? Who would have thought such glorious and hopefull beginnings should have vanished into Tyrannie? Who would have thought to have seen those men end in the persecution and imprisonment of persons whom their own Consciences tell them, to be men of known integritie to the Common-wealth; and which is so evident and demonstrative, that thousands in this Nation can bear Record thereof; and that those men should be so devillish, so tyrannicall and arbitrary, as after their imprisonment, to rake hell, and skim the Devill, to conjure out matter of Charge or accusation against them, that they might have their blood, as in our case they have done, sending abroad their blood-hounds to search and pry out in every corner, what could be made out against us, going up and down like roaring Lions seeking how they might devour us; one offering Mistris Prince her Husbands libertie, and the 1000 l. they owe him, if he will but discover what he knoweth (as they are pleased to imagine) against us; and not onely so, but some Members of the House (as Mr. Kiffin confess'd in respect of himself) negotiate with the principall Leaders of severall Congregations of religious people about the Town, to promote a petition, which was no other but in order to their bloudy designe against us; that those conscientious people (surprised by their fraudulent suggestions and craft) might (not truly understanding the business) appear in the disownment and discountenance of us; and in the approbation and furtherance of the prosecuters of their bloudy Votes of High-Treason, intentionally breathed out against us: for could they by their delusions overwhelm us once in the odium of religious people; with the venemous contagion of their malicious clamours, bug-bears, reproaches and lies, beget us under the Anathema of the Churches, then they think they may with ease and applause cut us off; for that's the venome lieth under the leafe, how finely soever they zeal it over; that so our friends and brethren (thus surprised and overtaken) may become our Butchers, and think they do God and their Country good service while they slay us; but let them beware how they contract the guilt of our bloud upon their heads; for assuredly the bloud of the Innocent will be upon them, and God will repay it; I speak not this to beg their mercy, I abhorre it, I bid defiance to what all the men and divels in earth or hell can do against me in the discharge of my understanding and Conscience for the good of this Common-wealth; for I know my Redeemer liveth, and that after this life I shall be restored to life and Immortality, and receive according to the innocency and uprightnesse of my heart: Otherwise, I tell you plainly, I would not thus put my life and wel-being in jeopardie, and expose my self to those extremities and necessities that I do; I would creaturize, be this or that or any thing else, as were the times, eat, drink, and take my pleasure; turn Judas or any thing to flatter great men for promotion: but blessed be the God of Heaven and Earth, he hath given me a better heart, and better understanding. But to proceed;

That which is most to our astonishment, we understand of a truth, That Master Kiffin (to whose Congregation my back-friend Axtel is a retainer) Master Spilsbury, Master Patience (who vilified the Book intituled, *The Second Part of Englands New Chains,* and yet confest he never saw it or heard it read, as by evidence can be made good) Mr. Fountain, Mr. Drapes, Mr. Richardson, Mr. Couset, Mr. Tomlins, and Mr. Wade the Scholmaster became their Pursuevants or bloud-hounds, to hunt us to the Bar of the House of Commons with a Petition (most evidently and cleerly in pursuance of our bloud) Intituled, *The humble Petition and Representation of the several Churches of God in London, commonly (though falsly) called Anabaptists,* April 2. 1649. tacitely and curiously in a most Religious vail pointing at, and reflecting upon us, as Interrupters of the Setlement of the Libertie and Freedom of this Common-wealth; headie, high-minded, unruly, disobedient, presumptuous, self-will'd, contemners of Rulers, Dignities and Civil Government, whoremasters, drunkares, cheaters, &c. as if it were not with those men, as with the Publican and Sinner, dis-owning the Book intituled, *The Second Part, &c.* which at that juncture of time, all circumstances dulie weighed, was an absolute justification of those Votes of High Treason, and of prosecution against us as Traytors, for the tendency of those Votes were vented at us, and that their own knowledge and Consciences tels them to be true, so that they could have done no more in Order to our bloud, then what they did in that matter, so as to hand it off fairly and covertly preserving to themselves the reputation of the Churches of God: and to adde unto their impiety against us, they juggle with the Churches, present it in the name of the Churches of God in London called Anabaptists, and in their names Remonstrate that they (meaning the Churches, as by the title they speak) neither had nor have heart nor hand in the framing, contriving, abetting, or promoting of the said Paper, which though read in several of our publick Meetings, we do solemnly professe, it was without our consent, being there openly opposed by us. Notwithstanding it is notoriously evident, That the generality of the People Dissented from their Petition against us; and as upon good intelligence I am informed, They had scarce ten in some Congregations to sign it, in some not above 2 or 3, in some none; and in the main they had not the Tythe of the people; and yet those men like a Consistory of Bishops, a Synod of Presbyters, or a New-England Classis, presume upon the Assumption of the name of Several Churches of God, as if to themselves they had purchased the Monopolie or Pattent thereof, or as if the persons of Mr. Kiffin, Mr. Patience, &c. were so many several Churches, (hence sprang the papal, Prelatical, and Presbyterial Supremacie over the Consciences of people) and therefore it behoveth the people to have a care of their Leaders.

We have had the name of King, the name of Parliament, the name of the Armie, &c. surprised, abused, and usurped against us by the hand of our exorbitant enemies; but never before, the name of Several Churches of God, and those stiled Anabaptists; Hear O Heavens, and judge O Earth! Was there ever the like Fact attempted or perpetrated amongst the Churches of God? such wickedness is not once to be named amongst them: And I do not doubt but the wel-minded Christian people of those several Churches presented by that Petition, will vindicate themselves from the Aspersion thereby laid upon them; For I cannot beleeve till I see it, That those people would do any thing, or own any thing that might but so much as seemingly tend to our bloud, or our imprisonment; I am confident they abhorre it: And they cannot in Conscience do less then to disavow that Bloudy Petition (as to its tendency against us) and till they do it, they will be sharers in the publick guilt of our imprisonment, yea, and of our Bloud, for (however God may divert the wicked purposes of men,) that Petition is guiltie of our Bloud.

I confesse, for my part, I am a man full of Sin, and personal Infirmities, and in that Relation I will not take upon me to cleer or justifie my self; but as for my Integrity and uprightnesse to the Common-wealth, to whatsoever my understanding tels me is for the good of mankind, for the safety, freedom, and tranquillity of my Country, happinesse and prosperity of my Neighbours, to do to my neighbor as I would be done by, and for the freedom and protection of Religious people: I say as to those things, (according to the weak measure of my understanding and judgment) I know my integrity to be such, that I shall freely (in the might of God) sacrifice my life to give witnesse thereunto; and upon that Accompt I am now in Bonds, a protestor against the Aristocratical Tyrannie of the Counsel of State, scorning their Mercy, and bidding defiance to their Crueltie, had they ten millions more of Armies, & Cromwels to perpetrate their inhumanities upon me; for I know they can pass but to this life; when they have done that, they can do no more; and in this case of mine, he that will save his life shall loose it; I know my life is hid in Christ, and if upon this accompt I must yeild it, Welcome, welcome, welcome by the grace of God.

And as for those reproaches and scandals like the

smoke of the bottomlesse pit, that are fomented against me; whereby too many zealous tender spirited people are prejudiced against my person, readie to abhorre the thing I do, though never so good, for my person sake; I desire such to remove their eies from persons to things: if the thing I do be good, it is of God; and so look upon it, and not upon me, and so they shall be sure not to mistake themselves, nor to wrong me: And I further desire such to consider, That tales, rumours, slanderings, backbitings, lyes, scandals &c. tost up and down like clouds with the wind, are not the fruits of the Spirit, neither are they weapons of Gods warfare, they are of the devil and corruption, and betray in the users of them an evil mind: It is a certain badge of a Deceiver to take up whisperings and tales of mens personal failings to inflect them to the cause those persons maintain, by such means to gain advantages upon them.

Consider whether the things I hold forth and professe as in relation to the Common-wealth, be not for the good of mankinde, and the preservation of Gods people: and if they be, my personal failings are not to be reckoned as a counter-balance against them. As I am in my self in respect to my own personall sins and transgressions; so I am to my self and to God, and so I must give an account; the just must stand by his own faith: But as I am in relation to the Common-wealth, that all men have cognizance of, because it concerns their own particular lives, livelihoods and beings, as well as my own; and my failings and evils in that respect I yeeld up to the cognizance of all men, to be righteously used against me. So that the businesse is, not how great a sinner I am, but how faithfull and reall to the Common-wealth; that's the matter concerneth my neighbour, and whereof my neighbour is only in this publick Controversie to take notice; and for my personall sins that are not of Civill cognizance or wrong unto him, to leave them to God, whose judgment is righteous and just. And till persons professing Religion be brought to this sound temper, they fall far short of Christianity; the spirit of love, brotherly charity, doing to all men as they would be done by, is not in them; without which they are but as a sounding brass, and a tinkling cymball, a whited wall, rottenness and corruption, let their ceremonial formall practice of Religion be never so Angel-like or specious.

There is a great noise of my sins and iniquities: but which of my Aspersers Oxe or Asse have I stollen? which of them have I wronged the value of a farthing? They taxe me with filthinesse, and strange impieties; but which amongst them is innocent? he that is innocent, let him throw the first stone; otherwise let him lay his hand on his mouth: I have heard of as odious failings, even of the same nature whereof they tax me (and it may be, upon better evidence) amongst them, laid open to me, even of the highest in present power, as well as amongst eminent persons in Churches; which I ever have counted unworthy to be used as an engine against them in the Controversie of the Common-wealth: But if they will not be quiet, I shall be forced, in honour to my own reputation, to open the Cabinet of my Aspersers infirmities, that the world may see what sort of men they are that say unto others, thou shalt not steal, and steal themselves: I shall be sorry to be forced to it; but if they will not be content, necessity hath no law, I shall (as Mr. John Goodwin said to Mr. Edwards, if he would not be quiet) make all their reputations as a stinking carcasse.

And although they think they have such firm matters against me, let them not be too hastie to pursue me with reproach any further, lest it recoil with a vengeance upon themselves: for it is an old and a true saying, One tale is good till another be told. Therefore let no man judge before the time, lest he be judged; for I am able to vindicate my self to all rationall men, as clear as the Sun at noon day, in what I have done.

Much I might have said as in relation to the illegality of our Apprehension, Commitment, &c. But for the present I shall omit it to further opportunity, or the engagement of some more abler pen: And so I shall commit my self and my wayes to God alone, with chearfulnesse and alacrity of spirit, rejoycing that he hath counted me worthy to bear witnesse once more against the Oppressours of the People, and to suffer for the sake of the poor, against the insulting tyrants of the times.

RICHARD OVERTON

From my Aristrocraticall
Captivity in the Tower
of London;
April 4,
1649.

Dulce est pro Patria mori.

Postscript

Courteous Reader, for thy better satisfaction concerning the infamous scandal raised by Lieutenant Colonel Axtel upon me, I thought meet to subjoin hereunto a Copie of an Affidavit concerning the Matter: But I have forborn the publishing of the Deponents name in print, upon his own desire; Yet those of my friends who are desirous, I shall be ready to shew unto them the Originall Copy: A transcript whereof is as followeth.

A. B. of the Parish of St. Anne Aldersgate, Citizen and Pewterer of London, aged thirty six years or thereabouts, maketh Oath, That whereas Lieutenant Colonel Axtel, upon his Apprehending of Mr. Richard Overton, upon Wednesday, between five and sixe of the clock in the morning, being the twenty ninth of March last past, 1649, by an Order from the Councell of State, did raise and make a Report, that he took the said Mr. Overton in bed with this Deponents Wife, that That Report was and is altogether false and scandalous; for that this Deponent and the said Mr. Overton, the Tuesday night next preceding the said Wednesday, did lie both together all that night in one and the self same bed; and this Deponents Wife and his little Childe in another bed of this Deponents house or lodgings. And that the next morning, before the said Lieutenant Colonel Axtel knocked at the door, this Deponent, with his Wife, with the said Mr. Overton, were all up and ready (saving that Mr. Overton had not put on his boots, band and cuffs) and were altogether in a chamber of this Deponents house, where this Deponents Wife was then suckling of her childe: and this Deponent hearing some body knock at the door, went down to open it; which was readily done by a girl of the same house. Whereupon the said Lieutenant Colonel Axtel (meeting this Deponent upon the stairs, and asking him if he were Mr. Overton; to which this Deponent replying, No;) commanded the Musketiers (who attended him) to take this Deponent into their custody, and he himself went directly up into the chamber with some Musketiers attending him. All which this Deponent affirmeth upon his oath to be true.

A. B.

Jurat. 4 Aprilis,
    1649.
Rob. Aylet.

FINIS.

XI

The English Souldiers Standard

[H. N. Brailsford (op. cit., p. 198) attributes this pamphlet to Walwyn, pointing out how closely the thinking resembles that of *The Bloody Project*. He may well be right, but it should be remembered that the four Leveller leaders were all imprisoned together at this time and any publication must have been fully discussed between them. This gives its statement of policy on Ireland a special importance. Notable also is the emphasis laid on Army-civilian unity and the need for the soldiers to win civilian support. Thomason dates it April 5th, 1649, so that it must have been one of the first tasks undertaken by the prisoners after their arrest. Since the other three must have been occupied with their parts of *A Picture* the likelihood that this pamphlet was at least drafted by Walwyn is increased.]

The English Souldiers

Standard

to repair to, for
Wisdom and Understanding
in these doleful
backsliding times.
To be read by every

honest Officer

to his

Souldiers,

and by the Souldiers
one to another.

It was most worthily said of you, in your Declaration of the 14 of June 1647, page 6, That you were not a meer mercenary Army, hired to serve any arbitrary power of a State; but were called forth, and conjured by the severall Declarations of Parliament, to the defence of your own and the peoples just Rights and Liberties: and so you took up Arms in judgment and conscience, to those ends.

Which expressions of yours, and the like, gave so great content and satisfaction to all sorts of well-minded people, that the meanest private Souldier amongst you was more honourable in their esteem, then the most glorious out-side man in the world: you had been their guard by day, and their defence by night; you delivered them from the Bear, and from the Lion; and when the Parliament began to turn Tyrants themselves, and would have broken you in pieces by dividing of you, and sending a part of you for Ireland, that so they might without obstacle have trampled upon the peoples Liberties, you resolved, as became an Army whom the Lord had blessed, to deliver the people also from those uncircumcised Philistims.

And when they would have terrified you from so doing, with urging, that you resisted Authority; you spared not to tell them (and that truly) That it is no resisting of Magistracy, to side with the just principles and Law of Nature and Nations: And that the Souldiery may lawfully hold the hands of the Generall who will turn his Canon (meaning his strength, power and authority) against his Army, on purpose to destroy (or enslave) them: And such (you say) were the proceedings of our Ancestours of famous memorie, to the purchasing of such Rights and Liberties as they have enjoyed through the price of their bloud; and we both by that, and the later bloud of our dear friends and fellow-souldiers (with the hazard of our own) do now lay claim to.

And truly friends, it will be necessary for you to look quickly about you, and that to purpose, and to be like unto our Ancestors, or like unto your selves in what you then declared: and to enquire, whether you and the rest of the people of this Nation are yet restored to those their Rights and Liberties: and accordingly to be satisfied in your Judgments and Consciences.

You have been many of you Country-men and know well what a miserable burthen Tythes and Free-quarter are: many of you have been Trades-men and laborious people, and can be sensible how intolerable the burthen of Excise, and Customs, and Monopolies in Trade are, Officers and Usurers running away with that which should pay you, and the poor labour for; to the ruine of Trade. You cannot but know what it is to live continually in prison, in penury and beggery, hearing and seeing the misery of such poor people in all places.

You know, we live under unknown Laws, written in canting French, vext and molested with a whole drove of corrupt Judges, Lawyers, Jaylors, and the like Caterpillers of the Common-wealth.

Your great Officers indeed have reduced the Supreme Authority into one Jurisdiction: but what are we or you the better, when it is used to set up new ways of tryals for our Lives and Liberties, new Courts of Justice, denying both you and us (when they please) the benefits of tryals by twelve sworn men: when already they have punish'd for matters of Religion, as other corrupt Parliaments use to do: and when they have erected a Councell of State that already examines men upon Interrogatories against themselves in criminall Cases: when they stop the Presse, that no information shall be given to you or the people, and imploy worse beagles to hunt after books, than the High-Commission or Star-Chamber ever did?

Nay Friends, where are you and our Liberties, when your Generall Councel of Officers make it so hainous a crime for Souldiers to petition Parliaments, without licence of their Officers. – It is but few years since that in London the Aldermen of the City endeavoured that no Citizens should petition the Parliament, but first they should passe the Common Councel.

But it was when those great men intended to grasp into their hands all power both of Parliament and people; as appeared soon after by their pernitious Remonstrances, and desperate Engagements; which we beleeve had done much more mischief, if honest and resolved Citizens had not made bold with their Greatships, and frequently visited the House with Petitions, which would as soon have past the fire, as the Common Councell.

And you had best look unto your selves, and to your and our Liberties, when as your Officers (many of them) begin to combine together, and punish men for petitioning; assure your selves, if they go on, your Liberties and ours are not long-lived; nay, are they not at last gasp, when they are grown so raging mad, as to importune for a Law to have power in themselves, to hang and put to death any person, though not of the Army, as shall hold any discourse with Souldiers about their own and the peoples just Rights and Liberties? – Pray friends, were these men any part of the Army when you published to the world, that you took up Arms in Judgment and Conscience, for the peoples just Rights and Liberties? or have those your Officers forgot themselves, and utterly lost their consciences, and all sense of their then promises, Declarations, and Remonstrances? if so, you shall do well to remember them, as you did those Officers of yours that made scruple to engage with you for your right of petitioning, and for the peoples Liberties at New-market.

Or are these Officers usurpers, and not properly the Councell that was then chosen by the Army? pray look to it, for your Declarations and their works differ exceedingly; the one tending to freedom, but the latter to such a bondage as all true English Souldiers will abhor; and if you find that you have not chosen them to deal with you in those affairs of the Common-wealth, which concern every private Souldier, as the greatest Commander: What have you then to do, but chuse out from amongst your selves, such faithfull men, whether Officers or Souldiers, as in these doubtfull staggering times, have stood firm to their first principles, and do evidence by their humility and resolution, that they took up arms in judgement and Conscience, for their own and the peoples just Rights, and Liberties: and such as rather then the Nation should be deprived thereof, being purchased with so vast expence of blood, durst hold the hands of the Generall, and all the Generall Officers, if they shall persist to turn their Cannons, their strength, power, and authority to the enslaving of the Common-wealth.

For what else is become of that judgment and Conscience, in which you took up armes? certainly your Consciences cannot be satisfied that your Generall, and Generall Officers, no nor the new Generall Councell of Officers, (which seldom exceeds three-score persons) shall after all your tedious strivings, and struglings for liberty, against all other parties, make both you and us, slaves to themselves in a Counsell of State, or their own packt Parliament? certainly Tyranny, Cruelty and continuance of oppression, is not the lesse because your Officers are now the Authors and continuers of it: but should rather be esteemed the greater and more abominable, by how much their promises have exceeded others. It cannot stand either with sound judgment, or good Conscience, that now you should be so far respecters of persons, as to beare with that wickedness, and treachery in your pretended friends and Commanders, which you have by many years war laboured to destroy and root out, in two great and powerfull parties.

You are seriously to consider that you have an alseeing God to give an account unto, and are not to please your Commanders in fulfilling their wils; but to be sure that you give satisfaction to your Conscience in the well pleasing of Almighty God.

And it will be no satisfaction at all to his justice, when he shall call you to an account for the killing and slaying of men, for you to say that you did it in obedience to the Commands of your Generall and Officers; for you must note that it is those just ends, the rights and liberties of the people, that only can acquit you from being murtherers in all you have done, so that you may at once highly please your commanders in killing and slaying of men, to make way for their greatness, wealth, and domination; and more highly displease God in being murtherers in so doing: nor can you escape his heavy Judgments, except you persevere and go on to those just ends, unto which you have made your way as through a Sea of Blood, and to be no respecters of persons, but to take whomsoever for an enemy that shall oppose you therein.

It is observed that you are very strict against your own fellow Souldiers, in case they offend, though in small matters, inflicting very severe punishments for particular offences; and why then look you not after and consider the ways of your Commanders, but let them pass with all their delusions of the Army, abusing the faith and credit thereof, with all sorts of people, breaking your Counsell of Agitators, corrupting and terrifying both Officers and Souldiers, to mould them to their own vile and unworthy ends: and are now in a ready way to make themselves, and their creatures in

Parliament, and elsewhere absolute Masters over the Common-wealth? Nay do you not help them in it for want of consideration? for why else are you so ready to execute their cruell sentences upon honest and faithfull Souldiers, as your shooting the man to death at Ware, and imprisoning of divers about the agreement of the people? And now also of late your forcing of five worthy Souldiers to ride the Horse, with their faces to the Horse tails, and breaking their swords over their heads, for standing to their and your Right in petitioning, and for presenting a letter to your cruell Counsell in justification thereof?

It seems it is a very true proverbe, that honors change manners, and is fully verified in your great Commanders, who in the fore recited Declaration of the 14 of June 1647, earnestly desired that the right and freedom of the people to present petitions to the Parliament might be cleared and vindicated, haveing made it before hainous crime in Hollis, and Stapleton, to hinder the Souldiers from petitioning; and yet now being in honor and power, judge, and sentence honest faithfull Souldiers, to base unworthy punishments, for but resolving to petition.

But truely friends, suffer this and suffer any thing; experience saith, he that takes one box on the ear invites another; and when Souldiers that should be men in all things, stand still and suffer their fellow Souldiers to be thus abused by a pack of Officers, no marvell if these officers turn Tyrants, and presume to do any thing to any man.

What right hath a Generall, Generall Officers, or a Counsell of Officers, to petition more then the meanest private Souldier? surely, to be a Generall is not to be above Law, except he make himself a Tyrant; is he or any Officer any other but a person under authority and accomptable for discharge of their trusts? nor is a private Souldier a slave because he is a private Souldier: but to have as full benefit of the Law, as clear a use of his liberty in petitioning, or otherwayes as his Generall, or Officers; and there is no surer mark to know a Tyrant by, or such as would be so, then for any to argue otherwise: And it will be good to mark such with a black coale.

Pray consider it, and lay it to heart: Is it not a shame that your fellow-souldiers should undergo so slavish, so severe and painfull punishment, as to ride the woodden horse, or run the gauntlet, and be whipt for small particular offences, and that you should suffer in the mean time your Officers and Commanders to turn Tyrants, and never punish them at all for it? Is this to take up Arms in Judgment and Conscience, when one man, being your Commander, may (as the proverb saith) steal a horse, and you will hang a private souldier for but looking over the hedge? for what comparison is there between a private souldiers offence, and an Officers turning a Bear, a Wolf, a Tyrant?

Beleeve it, if you look not to it speedily, your Officers are in a ready way to make you and the Commonwealth absolute slaves; for they mould and fashion the Army even how they please; preferring none to commands but flatterers and servile men, and catch at all advantages to turn all such out of command as are anyway sensible of the rights of the people; and have taken so absolute a power therein so long, that they have done very much of their work:

And do beleive all is formed to their own bent, and that's the reason they presume now to propose the sending of many of you for Ireland, pretending extraordinary necessity, and that that Nation otherwise will be utterly lost: — but surely all parties are not so soon agreed; 'twill not be amiss to make two words to such a bargain.

This you know is not the first fetch for Ireland; and you must note 'tis neither Ireland, nor Scotland, nor any other forces they fear, but the sting of their own consciences perpetually tels them they have dealt most perfideously, and Tyrannously with the Army, and Common-wealth; and they perceive by the many motions of Souldiers, and others, that the Army is likely to draw out Adjutators once more, whose morning they know will be the evening of their domination, and the next day they fear will prove their dooms day:

To avoid which, in all post haste they must be divided, and sent some one way, and some another; but if you be wise, stay a little, or you may perhaps never meet again. Certainly, before you go, it will be good for you to see those Rights and Liberties of the people, for which you took up Arms in judgment and conscience, cleared and secured, by a full and clear Agreement of the people; and not to leave them at the meer arbitrary mercy of a Councel of State, or a pack'd Parliament: for since they have dared to gull and cheat you to your faces, and whilest you are hereabouts, and together; what inhumane cruelties may they not do in your absence? especially, since they incline to raise more forces of a mercenary and servile nature, that shall make no questions for conscience sake about their Commands, as you have been used to do; and then fare-well the English Liberties for ever.

What-ever they may tell you, or however they may flatter you, there is no less danger lies at the bottom of this business for Ireland, and therefore it behoves every one of you to lay it to heart: and before you resolve upon a new Engagement, first see a new Representative of the Army established, by the free Election of every Regiment; and refer your selves to their Counsel and advice in all things, to be disposed of as they shall see cause; and neither admit of disbandings, nor of new listings, nor of any undertaking for Ireland, or any other service, but as that Councell shall advise.

For consider, as things now stand, to what end you

should hazard your lives against the Irish: have you not been fighting these seven years in England for Rights and Liberties, that you are yet deluded of? and that too, when as none can hinder you of them but your own Officers, under whom you have fought? and will you go on stil to kil, slay and murther men, to make them as absolute Lords and Masters over Ireland as you have made them over England? or is it your ambition to re-duce the Irish to the happinesse of Tythes upon trebble dammages, to Excise, Customs and Monopolies in Trades? or to fill their prisons with poor disabled prison-ers, to fill their Land with swarms of beggers; to enrich their Parliament-men, and impoverish their people; to take down Monarchical Tyranny, and set up an Aristo-cratical Tyranny; or to over-spread that Nation as this yet is, with such Wasps and Hornets as our Lawyers and their Confederates? Or if you intend not this, or would be sorry to see no better effects of your under-takings, it certainly concerns you in the first place, and before you go, to see those evils reformed here; that when occasion shall justly invite you thither, vou may carry a good platform in your hands, such a one as possibly they will never fight against: And it would be much more to be wished, that you might overcome them by just and equall offers, then by strength and force. And except you begin and proceed thus, how you will satisfie your consciences, is not discernable.

Therefore look to it, and be not surprised neither with the suddenness nor the plausibleness that may be put upon it by your General, or General Councels; the killing and slaying of men, or the making of a War, being a thing that every particular man of you must give a strict account to God for; in whose sight your Commanders are of as smal weight, when they come to be put into his just balance, as the meanest of you; and at whose great day, these will be found infallible truths, though now they will be called dividing doctrines.

But you must be stedfast to truths, and not be startled from your principles, nor from your promises and engagements, by the revilings of men: these being properly to be called Dividers, that forsake the society of honest men, because they stick close to their principles: it being also certainly good and justifiable to divide for good, rather then to unite for evill.

Labour by all means every man of you to preserve the love of the people toward you, and upon all occasions make it evident that it is for their good you continue in Arms, be courteous and gentle towards all you meet, whether in the streets, or upon the Roads; give them kind language and civil respects, without justling, or brushing, or bustling for the way; a thing which some proud Officers have cherish'd too much in some rude persons: and at your Quarters exercise your selves in harmless refreshments, without noise or lavish expence and give the preeminence to the Master and Mistris of the Family, whether rich or poor; and so you have food and raiment, be therewith content, without regard of bravery or delicateness; eat not but for hunger, which makes all things sweet; and cloath not but for health; and your happiness will not be far to seek.

Beware of entertaining il thoughts of any man, or of any condition of men without good proof; try and examine all things which shall be proposed unto you to act upon; and act or not act as you find the things good or evil; and be not diverted from your own understandings, by your respect to mens persons, nor terrified by aspersions cast upon the proposers, which from our Saviours time to this day hath ever been the obstructer of all good endevours: and if you mind the present proceedings, you will find it was never more practised then now; and it wil never go wel with the Publick, till you mark all aspersers as men that labour to deceive; and know what they have to alledge against the matter proposed, without reflection upon the persons that propose it, or you will never go on with any thing of worth.

Its come to a pretty pass with most of your great Officers: they would have you to obey their commands, though to the killing and slaying of men, without asking a reason: and as the Church of Rome holds the poor ignorant Papists in blind obedience, who are taught to beleeve as the Church beleeves; so would they have it with you, to be led this way, or that way (as men lead horses) into Ireland, or Scotland, or any whither, and as horses shall be whipped, or hanged as mutiniers, if you but dispute the cause, or but petition to have the cause stated before you go, that your judgments and consciences may be fully satisfied (as becometh honest men and Christians) in the lawfulness of whatsoever you undertake. But as there is no Tyrants like those of Rome, through the sottish ignorance of the Papists; so there is nothing will make your Officers so perfect tyrants, as this kind of blind obedience in you: nor wil any thing demonstrate that you took up arms in judgment and conscience, but that every one of you be satisfied in both, before you undertake or engage in any service: and that by sound consideration you wipe off that scandal which your great Officers have fixt upon you; that is, that if they but provide the Troopers good pay, they make no question but to command them any whither, and that they are then assured the Foot will follow the Horse whithersoever they go. T'is a sad storie, but it is frequent in their discourse, and no doubt you know it; and shews to what state they designe to bring you. On the other side, if any thing be proposed to you that is good in it self, and absolutely necessarie for the peace and freedom of the Common-wealth, how then do they bestir themselves, and even sweat with labor to perswade, that you see not to the bottom of it, that it is the most dangerous designe that ever was, that Jesuits at the least must be the authors of it, if not Levellers, who like Jack Cade, and Wat Tiler, and the Anabaptists of

Munster, would have all things common, wives and all.

But if you rightly consider, this doth but manifest unto you, that all Tyrants are directed by one and the same means; this being but the very same measure which was measured to the whole Army, a little before you past through the City, by those your opposers that were then setting up other Tyrannie.

Your General and Gen. Officers being then Jack Cade and Wat Tiler, that would have all things common; who now setting up for themselves, have packt a Parliament and a Councell of State for their purpose, must bestow the same language upon them that oppose those, as was bestowed upon themselves, and whilest you live you may confidently build upon, that none but those that would be Tyrants, will by aspersions go about to terrifie men from relying upon their own understandings.

You have had very much experience: and if you do but any thing consider and resolve, you shall very hardly be deceived; but assure your selves the great work in hand is how to deceive or corrupt you, it being impossible otherwise for them to become Masters of the Common-wealth.

And if they can but get a considerable part of you for Ireland before you see the Councell of State abolished, and this Nation set upon such sure foundations of Freedom, as shall not be in the power of future Parliaments to subvert, their work's done: nay if they cannot get you for Ireland as themselves much doubt thereof, and have cause enough considering the difficulties attending; yet if they can but get a good part of you in to Scotland before you see those Foundations of freedom setled firmly by an honest agreement of the people, nothing can hinder them of their designe.

Therefore be sure to see this Nation well settled first: keep together here and you may be confident none dare meddle with you from abroad, and when all things are to your mind at home, you may then safely cast your eys abroad, but not before, nor will it ever be good for you to meddle abroad but upon evident cause, upon good grounds, that you may engage upon sound judgement and good conscience; and not as most of the world doth through ambition, covetousness, and revenge, the fomenters of most of the wars that ever were; and tho religion, freedom, peace and prosperity of the people, have been ever in the tongue, yea though accompanied with fastings and prayings, and long preachings, yet your experiences cannot but tell you, ambition, covetousnesse, and revenge have ever been at the heart; and God is discovering it to the whole world.

And may every one of you, and your wel-minded Officers, be therein effectuall instruments to his glory, and in the accomplishment of the freedom, peace and happiness of this miserably abused Nation: And that you may be so, and neither be diverted nor terrified from setling yourselves thereunto, and that with all your might, cast your eys frequently on this your *Standard,* and be diligent in searching into your own Consciences, and swerve not from what you find to be your duty; prefer your Officers before others, if they inform your Judgements aright, and lead you to nothing but what is evidently just, obey them exactly after you are resolved of the Justnesse of the cause, but not before.

For he that runs to kill men meerly upon Authority, or others Judgments, or for money, is condemned of himself, in his Conscience, as a murtherer, be the cause what it will; and first or last shall not escape the Judgments of God.

FINIS.

XII

A Manifestation

[Though signed by all four Leveller leaders, *A Manifestation,* both at the time and since, has usually been regarded as mainly Walwyn's. *Walwins Wiles* says that its "devout, specious, meek, self-denying, soft and pleaseant lips savours much of the sligh, cunning and close subtlety . . . of Mr. William Walwyn . . . of whose curious spinning we have several reasons to presume this piece." Walwyn, as he was bound to do, denies this, saying, "all our four heads, and hands were nigh equally employed." Yet the style suggests that if all heads were employed the hand was mainly his. *A Manifestation* is dated from the Tower, April 14th and was probably printed at once.

H. and D., pp. 276–284.]

A
MANIFESTATION

FROM

Lieutenant Col. John Lilburn, Mr William
Walwyn, Mr Thomas Prince, and
Mr Richard Overton,
(Now Prisoners in the TOWER of London)
And others, commonly (though unjustly)

STYLED

LEVELLERS.

Intended for their

FULL VINDICATION

FROM

The many aspersions cast upon them, to
render them odious to the World, and unserviceable
to the Common-wealth.
And to satisfie and ascertain all MEN
whereunto all their Motions and Endeavours
tend, and what is the ultimate Scope of
their Engagement in the

PUBLICK AFFAIRES.

They also that render evill for good, are Our adversaries:
because We follow the thing that good is.

Printed in the year of our LORD, 1649.

SINCE no man is born for himself only, but obliged by the Laws of Nature (which reaches all) of Christianity (which ingages us as Christians) and of Publick Societie and Government, to employ our endeavours for the advancement of a communitive Happinesse, of equall concernment to others as our selves: here have we (according to that measure of understanding God hath dispensed unto us) laboured with much weaknesse indeed, but with integrity of heart, to produce out of the Common Calamities, such a proportion of Freedom and good to the Nation, as might somewhat compensate its many grievances and lasting sufferings: And although in doing thereof we have hitherto reaped only Reproach, and hatred for our good Will, and been faine to wrestle with the violent passions of Powers and Principalities; yet since it is nothing so much as our Blessed Master and his Followers suffered before us, and but what at first we reckoned upon, we cannot be thereby any whit dismayed in the performance of our duties, supported inwardly by the Innocency and evennesse of our Consciences.

'Tis a very great unhappinesse we well know, to be alwayes strugling and striving in the world, and does wholly keep us from the enjoyment of those contentments our severall Conditions reach unto: So that if we should consult only with our selves, and regard only our own ease, Wee should never enterpose as we have done, in behalfe of the Common-wealth: But when so much has been done for recovery of our Liberties, and seeing God hath so blest that which has been done, as thereby to cleer the way, and to afford an opportunity which these 600 years has been desired, but could never be attained, of making this a truly happy and wholly Free Nation; We think our selves bound by the greatest obligations that may be, to prevent the neglect of this opportunity, and to hinder as much as lyes in us, that the bloud which has been shed be not spilt like water upon the ground, nor that after the abundant Calamities, which have overspread all quarters of the Land, the change be onely Notionall, Nominall, Circumstantiall, whilst the reall Burdens, Grievances and Bondages, be continued, even when the Monarchy is changed into a Republike.

We are no more concern'd indeed then other men, and could bear the Yoke we believe as easily as others; but since a Common Duty lyes upon every man to be cautious and circumspect in behalfe of his Country, especially while the Government thereof is setling, other mens neglect is so far we thinke from being a just motive to us of the like sloath and inanimadvertency, as that it rather requires of us an increase of care and circumspection, which if it produces not so good a settlement as ought to be, yet certainly it will prevent its being so bad as otherwise it would be, if we should all only mind our particular callings and imployments.

So that although personally we may suffer, yet our solace is that the Common-wealth is therby some gainer, and we doubt not but that God in his due time wil so cleerly dispel the Clouds of Ignominy and Obloquy which now surround us by keeping our hearts upright and our spirits sincerely publike, that every good man will give us the right hand of fellowship, and be even sorry that they have been estranged, and so hardly opinionated against us: We question not but that in time the reason of such misprisions will appeare to be in their eyes and not in our Actions, in the false Representation of things to them and improper glosses that are put upon every thing we do or say: In our own behalfs we have as yet said nothing, trusting that either shame and Christian duty would restraine men from making so bold with others good Name and Reputation, or that the sincerity of our actions would evince the falshood of these scandals, and prevent the Peoples Beliefe of them; But we have found that with too much greedinesse they suck in Reports that tend to the discredit of others, and that our silence gives encouragement to bad Rumors of us; so that in all places they are spread, and industriously propagated as well amongst them that know us, as them that know us not, the first being fed with Jealousies that there is more in our designs then appeares, that there is something of danger in the bottom of our hearts, not yet discovered: that we are driven on by others, that we are even discontented and irresolved, that no body yet knowes what we would have, or where our desires will end; whilst they that know us not are made believe any strange conceit of us, that we would Levell all mens estates, that we would have no distinction of Orders and Dignities amongst men, that we are indeed for no government, but a Popular confusion; and then againe that we have bin Agents for the King, and now for the Queen; That we are Atheists, Antiscripturists, Jesuites and indeed any thing, that is hatefull and of evill repute amongst men.

All which we could without observance pass over, remembring what is promised to be the Portion of good men, were the damage only personall, but since the ends of such Rumors are purposely to make us uselesse and unserviceable to the Common-wealth, we are necessitated to open our breasts and shew the world our insides, for removing of those scandalls that lye upon us, and likewise for manifesting plainly and particularly what our desires are, and in what we will center and acquiess: all which we shall present to publike view and consideration, not pertinatiously or Magisterially, as concluding other mens judgements, but manifesting our own, for our further vindication, and for the procuring of a Bond and lasting establishment for the Commonwealth.

First, Then it will be requisite that we express our selves concerning Levelling, for which we suppose is commonly meant an equalling of mens estates, and taking away the proper right and Title that every man has to what is his own. This as we have formerly declared against, particularly in our petition of the 11 of Sept. so do we again professe that to attempt an inducing the same is most injurious, unlesse there did precede an universall assent thereunto from all and every one of the People. Nor doe we, under favour, judge it within the Power of a Representative it selfe, because although their power is supreame, yet it is but deputative and of trust, and consequently must be restrained expresly or tacitely, to some particulars essential as well to the Peoples safety and freedom as to the present Government.

The Community amongst the primitive Christians, was Voluntary, not Coactive; they brought their goods and laid them at the Apostles feet, they were not enjoyned to bring them, it was the effect of their Charity and heavenly mindednesse, which the blessed Apostles begot in them, and not the Injunction of any Constitution, which as it was but for a short time done, and in but two or three places, that the Scripture makes mention of, so does the very doing of it there and the Apostles answer to him that detained a part, imply that it was not esteemed a duty, but reckoned a voluntary act occasioned by the abundant measure of faith that was in those Christians and Apostles.

We profess therefore that we never had it in our thoughts to Level mens estates, it being the utmost of our aime that the Common-wealth be reduced to such a passe that every man may with as much security as may be enjoy his propriety.

We know very well that in all Ages those men that engage themselves against Tyranny, unjust and Arbitrary proceedings in Magistrats, have suffered under such appellations, the People being purposely frighted from that which is good by insinuations of imaginary evill.

But be it so, we must notwithstanding discharge our Duties, which being performed, the successe is in Gods hand to whose good pleasure we must leave the cleering of mens spirits, our only certainty being Tranqillity of mind, and peace of Conscience.

For distinction of Orders and Dignities, We think them so far needfull, as they are animosities of vertue, or requisite for the maintenance of the Magistracy and Government, we thinke they were never intended for the nourishment of Ambition, or subjugation of the People but only to preserve the due respect and obedience in the People which is necessary for the better execution of the Laws.

That we are for Government and against Popular Confusion, we conceive all our actions declare, when rightly considered, our aim having bin all along to reduce it as near as might be to perfection, and certainly we know very well the pravity and corruption of mans heart is such that there could be no living without it; and that though Tyranny is so excessively bad, yet of the two extreames, Confusion is the worst: Tis somewhat a strange consequence to infer that because we have laboured so earnestly for a good Government, therefore we would have none at all, Because we would have the dead and exorbitant Branches pruned, and better sciens grafted, therefore we would pluck the Tree up by the roots.

Yet thus have we been misconceived, and misrepresented to the world, under which we must suffer, till God sees it fitting in his good time to cleer such harsh mistakes, by which many, even good men keep a distance from us.

For those weake suppositions of some of us being Agents for the King or Queen, we think it needful to say no more but this, That though we have not bin any way violent against the persons of them, or their Partie, as having aimed at the conversion of all, and the destruction of none, yet doe we verily beleeve that those Principles and Maxims of Government which are most fundamentally opposite to the Prerogative, and the Kings interest, take their first rise and originall from us, many whereof though at first startled at, and disown'd by those that professed the greatest opposition to him, have yet since been taken up by them and put in practise: and this we think is sufficient, though much more might be said to cleer us from any Agency for that Party.

It is likewise suggested that we are acted by others, who have other ends then appear to us; we answer, That that cannot be, since every thing has its rise amongst our selves, and since those things we bring to light cannot conduce to the ends of any but the publike weale of the Nation.

All our Desires, Petitions and Papers are directly opposite to all corrupt Interests; nor have any credit with us but persons well known, and of certain aboads, and such as have given sound and undeniable testimonies of the truth of their affection to their Country: Besides, the things we promote, are not good onely in appearance, but sensibly so: not moulded nor contrived by the subtill or politick Principles of the World, but plainly produced and nakedly sent, without any insinuating arts, relying wholly upon the apparent and universall beleefe they carry in themselves; and that is it which convinces and engages us in the promotion thereof. So that that suggestion has not indeed any foundation in it self, but is purposely framed, as we conceive, to make us afraid one of another, and to disable us in the promotion of those good things that tend to the freedom and happinesse of the Common-wealth.

For our being Jesuits, either in Order or Principles, as 'tis severally reported of us; Though the easiest Negative is hardly proved; yet we can say, That those on whom the first is principally fix'd, are married, and were never over Sea: and we think Marriage is never dispenc'd withall in that Order, and that none can be admitted into the Order but such as are personally present. 'Tis hard that we are put to expresse thus much; and haply we might better passe such reports over in silence; but that we beleeve the very mentioning of them publickly, will be an answer to them, and make such as foment them asham'd of such generally condemned wayes of discrediting and blasting the Reputation of other men. For the principles of Jesuits, we professe we know not what they are; but they are generally said to be full of craft and worldly policy; and therefore exceedingly different from that plainness and simplicity that is apparantly visible in all our proceedings.

Whereas its said, we are Atheists and Antiscripturists, we professe that we beleeve there is one eternall and omnipotent God, the Author and Preserver of all things in the world. To whose will and directions, written first in our hearts, and afterwards in his blessed Word, we ought to square our actions and conversations. And though we are not so strict upon the formall and Ceremonial part of his Service, the method, manner, and personall injunction being not so clearly made out unto us, nor the necessary requisites which his Officers and Ministers ought to be furnished withall as yet appearing to us in any that pretend thereunto: yet for the manifestation of Gods love in Christ, it is cleerly assented unto by us; and the practicall and most reall part of Religion is as readily submitted unto by us, as being, in our apprehensions, the most eminent and the most excellent in the world, and as proceeding from no other but that God who is Goodnesse it self: and we humbly desire his Majesty daily more and more to conform our hearts to a willing and sincere obedience thereunto.

For our not being preferred to Offices and Places of profit and credit, which is urged to be the ground of our dissatisfaction, we say, That although we know no reason why we should not be equally capable of them with other men, nor why our publick Affection should be any barr or hinderance thereunto: Yet on the other side, we suppose we can truly say of our selves, that we have not been so earnest and solicitous after them as others: and that in the Catalogue of Sutors, very few that are reckoned of us, are to be found. We are very sorry that so general a change of Officers is proposed, which we judge of no small disparagement to our Cause; and do think it best, that in removals of that kinde, the ground should not be difference in opinion, either in Religious or Civil Matters, but corruption or breach of Trust; considering the misery which befalls whole Families upon such Changes; and that discontents are thereby increased: Whereas we hold it necessary that all wayes of composure and acquieting those storms which the preceding differences and distractions have begotten, be with utmost care and prudence endeavoured.

And whereas 'tis urged, That if we were in power, we would bear our selves as Tyrannically as others have done: We confess indeed, that the experimentall defections of so many men as have succeeded in Authority, and the exceeding difference we have hitherto found in the same men in a low, and in an exalted condition, makes us even mistrust our own hearts, and hardly beleeve our own Resolutions of the contrary. And therefore we have proposed such an Establishment, as supposing men to be too flexible and yeelding to worldly Temptations, they should not yet have a means or opportunity either to injure particulars, or prejudice the Publick, without extreme hazard, and apparent danger to themselves. Besides, to the objection we have further to say, That we aim not at power in our selves, our Principles and Desires being in no measure of self-concernment: nor do we relie for obtaining the same upon strength, or a forcible obstruction; but solely upon that inbred and perswasive power that is in all good and just things, to make their own way in the hearts of men, and so to procure their own Establishment.

And that makes us at this time naked and defencelesse as we are, and amidst so many discouragements on all hands to persevere in our motions and desires of good to the Nation; although disowned therein at such a time when the doing thereof can be interpreted no other but a politick delivering us up to slaughter, by such as we took for Friends, our brethren of severall Churches; and for whom with truth of affection we have even in the most difficult times done many Services: all which, and whatsoever else can be done against us, we shall reckon but as badges of our sincerity, and be no whit discouraged thereby from the discharge of our duties.

For the dis-satisfactions that be upon many good mens spirits, for that they are not ascertained whereunto all our motions tend, and in what they will center,

Though, we conceive, they may have received some general satisfaction from what we have formerly at severall times propounded; yet since they were not disposed into such a form and condition as to become practicable; we have, with the best care and abilities God hath afforded us, cast the same into a Modell and Platform, which we shall speedily present unto the view and consideration of all, as the Standard and ultimate scope of our Designes, that so (in case of approvall) it may be subscribed and returned as agreed upon by the People. And thus far, we conceive, we may without offence or prejudice to Authority, proceed; and which we the rather do, because we know no better, and indeed no other way or means (but by such an Agreement) to remove (as much as may be) all disgusts and heart-burnings, and to settle the Common-wealth upon the fairest probabilities of a lasting Peace, and contentfull Establishment.

The agreement of the People which was presented by his Excellency and the Officers of the Army to the Right Honourable the Commons in Parliament, although in many things short (according to our apprehensions) of what is necessary for the good of the Commonwealth, and satisfaction of the People; particularly, in that it containeth no provision for the certain removall of notorious and generally complained of grievances: And although it hath some things of much hazard to the Publick, − yet, had it been put in execution, we should scarcely have interrupted the proceedings thereof, since therein is contained many things of great and important concernment to the Common-wealth. But seeing the time proposed therein for reducing the same into practice, is now past, and that likewise the generality of the people have not, or do not approve of the same, for the reasons (as we suppose) fore-mentioned: We have thought fit to revise it, making onely such alterations therein as we conceive really necessary for the welfare, security and safety of the People, together with additionall Provisions for the taking away of those Burdens and Grievances which may without reall prejudice to the Management of publick Affairs be removed.

And because it is essentiall to the nature of such an Agreement to take its rise from the People, we have therefore purposely declined the presentment thereof to the Parliament: and conceive it may speedily proceed to Subscription, and so to further practice, without any interruption to this Representative, untill the season prefix'd in the Agreement, for the assembling another: By whose immediate succession, without any intervall, the Affairs of the Common-wealth may suffer no stop or intermission.

Lastly, We conceive we are much mistaken in being judged impatient, and over-violent in our motions for the publick Good. To which we answer, That could we have had any assurance that what is desired should have otherwise, or by any have been done; and had not had some taste of the relinquishment of many good things that were promised, we should not have been so earnest and urgent for the doing thereof.

Though we know likewise it hath been very customary in such heretofore as never intended any freedom to the Nation, to except only against the season, and to protract the time so long, till they became sufficiently impowred to justifie the totall denyall and refusall thereof. However, the main reason of our proceeding as we do, is, because we prefer the way of a settlement by an Agreement of the People before any other whatsoever.

And thus the world may clearly see what we are, and what we aym at: We are altogether ignorant, and do from our hearts abominate all designes and contrivances of dangerous consequence which we are said (but God knows, untruly) to be labouring withall. Peace and Freedom is our Designe; by War we were never gainers, nor ever wish to be; and under bondage we have been hitherto sufferers. We desire however, that what is past may be forgotten, provided the Common-wealth may have amends made it for the time to come. And this from our soul we desire.

Having no mens persons in hatred, and judging it needfull that all other respects whatsoever are to give way to the good of the Common-wealth, and this is the very truth and inside of our hearts.

From the Tower
April 14. 1649.

JOHN LILBURNE
WILLIAM WALWYN
THOMAS PRINCE
RICHARD OVERTON.

XIII

An Agreement of the Free People of England

[This final version of the *Agreement* was one of the few Leveller pamphlets to be printed legally with an official licence. Its printer, Giles Calvert, published many radical books, including works by Saltmarsh, Winstanley, Clarkson, and, later, many Quakers. Mabbott, the licencer most friendly to the radicals, and editor of *The Moderate,* was dismissed from his post for allowing the publication of *An Agreement.* Copies were also attached to William Thompson's *Englands Standard Advanced* (May 6th) and *The Levellers Vindicated* [XV]. It is dated May 1st, 1649 and was published very soon after that date.

Wolfe, pp. 400–410. H. and D., pp. 318–328.]

AN
AGREEMENT
OF THE
Free People of
England.

Tendered as a Peace-Offering to
this distressed Nation.

BY

Lieutenant Colonel John Lilburne,
Master William Walwyn, Master Thomas Prince,
and Master Richard Overton,
Prisoners in the Tower of London,
May the 1. 1649.

Matth. 5. verse 9.
Blessed are the Peace-makers for they shall be
called the children of God.

A Preparative to all sorts of people.

IF AFFLICTIONS make men wise, and wisdom direct to happinesse, then certainly this Nation is not far from such a degree therof, as may compare if not far exceed, any part of the world: having for some yeares by-past, drunk deep of the Cup of misery and sorrow. We blesse God our consciences are cleer from adding affliction to affliction, having ever laboured from the beginning, of our publick distractions, to compose and reconcile them: & should esteem it the Crown of all our temporal felicity that yet we might be instrumentall in procuring the peace and prosperity of this Commonwealth the land of our Nativity.

And therefore according to our promise in our late *Manifestation* of the 14 of Aprill 1649. (being perswaded of the necessitie and justnesse thereof) as a Peace-Offering to the Free people of this Nation, we tender this ensuing Agreement, not knowing any more effectuall means to put a finall period to all our feares and troubles.

It is a way of settlement, though at first much startled at by some in high authority; yet according to the nature of truth, it hath made its own way into the understanding, and taken root in most mens hearts and affections, so that we have reall ground to hope (what ever shall become of us) that our earnest desires and indeavours for good to the people will not altogether be null and frustrate.

The life of all things is in the right use and application, which is not our worke only, but every mans conscience must look to it selfe, and not dreame out more seasons and opportunities. And this we trust will satisfie all ingenuous people that we are not such wilde, irrationall, dangerous Creatures as we have been aspersed to be; This agreement being the ultimate end and full scope of all our desires and intentions concerning the Government of this Nation, and wherein we shall absolutely rest satisfied and acquiesce; nor did we ever give just cause for any to beleeve worse of us by any thing either said or done by us, and which would not in the least be doubted, but that men consider not the interest of those that have so unchristian-like made bold with our good names; but we must bear with men of such interests as are opposite to any part of this Agreement, when neither our Saviour nor his Apostles innocency could stop such mens mouthes whose interests their doctrines and practises did extirpate; And therefore if friends at least would but consider what interest men relate to, whilst they are telling or whispering their aspersions against us, they would find the reason and save us a great deale of labour in clearing our selves, it being a remarkable signe of an ill cause when aspersions supply the place of Arguments.

We blesse God that he hath given us time and hearts to bring it to this issue, what further he hath for us to do is yet only knowne to his wisedom, to whose will and pleasure we shall willingly submit; we have if we look with the eyes of frailty, enemies like the sons of Anak, but if with the eyes of faith and confidence in a righteous God and a just cause, we see more with us then against us.

JOHN LILBURN.   WILLIAM WALWYN.
THOMAS PRINCE.   RICHARD OVERTON.

From our causelesse captivity
in the Tower of London, May
1. 1649.

The Agreement it selfe thus followeth.

After the long and tedious prosecution of a most unnaturall cruell, homebred war, occasioned by divisions and distempers amongst our selves, and those distempers arising from the uncertaintie of our Government, and the exercise of an unlimited or Arbitrary power, by such as have been trusted with Supreme and subordinate Authority, wherby multitudes of grievances and intolerable oppressions have been brought upon us. And finding after eight years experience and expectation all indeavours hitherto used, or remedies hitherto applyed, to have encreased rather then diminished our distractions, and that if not speedily prevented our falling againe into factions and divisions, will not only deprive us of the benefit of all those wonderful Victories God hath vouchsafed against such as sought our bondage, but expose us first to poverty and misery, and then to be destroyed by forraigne enemies.

And being earnestly desirous to make a right use of that opportunity God hath given us to make this Nation Free and Happy, to reconcile our differences, and beget a perfect amitie and friendship once more amongst us, that we may stand clear in our consciences before Almighty God as unbyassed by any corrupt Interest or particular advantages, and manifest to all the world that our indeavours have not proceeded from malice to the persons of any, or enmity against opinions; but in reference to the peace and prosperity of the Common-wealth, and for prevention of like distractions, and removall of all grievances; We the free People of England, to whom God hath given hearts, means and opportunity to effect the same, do with submission to his wisdom, in his name, and desiring the equity thereof may be to his praise and glory; Agree to ascertain our Government, to abolish all arbitrary Power, and to set bounds and limits both to our Supreme, and all Subordinate Authority, and remove all known Grievances.

And accordingly do declare and publish to all the world, that we are agreed as followeth,

I. That the Supreme Authority of England and the Territories therewith incorporate, shall be and reside henceforward in a Representative of the People consisting of four hundred persons, but no more; in the choice of whom (according to naturall right) all men of the age of one and twenty yeers and upwards (not being servants, or receiving alms, or having served the late King in Arms or voluntary Contributions) shall have their voices; and be capable of being elected to that Supreme Trust, those who served the King being disabled for ten years onely. All things concerning the distribution of the said four hundred Members proportionable to the respective parts of the Nation, the severall places for Election, the manner of giving and taking of Voyces, with all Circumstances of like nature, tending to the compleating and equall proceedings in Elections, as also their Salary, is referred to be setled by this present Parliament, in such sort as the next Representative may be in a certain capacity to meet with safety at the time herein expressed: and such circumstances to be made more perfect by future Representatives.

II. That two hundred of the four hundred Members, and not lesse, shall be taken and esteemed for a competent Representative; and the major Voyces present shall be concluding to this Nation. The place of Session, and choice of a Speaker, with other circumstances of that nature, are referred to the care of this and future Representatives.

III. And to the end all publick Officers may be certainly accountable, and no Factions made to maintain corrupt Interests, no Officer of any salary, Forces in Army or Garison, nor any Treasurer or Receiver of publick monies, shall (while such) be elected a Member for any Representative; and if any Lawyer shall at any time be chosen, he shall be uncapable of practice as a Lawyer, during the whole time of that Trust. And for the same reason, and that all persons may be capable of subjection as well as rule.

IV. That no Member of the present Parliament shall be capable of being elected of the next Representative, nor any Member of any future Representative shall be capable of being chosen for the Representative immediately suceeding: but are free to be chosen, one Representative having intervened: Nor shall any Member of any Representative be made either Receiver, Treasurer, or other Officer during that imployment.

V. That for avoyding the many dangers and inconveniences apparantly arising from the long continuance of the same persons in Authority; We Agree, that this present Parliament shall end the first Wednesday in August next 1649, and thenceforth be of no power or Authority: and in the mean time shall order and direct the Election of a new and equall Representative, according to the true intent of this our Agreement: and so as the next Representative may meet and sit in power and Authority as an effectuall Representative upon the day following; namely, the first Thursday of the same August, 1649.

VI. We agree, if the present Parliament shall omit to order such Election or Meeting of a new Representative; or shall by any means be hindered from performance of that Trust:

That in such case, we shall for the next Representative proceed in electing thereof in those places, & according to that manner & number formerly accustomed in the choice of Knights and Burgesses; observing onely the exceptions of such persons from being Electors or Elected, as are mentioned before in the first, third, and fourth Heads of this Agreement: It being most unreasonable that we should either be kept from new, frequent and successive Representatives, or that the su-

269

preme Authority should fall into the hands of such as have manifested disaffection to our common Freedom, and endeavoured the bondage of the Nation.

VII. And for preserving the supreme authority from falling into the hands of any whom the people have not, or shall not chuse,

We are resolved and agreed (God willing) that a new Representative shall be upon the first Thursday in August next aforesaid: the ordering and disposing of themselves, as to the choice of a speaker, and the like circumstances, is hereby left to their discretion: But are in the extent and exercise of Power, to follow the direction and rules of this agreement; and are hereby authorised and required according to their best judgements, to set rules for future equall distribution, and election of Members as is herein intended and enjoyned to be done, by the present Parliament.

VIII. And for the preservation of the supreme Authority (in all times) entirely in the hands of such persons only as shal be chosen thereunto – we agree and declare: That the next & al future Representatives, shall continue in full power for the space of one whole year: and that the people shall of course, chuse a Parliament once every year, so as all the members thereof may be in a capacity to meet, and take place of the foregoing Representative: the first Thursday in every August for ever if God so please; Also (for the same reason) that the next or any future Representative being met, shall continue their Session day by day without intermission for four monthes at the least; and after that shall be at Liberty to adjourn from two monthes to two months, as they shall see cause untill their yeer be expired, but shall sit no longer then a yeer upon pain of treason to every member that shall exceed that time: and in times of adjurnment shall not erect a Councel of State but refer the managing of affairs in the intervals to a Committee of their own members, giving such instructions, and publish them, as shall in no measure contradict this agreement.

IX. And that none henceforth may be ignorant or doubtful concerning the power of the Supreme authority, and of the affairs, about which the same is to be conversant and exercised: we agree and declare, that the power of Representatives shall extend without the consent or concurrence of any other person or persons,

1 To the conservation of Peace and commerce with forrain Nations.

2 To the preservation of those safe guards, and securities of our lives, limbes, liberties, properties, and estates, contained in the Petition of Right, made and enacted in the third year of the late King.

3 To the raising of moneys, and generally to all things as shall be evidently conducing to those ends, or to the enlargement of our freedom, redress of grievances, and prosperitiy of the Common-wealth.

For security whereof, having by wofull experience found the prevalence of corrupt interests powerfully inclining most men once entrusted with authority, to pervert the same to their own domination, and to the prejudice of our Peace and Liberties, we therefore further agree and declare.

X. That we do not impower or entrust our said representatives to continue in force, or to make any Lawes, Oaths, or Covenants, whereby to compell by penalties or otherwise any person to any thing in or about matters of faith, Religion or Gods worship or to restrain any person from the profession of his faith, or exercise of Religion according to his Conscience, nothing having caused more distractions, and heart burnings in all ages, then persecution and molestation for matters of Conscience in and about Religion:

XI. We doe not impower them to impresse or constrain any person to serve in war by Sea or Land every mans Conscience being to be satisfied in the justness of that cause wherein he hazards his own life, or may destroy an others.

And for the quieting of all differences, and abolishing of all enmity and rancour, as much as is now possible for us to effect.

XII. We agree, That after the end of this present Parliament, no person shall be questioned for any thing said or done in reference to the late Warres, or publique differences; otherwise then in pursuance of the determinations of the present Parliament, against such as have adhered to the King against the Liberties of the people: And saving that Accomptants for publick moneys received, shall remain accomptable for the same.

XIII. That all priviledges or exemptions of any persons from the Lawes, or from the ordinary course of Legall proceedings, by vertue of any Tenure, Grant, Charter, Patent, Degree, or Birth, or of any place of residence, or refuge, or priviledge of Parliament, shall be henceforth void and null; and the like not to be made nor revived again.

XIV. We doe not impower them to give judgment upon any ones person or estate, where no Law hath been before provided, nor to give power to any other Court or Jurisdiction so to do, Because where there is no Law, there is no transgression, for men or Magistrates to take Cognisance of; neither doe we impower them to intermeddle with the execution of any Law whatsoever.

XV. And that we may remove all long setled Grievances, and thereby as farre as we are able, take away all cause of complaints, and no longer depend upon the uncertain inclination of Parliaments to remove them, nor trouble our selves or them with Petitions after Petitions, as hath been accustomed, without fruit or benefit; and knowing no cause why any should repine at our removall of them, except such as make advantage by their continuance, or are related to some corrupt Interests, which we are not to regard.

We agree and Declare,

XVI. That it shall not be in the power of any Representative, to punish, or cause to be punished, any person or persons for refusing to answer to questions against themselves in Criminall cases.

XVII. That it shall not be in their power, after the end of the next Representative, to continue or constitute any proceedings in Law that shall be longer then Six months in the final determination of any cause past all Appeal, nor to continue the Laws or proceedings therein in any other Language then English, nor to hinder any person or persons from pleading their own Causes, or of making use of whom they please to plead for them.

The reducing of these and other the like provisions of this nature in this Agreement provided, and which could not now in all particulars be perfected by us, is intended by us to be the proper works of faithful Representatives.

XVIII. That it shall not be in their power to continue or make any Laws to abridge or hinder any person or persons, from trading or merchandizing into any place beyond the Seas, where any of this Nation are free to Trade.

XIX. That it shall not be in their power to continue Excise or Customes upon any sort of Food, or any other Goods, Wares, or Commodities, longer then four months after the beginning of the next Representative, being both of them extreme burthensome and oppressive to Trade, and so expensive in the Receipt, as the moneys expended therein (if collected as Subsidies have been) would extend very far towards defraying the publick Charges; and forasmuch as all Moneys to be raised are drawn from the People; such burthensome and chargeable wayes, shall never more be revived, nor shall they raise Moneys by any other ways (after the aforesaid time) but only by an equal rate in the pound upon every reall and personall estate in the Nation.

XX. That it shall not be in their power to make or continue any Law, whereby mens reall or personall estates, or any part thereof, shall be exempted from payment of their debts; or to imprison any person for debt of any nature, it being both unchristian in it self, and no advantage to the Creditors, and both a reproach and prejudice to the Common-wealth.

XXI. That it shall not be in their power to make or continue any Law, for taking away any mans life, except for murther, or other the like hainous offences destructive to humane Society, or for endevouring by force to destroy this our Agreement, but shall use their uttermost endeavour to appoint punishments equall to offences: that so mens Lives, Limbs, Liberties, and estates, may not be liable to be taken away upon trivial or slight occasions as they have been; and shall have speciall care to preserve, all sorts of people from wickedness misery and beggery: nor shall the estate of any capitall offendor be confiscate but in cases of treason only; and in all other capitall offences recompence shall be made to the parties damnified, as well out of the estate of the Malifactor, as by loss of life, according to the conscience of his jury.

XXII. That it shall not be in their power to continue or make any Law, to deprive any person, in case of Tryals for Life, Limb, Liberty, or Estate, from the benefit of witnesses, on his, or their behalf; nor deprive any person of those priviledges, and liberties, contained in the Petition of Right, made in the third yeer of the late King Charls.

XXIII. That it shall not be in their power to continue the Grievance of Tithes, longer then to the end of the next Representative; in which time, they shall provide to give reasonable satisfaction to all Impropriators: neither shall they force by penalties or otherwise, any person to pay towards the maintenance of any Ministers, who out of conscience cannot submit thereunto.

XXIV. That it shall not be in their power to impose

Ministers upon any the respective Parishes, but shall give free liberty to the parishioners of every particular parish, to chuse such as themselves shall approve; and upon such terms, and for such reward, as themselves shall be willing to contribute, or shall contract for. Provided, none be chusers but such as are capable of electing Representatives.

XXV. That it shal not be in their power, to continue or make a law, for any other way of Judgments, or Conviction of life, limb, liberty, or estate, but onely by twelve sworn men of the Neighbor-hood; to be chosen in some free way by the people; to be directed before the end of the next Representative, and not picked and imposed, as hitherto in many places they have been.

XXVI. They shall not disable any person from bearing any office in the Common-wealth, for any opinion or practice in Religion, excepting such as maintain the Popes (or other forraign) Supremacy.

XXVII. That it shal not be in their power to impose any publike officer upon any Counties, Hundreds, Cities, Towns, or Borroughs; but the people capable by this Agreement to chuse Representatives, shall chuse all their publike Officers that are in any kinde to administer the Law for their respective places, for one whole yeer, and no longer, and so from yeer to yeer: and this as an especial means to avoyd Factions, and Parties.

And that no person may have just cause to complain, by reason of taking away the Excise and Customs, we agree,

XXVIII. That the next, and all future Representatives shall exactly keep the publike Faith, and give ful satisfaction, for all securities, debts, arrears or damages, (justly chargeable) out of the publike Treasury; and shall confirm and make good all just publike Purchases and Contracts that have been, or shall be made; save that the next Representative may confirm or make null in part or in whole, all gifts of Lands, Moneys, Offices, or otherwise made by the present Parliament, to any

Member of the House of Commons, or to any of the Lords, or to any of the attendants of either of them.

And for as much as nothing threateneth greater danger to the Common-wealth, then that the Military power should by any means come to be superior to the Civil Authority,

XXIX. We declare and agree, That no Forces shal be raised, but by the Representatives, for the time being; and in raising thereof, that they exactly observe these Rules, namely, That they allot to each particular County, City, Town, and Borrugh, the raising, furnishing, agreeing, and paying of a due proportion, according to the whole number to be levyed; and shall to the Electors of Representatives in each respective place, give Free liberty, to nominate and appoint all Officers appertaining to Regiments, Troops, and Companies, and to remove them as they shall see cause, Reserving to the Representative, the nominating, and appointing onely of the General, and all General-Officers; and the ordering, regulating, and commanding of them all, upon what service shall seem to them necessary for the Safety, Peace, and Freedom of the Common-wealth.

And in as much as we have found by sad experience, That generally men make little or nothing, to innovate in Government, to exceed their time and power in places of trust, to introduce an Arbitrary, and Tyrannical power, and to overturn all things into Anarchy and Confusion, where there are no penalties imposed for such destructive crimes and offences,

XXX. We therefore agree and declare, That it shall not be in the power of any Representative, in any wise, to render up, or give, or take away any part of this Agreement, nor level mens Estates, destroy Propriety, or make all things Common: And if any Representative shall endevor, as a Representative, to destroy this Agreement, every Member present in the House, not entering or immediately publishing his dissent, shall incur the pain due for High Treason, and be proceeded against accordingly; and if any person or persons, shall by force endevor or contrive, the destruction thereof, each person so doing, shall likewise be dealt withal as in cases of Treason.

And if any person shal by force of Arms disturb Elections of Representatives, he shall incurr the penalty of a Riot; and if any person not capable of being an Elector, or Elected, shal intrude themselves amongst those that are, or any persons shall behave themselves rudely and disorderly, such persons shal be liable to a presentment by a grand Inquest and to an indictment upon misdemeanor; and be fined and otherwise punish'd according to the discretion and verdict of a Jury. And all Laws made, or that shall be made contrary to any part of this Agreement, are hereby made null and void.

Thus, as becometh a free People, thankfull unto God for this blessed opportunity, and desirous to make use thereof to his glory, in taking off every yoak, and removing every burthen, in delivering the captive, and setting the oppressed free; we have in all the particular Heads fore-mentioned, done as we would be done unto, and as we trust in God will abolish all occasion of offence and discord, and produce the lasting Peace and Prosperity of this Common-wealth: and accordingly do in the sincerity of our hearts and consciences, as in the presence of Almighty God, give cleer testimony of our absolute agreement to all and every part hereof by subscribing our hands thereunto. Dated the first day of May, in the Yeer of our Lord 1649.

April 30. 1649.
Imprimatur.

JOHN LILBURN.
WILLIAM WALWYN.
THOMAS PRINCE.
RICHARD OVERTON.

GILBERT MABBOT

finis.

London, Printed for Gyles Calvert at the black spread-Eagle at the West end of Pauls.

XIV

The Baiting
of the Great Bull of Bashan

[This was Overton's last pamphlet and his last effort
to rouse the activists of the Leveller Party to renew the
struggle. In it he replied to critics of *Overtons Defyance of the Act of Pardon*. Dated by Thomason July
16th, 1649.]

THE BAITING OF THE GREAT

BULL *of* BASHAN

Unfolded and
Presented to the Affecters and approvers
of the PETITION of the
11 *Sept.* 1648.

Especially, to the *Citizens* of London usually
meeting at the *Whale-bone* in LOTHBURY
behind the Royal Exchange, Commonly
(though unjustly) styled

LEVELLERS.

By *Richard Overton* Close-prisoner in the
Tower of LONDON.

Psal. 22. 12. 13. Psal. 68. 28. 30.

*Many Bulls have compassed me: strong Buls of Bashan
have beset me round.*

*They opened their mouths against me, as a ravening and a
roaring Lion.*

Strengthen O God that which thou hast wrought for us.

*Rebuke the Company of Spearmen, the multitude of the
Bulls, with the Calves of the people, til every one
submit. Scatter thou the people that delight in war.*

Imprinted at *London*, 1649.

Gentlemen,

BEING necessitated (by some over-sudden misdeemings from amongst you) some few dayes since to assert and avow the continuance of my integrity to those sure foundations of Peace and Freedom, offered to the people of this Nation under the forme or draught of an Agreement of the People, May 1. 1649.

It hath happened with me, as with other adventurers into the publick: All pallates are not pleased with that Sheet intituled *Overtons Defiance &c.* yet falleth it out no other wise then I expected; it seems many are weak and as many are offended, and chiefly with that figurative passage of the Bull; especially at the word Pox; but they need not much, did they but also take into their thoughts, the adulterous and wicked generation, on whom that Metaphor is made good, a people whose heart is waxed grosse, and their ears dull of hearing, having closed their eyes, least at any time they should see, hear, understand and be converted.

To such a people Christ spake not but in Parables: why then to such might not I use the Figure of the Bull of Bason, or rather of the Bull-baiting, with all the circumstances *Emphasis Gratia* thereunto appertaining? But ther's uncivill language, such as becommeth not the Gospell of Christ. I answer (my Brethren) he or she (how pure or nice soever to the eye) that is not guilty of reall grosse incivilities both in word and deed, let him or her throw the first stone at that seeming incivillity, for at most you can make it but so in appearance, and no like is the same. The figure is but the shell; will you not crack the shell to take out the kernell? passe through the Parable to the Morall thereof? I, but it jears and thats not the language of Canaan; and be it so: Is it not recorded that Eliah mocked the Priests of Baal, and said, Cry aloud for he is god, either he is talking or he is pursuing his Enemy, or he is in a journey, or peradventure he sleepeth, and must be waked,

Sure this was a jear to some purpose: here Eliah bid them cry aloud &c. and 'tis justified; then why now may I not cry ha-looe-ha-looe-&c. and not be condemned? What if I had turn'd Fidler in that Paper, Christ himselfe useth the simile of a Piper, saying, we have Piped unto you and ye have not danced (*Mat*. 11. 17.) And truly I think we (the four poor Sea-green Fidlers in the Tower) may take up the same saying, We have Piped unto you ever since the first of May, the most pleasant tune of the AGREEMENT of the PEOPLE, but yee have not danced up so roundly as so sprightly a tune deserves. But you will say (it may be) I am still in the language of Ashdod (as perchance you may take it) or that this Dialect is of Consanguinity with the other: Tis true; things (however in themselves) are to others as they are taken. He that should take the Parable of Dives and Lazarus in the bare letter (how known Cannonical soever in its own genuine sence) he must explode[1] it the Scriptures and at best give it but a place in the Apocrypha, for the Letter or character thereof (if that must be the sense) is contradictory to the body of divinity, except you wil say, to beleeve that the rich Glutton and the Begger left not their eyes, tongues, fingers, &c. in the grave is Orthodox. And so of my Metaphor of the Bull, the use of the word Genitals, Pox, &c. you may say is uncivill in the Letter, but how uncivill I pray in the Morall? Know yee not that whosoever shall but fasten on the Genitors or Parents of the peoples ruine, so, as to pinch the grand Imposters and deluders of the

[1] expel (ed.)

times, he burns his Fingers, is smit with the *Morbus Gallicus* of the enslaving Sword; For, what's he, that is precisely honest to the Common-wealth, that can scape persecution? As it hath been of old and is still in things spirituall, He that will live godly in Christ Jesus shall suffer persecution; so he now, that will but faithfully discharge his duty to the publick, shall be sure to be cast upon the Fiery Tryall, that Dogs mouth (as after the Metaphor) shall be sure to be burnt, and tis well he scapes hanging as the time goes.

Now I pray, to how much incivility doth this amount? Is it so worthy your second condemnings as it may not be indulg'd with a favourable eye? Love envyeth not, it judgeth the best; I had thought with two or three merry Jiggs to attempt an uproar in all the laughers in England, but I see you are a company of dull souls, mirth with you is like a Shoulder of Mutton to a sick Horse, or worse, you strait convert into malancholy, trample it under your feet, turne againe, and are (some of you) ready to rent me; He that had cast Pearls before Swine could have expected no lesse,

Indeed, you looked (many of you) upon me as in a Sownd at my close Imprisonment; but truly, when I came abroad with that ignorant Sheet, it found you in a dead sleep, as men in a Trans, portending, as if the Champions of the Eleventh of September had been Sparrow-blasted with the businesse of Burford: and I essayed, to put you out of your dumps, and mind you of the *Agreement of the People* as the center, or *ne plus ultra* of all our Engagements; but it seems it proved but as musick to the house of Mourning: yet however, it hath so far gained its end; if by it you wil not be provoked to your duties equally with us, it hath awaked you into a little discourse *pro & con,* though it be but to point at my weaker parts, and that's better then nothing, if rightly applyed, for *ex nihilo nil fit:* by this you may take notice of your own infirmities in so wire-drawing

285

of mine: Certainly, it may provoke you to consider of what spirits you are, not unlike such as strain at a Gnat & swallow a Camel, that usually in any discourse passe over what concerneth themselves, though of never so serious and weighty consideration in point of their duties, and betake themselves wholly to spye out the spots and infirmities thereof, and of the Author, and fall foul thereupon, and so sleight their duties, stifle and smother the thing that is good: And now (my tender friends) I pray tell me what Spirit is this? 'tis a foul spirit, away with't for shame; go purge, goe purge; one penniworth of the *Agreement of the people*, with a little good resolution taken morning and evening, will work out this corruption, cleanse and purifie the bloud, and put a period to this distinction of parties, allay the feude and division of the people, and state us in firme Freedom, Safety and Peace; and then there will be none of this catching and carping, this lying in wait to snap at infirmities; and till the Agreement be setled, this is not to be expected.

I have known, when things as unserious as my last sheet, drest out in the youthfull attire of mirth, hath found a very large acceptance not only with you, but even with this generation of men, that are now the Enemies of the People; and I think if I have not forgot the *Arraignment of Persecution,* and some other things of that nature, that I myself have been one of those who have had the honour of such acceptances: But *O tempora! O Mores!* how few are the same yesterday and to day? successe changeth mens minds as the wind doth the weathercock.

But (my friends) your gravity (which I am affraid hath too much of Melancholy in it) cannot more move me to a more serious Dialect, then my own affections incline me, I prize both in their places; as I affect the one, I respect the other: for sure, modest mirth tempered with due gravity makes the best composition, most naturall and harmonious: God in the temper of our natures as he hath made us Earth, so hath he enlivened that dull lump with the Element of Fire, which is the *forma formans*, the giver and preserver of being and motion, and the Original of that habit of laughter: Therefore Mirth sure is of Divine instinct, and I think I may boldly say, more naturall then Melancholy, and lesse savours of the Curse. Nature in its Creation was pure and good, void of corruption, or any thing obnoxious or destructive: all misery and mischiefe came in with the fall, as a Curse upon the Creature, as Death, sorrow, tears, pains, &c, in which number you may reckon Melancholy, for 'tis both unnaturall and destructive to nature, and so fitly reputed a branch of the Curse, and 'tis the root of the root of all wickednesse, Coveteousnesse; for where have you seen a Melancholy man that's not covetous? and a covetous man seldom proves a good Common-wealths man: yet this ill Weed is gotten into so religious an esteem that all our Religion is turn'd into Melancholy; that, he that cannot whine, pipe, weep and hang down his head like a Bulrush and seem sad unto men, is prophane, light, hath not any thing of God in him, is a Reprobate, is condemned and censured of all, as neither fit for Church nor Common-wealth; And thus comes it to passe; my mirth is heightened to such a transgression, even to cast me under the present *Anathama* of the now godly party.

But my Brethren of the Sea green Order, take a little wine with your water, and Ile take a little water with my wine, and it will temper us to the best constitution. I wonder what meaneth your late dulnesse of motion, appearing as men in a dream, or as if you were another sort of people then the Authors, promoters, approvers and presenters of the Petition of the 11 of Sept. that people use to be the most active and vigorous People in England for publick Freedom and safety, they use to fear no colours, the more they were prest down the more they prest forward, and the more they encreased; few months have passed that they have not in point of Common-Right produced some eminent peece: but your heads have drooped of late, nothing hath appeared, not one punctilio in supportation and promotion of the *Agreement;* deep silence hath covered you; fie, fie; be not cow'd out of your abilities and principles by the present rage of the wicked: compare but the strength of your principles and the strength of an Army, and tell me which is stronger: How many persecuting powers have fallen before your principles as Dagon before the Ark? and who hath been able to stand before them, even from Episcopacy to this whited and Jesabel like painted Independency? Think you, that this unparallell'd tyranny, under this new name, more fierce and cruel then his fellows, trampling the residue under its feet, that it shall scape the vengeance of Gods wrath more than its Predecessors? no, no; Gods Motto is *Semper Idem.* Be not therefore dismayed or daunted at the height and magnificence of this insolent faction, the new sons of Perdition, that are set up to deceive if it were possible the very Elect.

It is your own evill and weaknesse, and of those that are Professors and pretenders to the same principles with you, that our Cause is thus under a Cloud: would you all act together, all suffer together, all be as one; and not thus (as some amongst you Commonally use) hang back in the adversity, and be seen in the Van of Prosperity (not daring when the storme rageth, to peep into the tempest for fear of being blowne away) we should not be at this passe with our Cause.

Where there is any thing of venture or hazard, while 'tis in the *Embrio*, who's not then busie and forward? but when 'tis put upon the personall test for execution, O then one hath bought a piece of ground, and must be excused; another a yoke of Oxen, and he must goe see them; and a third hath marryed a wife and therefore must please her.

Friends, be not offended, this is a crime deserves your repentance; I condemn you not all, it is but some few; A little Leaven you know leaveneth the whole Lump; therefore do ye beware of the Leaven of the pharisees; it much retardeth your motions and blasteth their fruits; the publick is a loser thereby, and your Cause receiveth dammage: let those whom this pincheth, be thereby provoked to amendment, it is worthy their care: For know you not, that it is many hands make light work? If the stresse or weight of the work be laid upon one, or some 3 or 4, it must needs goe on slowly: Why, is not he that's most backward as forward as the best? it is his Cause as much as it is any mans, and thereto in duty as much obliged as any. We are no more concerned than your selves, 'tis but upon the point of common duty (which binds all) to our Country, that we suffer, and we count it our Joy, for that we know we suffer for well-doing, and though we perish in the Work, our Reward shall goe with us, for our Redeemer liveth, and that is our stay. Therefore why stand you still, and are not provoked to this good Emulation; be as active and vigilant, and you shall share in the rejoycing, and 'tis such (I must tell you my Friends) is worth your having; *Dulce est pro patria pati.*

Fear not those Hils and Mountains that are in your way; it is but your want of faith that they are not removed, and cast into the bottome of the sea: While you lift up your heads, are vigorous and active, your principles present you as Steeples above the rest of the people; every man is a strong Barricado in the way of the Enemy, and your principles flourish and get ground, but when you are fearfull, are flat or remisse, then they retire and fade; for they are said to increase or diminish, as they get or lose ground in the understanding or acceptance of others: And this ever take as a sure Rule, That the most vertuous and saving principles in a person most undaunted and faithfull, the more they are suprest, and the more he is persecuted, the more they prosper and spread; of so mighty an efficacy are his sufferings and testimony; as, in the case of Paul is witnessed, Now I would (saith he) ye should understand, Brethren, that the things that hapned unto me, have faln out rather to the furtherance of the Gospel; so that my bonds in Christ are manifest in all the Pallace, and in all other places, and many of the Brethren in the Lord waxed confident by my Bonds, are much-more bold to speak the Word without fear: And this is all the persecutor gaineth upon the undaunted Asserters of righteousness; his own sword is turned into his own bowels: persecution, as the Viper, devoureth its own parent. Then faint ye not (my friends) rouse up your heads and be valiant; lift up your *Agreement of the people* again, and put it upon the publick stage for promotion and subscription, and doubt not: What man that there is amongst you, that is fearfull and faint-hearted, let him depart your Meetings, and return to his house: the more the Enemy stormeth, the more resolute and vigorous be ye; give them enough of persecution; the more they persecute, the more doe ye appear, that your Bands may be famous; for with fetters, Irons, and prison-walls you may shake them to pieces; 'tis their tyrannies, cruelties and oppressions must be their Fall, through which you must eat your way for the *Agreement*.

I highly honor the fidelity and valor of Mr. Chrestopher Chisman, who notwithstanding his Imprisonment, his abuses and sufferings, hath not wrapt up his talent in a napkin, but like a good and faithful servant hath improv'd his imprisonment to the publick advantage; see his Book, entituled, *The Lamb contending with the Lion,* 'tis worthy your imitation. Let your light (as his) so shine before men, that they may see your good Works, and glorifie your Cause; fear no dangers; the high and mighty Cedars are never able to overtop your principles; what though Ambition hath mounted to the title of Lord Govenour (forsooth) hath not your vigorous principles slain both the Lyon and the Bear, and shall not this uncircumcised Philistine be as one of them?

But (my friends) I am informed those painted Sepulchers of Independency desire your complyance and treaty with them: But touch pitch, and you shall be defiled, have nothing to do with them; touch not, tast not, handle not, which all are to perish with the using; Remember the fidelity of Uriah to David: The Ark, and Israel, and Judah abide in Tents, and my Lord Joab, and the servants of my Lord are encamped in the open fields, shall I then go into my house, to eat and to drink, and to lye with my wife? As thou livest and as thy soul liveth, I wil not do this thing. Your *Agreement* lyeth half dead in the streets, your friends and its assertors are in prison, with sentinels at their doors, denied the access and visitation of friends, have the catch-poles of the Counsel of State enter their chambers when they are in bed, with Musketteers at their heels, search, rifle, catch and take away any thing that any way they may wrest unto their bloody ends against them, as formerly, and now, the other day (July 4.) they have done, and all the land mourneth and groaneth at the calamity and miseries upon it for want of the settlement of a just constitution of Government; and shall you go unto them (those pests and vipers of the Nation) to treat or comply? As you live and as your soul liveth you must not do this thing:

While your agreement is trod under their feet, your freinds under their cruel captivity, &c. let him that treateth with them amongst you, or with any of their creatures, or keepeth any correspondency with them, be to you as a Reprobate, let the Marke of Cain be set upon him, that every finger may point at him for a Traytor, and a Judas to the people that meeteth him.

If a wife or child be like to be destroyed by fire, water, or thieves, he accounts himself base that dare not venture his own life to save theirs: our cause is of a more transcendent value, and we suffer for it; and can you see it destroyed in us, and we for it, and not be as naturall as in a private relation? the lives, liberties, and freedomes of all is contained in it? If your neighbours Oxe or his Asse were in a ditch, it is a shame to passe by and not to help; and behold, here's all in the ditch, then, why venture you not your time, your labours, your monies, &c. to redeeme out all, our Cause, the nation, and us in it, and with it.

I confesse no people in England have been more vigorous, more active and diligent, and more adventurous for the Cause of the Nation, and for our Liberties than most of you: we have been as precious to you as the apple of your eye; you have spared no hazard, no toyle or time to get us at freedome, and I hope we shall never be so ungratefull as not thankfully to remember that service of Love: To you we are obliged in the deepest obligations of any others in England.

But now considering the extream necessity of your still constant unwearied prosecution, I have emboldened my self to presse you forward to the good work of the people, that at this time you may be as vigilant and industrious as at any other, that publick life and spirit may still be preserved and encreased in our cause, even in these worst of times.

And if I have been a little too sharp in my advice, and admonishment, impute it I pray you to the heat of my zeal and ardent affections to the promotion of that Cause; for truly to me it is as the life of my life; without it I'm nothing, with it I live, and therein am

Yours and every mans as my own
RICHARD OVERTON

From my close imprisonment
in the tower of London
July the ninth, 1649.

FINIS.

XV

The Levellers Vindicated

[This is the soldiers' own story of the mutiny that ended at Burford. It is signed by six troopers of the regiments involved and many of the facts it contains can only have come from them. It is not possible to say what help they had in drawing up their account, but it must have been substantial. It may be significant that much in the style and arguments recalls *The English Souldiers Standard*.

THE
LEVELLERS
(Falsly so called)
Vindicated,
OR THE CASE

Of the twelve Troops
(which by Treachery in a Treaty)
was lately surprised, and defeated at
Burford, truly stated, and offered to the
Judgment of all unbyassed, and wel-minded
People, especially of the Army, their
fellow Souldiers, under the Conduct
of the Lord *Fairfax.*
By a faithful remnant, late of
Col. *Scroops,* Commissary General *Iretons,*
and Col. *Harrisons* Regiments, that hath
not yet bowed their knee unto *Baal,*
whose names (in the behalf of themselves,
and by the appointment of the rest
of their Friends) are hereunto
subscribed.

IT IS wel known, and yet fresh in the publike memory, with what monstrous and hateful defamations, as Anti-Scripturists, Libertines, Atheists, Mutiniers, Levellers, &c. we have most falsly and maliciously been deciphered out to the people and Army, on purpose to bury us under the rage and odium of our fellow-souldiers; and utterly to blast, and prejudice the common acceptance, against our late, lawful, and consciencious Undertaking: And seeing the equity of all transactions is most commonly measured by the event, and success that befals them; few considering how God many times suffereth unjust men to prosper, and spred themselves in the world, like the Green Bay Tree; and the just (for their correction and proof) to be subdued and trod under foot for a season. We are thereby at so great a seeming disadvantage amongst men, That in every thing we are fore-spoken, our truths (how palpable and evident soever) are rendred as incredible, and regardless, strength and power being on their side to countenance their actions, our enemies over awing all judgments, and forcing by the might of their lawless Sword, a credit or subjection to their own most perfidious and deceitful ways; so that, as for the fruit or success that we expect, we could still have sat in patience, and not have uttered a word, but the dishonest and treacherous dealings received, with the woful ruine of the Nation, therewith sustained in ours (evidently appearing) do so boyl at our hearts, and so prevalently press upon our consciences, that we are not able longer to rest in silence; but let the hazard to us be what it will, we shall so far presume

297

upon the publike view, as faithfully and impartially, to set down the true state and maner of our whole proceedings in that our late undertaking, hitherto most falsly and deceitfully represented by the ruling Faction of the Army, and so leave the same to the judgment and timely consideration of all honest and consciencious people, especially of the Army, our fellow-souldiers, under the conduct of the Lord Fairfax, and amongst them in a special maner, all those that really in judgment and conscience, took up Arms for the Rights and Liberties of their Native Country, as the whole Army in their Declaration of the 14 of June, 1647. declare they all did. Thus then understanding, that we the Souldiers of Col. Scroops Regiment, and others, were allotted for the service of Ireland, without our consent; or of any of our fellow-souldiers in Counsel for us, we fell into serious debate (as in reason and honesty we could do no less, considering likewise our late solemn Engagement), whether we could lawfully, in safety to ourselves, and our own Native Rights in England, submit unto that forraign Service, or no? And finding by that our old solemn Engagement at New Market, and Triplo Heaths, June 5. 1647. with the manifold Declarations, Promises, and Protestations of the Army, in pursuance thereof, were all utterly declined, and most perfidiously broken, and the whole fabrick of the Common-wealth faln into the grossest and vilest Tyranny that ever English men groaned under; all their Laws, Rights, Lives, Liberties and Properties, wholly subdued (under the vizard and form of that Engagement) to the Boundless wills of some deceitful persons, having devolved the whole Magistracy of England into their Martial Domination, ruling the people with a Rod of Iron, as most mens woful experience can clearly witness; which, with the consideration of the particular, most insufferable abuses and dis-satisfactions put upon us, moved us to an unanimous refusal to go, till our

Conscience were discharged in the faithful fulfilment of our said Solemn Engagement to our Native Country; in which Engagement, we were expressly and particularly obliged against the service of Ireland, till full satisfaction and security were given to us, as Souldiers and Commoners, by a Councel of our own free Election, according to the rule and tenor of that Engagement, recorded in the Armies Book of Declarations pag. 23, 24, 25, 26, 27. Whereupon we drew up a Paper of some Reasons, by way of Declaration, concerning our said refusal, to deliver to our Colonel; unto which we all chearfully subscribed, with many of our Officers (especially Cornet Den, who then seemingly was extream forward in assisting us to effect our desires) which being delivered a day or two after, immediately our Officers caused a Rendezvous near unto Salisbury, where they declared, That the General intended not to force us, but that we might either go or stay; and so testifying our intents to stay, we were all drawn into the Town again, and the Colonell, with the rest of the Officers, full of discontent, threatened us the Souldiers; and because we were all, or most of one minde, he termed our Unity a Combination, or Mutiny; yet himself upon our request to know, told us, That he could not assure us, that he would go. Which fore-mentioned Paper, with a Letter, we sent to Commissary General Iretons Regiment, who took it so well, That they were immediately upon their march towards our quarters, to joyn with us, for the making good of their and our Engagement, which we, they, and the rest of the Army had engaged at New-Market and Triplo Heaths.

After this, all politike means that could be thought upon, were put in practice to work us off from our Resolutions, as severing the Troops, and dealing with them apart, not suffering the Souldiers of one Troop to come to any of the other, employing Agents and Preaching Officers from Troop to Troop, to work us to that Service; and craftily, and lyingly, telling each Troop, That the other Troops were listed for the Irish Service, surrupticiously to over-reach, and gain us by that deceit. A crime they most maliciously fix upon others, whom they would make the world believe drew us to that undertaking, as in their Declaration of their proceedings against us, published last May 22. is to be seen, where page 6. speaking scandalously of some persons, naming none, yet strongly implying our four worthy Friends in the Tower, they say of them, That they sent their Emissaries and Agents into all parts, pretending from one Regiment to another, that each Regiment had declared, That so by that Artifice, they might draw each to declare. To the Forces in Wales, and the west, they gave assurances, that the forces about London would revolt; to those about London, that those in Wales, and the west, would do the same. Thus to shroud their own vildness, and to effect their own evil ends, they are not sparing to blast innocent persons with their own wicked devices themselves are so apparently and foully guilty of; and yet wipe their mouths, as if no speck or stain were upon them, and raise the report upon others.

All those devices working nothing upon us (there being no satisfaction given to our just exceptions) our Colonel fell to violent threats, and commanded us to put our Horses in a Field two miles from our Quarters; which though at first we did, yet finding the bitterness of his spirit to encrease, and that upon his information, That the General, and Lieutenant General were preparing a force against us: what could we do less, then put our selves into the best posture we could to preserve our selves, which we immediately did (and in this no man was more forward, and violently earnest, then that perfidious Apostate, Cornet Den.) And for our justification therein, we need go no further then their own words in the Armies Declaration of the 14 of June,

1647. where to justifie their own opposition and rebellion to the Orders of a full, free, unforced, unravished and untwice purged Parliament, they tell us, That the Parliament hath declared it no resisting of Magistracy, to side with the just principles, and Law of Nature and Nations, being that Law upon which the Army assisted; and that the Souldiers may lawfully hold the hands of the General that will turn his Cannon against his Army, on purpose to destroy them.

This being done, we had further Intelligence of the greatness and speediness of the Generals preparations against us, and that, Though what we had done, did not amount to so much, as the Army had formerly done at Saffron Walden, upon the Parliaments commanding them for Ireland, yet were we strangely represented to our fellow Souldiers, by the Lieutenant General in Hide Park, under the notion of Mutiniers, Levellers, and denyers of the Scriptures, of purpose to make them engage against us;* so that now we saw, there was no way of safety left us, but by standing upon our Guard, and capitulating with our Sword in our hands, being encouraged thereto, as well by our own innocency, and the equity of those things, upon which we had grounded our Resolutions: As also for that we could not think our fellow Souldiers of the Army, who with us engaged at New-Market Heath, would fight against us, for upholding the said solemn Engagement, wherein they were equally concerned and obliged with us, both as Soul-

---

* Though none act more directly against the tenor thereof then themselves, as is too manifest by their frequent breaking of all Faith, and Premises, making nothing of Treachery, dissembling, yea, and lying too (which is not once to be mentioned amongst Saints, as they would have men think of them.) O abominable Hypocrites! know ye not, that dissembling Piety is double Iniquity; but we fear, while ye pretend to Scripture, ye believe neither it, nor the Resurrection: For if ye did, ye would not condemn the Innocent, against Knowledg and Conscience, of those things your selves are guilty. Repent betimes, or else your portion will be with Hypocrites.

diers and Commoners to each other, to us, and the whole Nation, with whom it was made. But indeed, this Treacherous Tragedy was principally managed and acted by (that Turn Coat) Reynolds, and his Regiment; who for the most of them were strangers to that Engagement. A Company of Blood-thirsty Rogues, Murderers, Theeves, High-way-men, and some that were taken in Colchester, and such as were cashiered out of other Regiments, for high misdemeanors, being entertained therein. And these were the men principally designed, and to be trusted against us, as most fittest to fight for the truth of the Scriptures, and such Saints as the Lieutenant General.*

But to return. Hereupon our Officers leaving us, we choose new ones, and disposed of our Colours, and immediately drew up a Declaration, wherein we signified the Resolutions of the General (upon our refusal to go for Ireland) in a slight and unworthy maner to disband us, after our so many yeers hard and faithful Services; which we then knew to have been practised upon many of our fellow Souldiers in Colonel Huesons, and Cooks Regiments; and thereupon, we resolved to stand to our former Engagements made at New-Market; which the proceedings of the General and our Officers, did expressly contradict and make voyd. This Declaration was publikely read at our Rendezvous in old Sarum, where four Troops of Commissarie General Iretons met us, and unanimously assented to by both Regiments: whereupon our conjunction we advanced to Marlborough, and so to Wantage, where Commissioners from the General met us, to wit. Major White, Captain Scotten,

* These are of the men that usually asperce the Peoples best Friends with such Language, as Atheists, Levellers, Anti-Scripturists, and who lives more like such, then they? for it is they who ruine all, and destroy Propriety, by their Arbitrary and Lawless Power; and who more like Jesuites then themselves for crafty Policy, Lying, and Treachery? and certainly these be the effects, or fruits of Atheism: For by their works you shall know them.

Captain Peveral, and Captain Lieutenant Baily, with whom that day we did nothing, but agreed to meet at Stamford Green, the next morning by eight of the Clock, where we were all according to appointment, but the Commissioners not coming, we marched out of the field, on our way towards Abbington; and as we were upon our march the Commissioners came posting after us, and we presently made a Hault; then they overtaking us, and told us, They had Order from the General, and Lieutenant General, to heare our Desires, and endevor the Composure of our Differences; then they read a Letter unto us from the General, which took but little effect upon our Spirits; and so marching a little further, two of Col. Harrisons Troops, to wit, Cap. Pecks and Captain Winthrops were marching to their Quarters, where Cornet Den and divers others met them, And read a Declaration to them, and used many glorious invitations of them to desire them to come and joyn with us, making appeare the lawfulnesse of our cause, telling them that we were resolved to stand to our first principles, and that if there were but ten men that would stand for those just things, he would make the eleventh, with divers such like expressions, the two Troops being very willing to be satisfied in the lawfulnesse of the engagement, telling us they were marching to Thame, and the next morning we should know their resolutions: But as we were marching back againe, before we were half out of the field, we spied a partie of horse, which it seemed was the Apostate Reynolds with his mercenary damme crew (such as in our hearing most desperately swore, That if the Devil would come from hell and give them a groat a day more then the State, they would fight for him against the Levellers or any others) well, upon this we drew out a Forlorne hope, and thereupon two Troops of Colonel Harrisons marched with us towards them; they retreated towards New-bridge and kept it by force against us, but we [were] unwilling to shed blood, or to be the original occasion of a new war (though they have often branded us with it as if we wholy fought it) but our actions did then cleerly manifest the contrary; for we seeing Souldiers, coming in a Hostile manner against us as aforesaid, did meet them, having forty or fifty of them at our mercy, and could have destroyed them, for we had them two miles from the foresaid bridg, but we did not then in the least offer them any violence or deminish a hair of their heads, but let them go to their body againe, and withall marched to a Ford, because we would not in the least be an occasion of any blood-shed; and having marched through the Ford into the Marsh on the other side, we called our Councel together, who referred the appointment of our quarters to Lieut. Ray, and Cornet Den, who designed us for Burford, where being in the Treatie with the Commissioners, and having intelligence, that the General and Lt. Generall were upon their march towards us, many of us severall times, urged to Major White, and prest upon him, that he came to betray us, to which he replyed, That the Generall and Lieutenant Generall had engaged their Honours not to engage against us in any Hostile manner till they had received our Answer, no not so much as to follow their Messengers or Commissioners with force, and being too credulous to the Generals words, knowing that he never broak ingagement with the Cavaleers in that kind; We gave the more credit to the Major, who seemed extream forward and hastie to make the Composure, pretending so far to approve of our standing for the things contained in our engagement at Triplo-Heath, that himself with our consents drew up a Paper in Answer to the Generall for us, so fully according to our desires as that it gave us satisfaction, so that the Agreement betwixt the Generals Commissioners and us, seemed to be even concluded and at an end; And for full satisfaction take Copie of the said Letter which is as followeth:

May it please your Excellency,

Wee are your Excellencies Souldiers, who have engaged our lives under your Excellencies conduct, through all difficulties and hazards in order to the procurement of Freedom Safety and Peace to this Nation, and our selves as Members thereof, and being lately designed by lot to be divided, and sent over into Ireland for the prosecution of that service, in order to the Peace and safety of this Common-wealth, which we think necessary to be performed, but looking back to take a view of our former proceeding, we finde that we cannot in conscience to ourselves, in duty to God, this Nation, and the rest of our fellow souldiers undertake that service, but by such a decision as is Agreeable to our solemn Engagement made at New-market Heath, the 5 of June 1647. where we did in the presence of God, with one consent solemnly engage one to another, not to disband nor divide, nor suffer our selves to be disbanded nor divided, Untill satisfaction and security was received by the judgment of a counsell consisting of two Officers and two Souldiers together with the Generall Officers that did concur, such satisfaction and security as that engagement refers unto; And being now departed from our obedience to you because you keep not Covenant with us: yet we shall not in the least harber any evill thought or prejudice against you, nor use any act of hostility, unlesse necessitated thereunto in our own defence, which we desire God to prevent; All that we desire (and we speak it in the presence of God, who knowes our hearts) is, that your Excellency will call a Generall Councell according to the solemn Engagement. In the Judgment whereof we will acquiesse, and refer ourselves to them to take an account of our late actions. This being assured we will every man with cheerfulnesse returne to our obedience, and submit to your Excellency and the Judgment of that Councell in all matters that concern us as Souldiers, or Members of this Common-wealth; this we beg of your Excellency to grant, out of the respect of your duty to God, this Nation, and the Army, that we may therby retain our peace with him and procure the happinesse of this Nation under him, which is the desire of our soules: If you shall deny us this, we must lay at your door all the Misery, Bloodshed and Ruine that will fall upon this Nation and Army; for we are resolved as one man by Gods assistance to stand in this Just desire, and although our bodies perish, yet we shall keep our consciences cleer, and we are confident our soules will be at peace; now till we have a full determination herein, we desire your Excellency will forbear all manner of hostility, or marching towards us for avoyding any inconveniencies that may come to our selves or the Country; these desires with affection being granted, we hope the falling out of friends will be the renewing of love, And we shall subscribe and manifest our selves your Excellencies faithfull Souldiers, and servants to this Common-wealth.

But to returne, during the time of treaty, while the Commissioners thus assured us all security, one of them, to wit, Captain Scotten privately slipt from us, and two others, to wit, Captain Bayley and Peverill left notes at every Town of our strength and condition, whilst Major White held us in hand, and told us, that if they fell upon us, he would stand between the bullets and us: So that when notice had been sufficiently given, and we with all the meanes that could be used, wrought into a secure condition at Burford, and after the setting of our Guard, which was commanded by Quarter-Master More who was thereupon appointed, by his Brother Traytor, Cornet Den (who himself) since his coming to London hath avowedly declared to Ma. W. W. to this effect that his beginning, and continuing with the Burford Troops was out of premeditated and complotted designe, that so at last he might the easier bring on their destruction, holding all the time he was with them, correspondency with the Generalls creatures, which said Quarter-Master More after he had set the Guard in this slight manner, and possest us with as much security as he could, and under the pretence of going to refresh himself and horse, did most villanously and treacherously leave the guard without any Orders, and himself in person posted away to the Generals forces and brought them in upon us, marching in the head of them with his sword drawn against us; And Quarter-Master More being afterward called Traitor by some of the Souldiers, Cap. Gotherd of Scroops Regiment made answer, he was none, for that he did nothing but what he was sent to do; so that most Treacherously, that same night the Generals forces came pouring on both sides of the Towne of Burford, where we had not been above three houres, swearing, Damme them and sink them, and violently fell upon us, and so by a fraudulent and Treacherous surprize defeated us, not expecting it during the Treatie, especially from them with whom we had joyned these seven years for the defence of Englands Liberties and Freedoms, and though divers of us had faire quarter promised us by Colonel Okey, Major Barton and the rest of the Officers then with them, as that not a hair of our heads should perish, yet did they suffer their souldiers to plunder us, strip us, and barbarously to use us, worse then Cavaliers, yea Cromwell stood by to see Cornet Tomson, Master Church and Master Perkins murthered, and we were all condemned to death, although Colonel Okey, Major Barton and others of the Grandees had ingaged that not a hair of our heads should perish, when they surrendred themselves unto them, Tompson being then at the head of a party of two Troops of horse, and the other with their fellow Souldiers made good their Quarters while they had the conditions promised them, and then Cromwel after this horrid murther was committed upon the three

forementioned, contrary to Okeys, Bartons and others
of their promises at their taking them, came to us in the
Church, and making his old manner of dissembling
speeches, told us it was not they that had saved our
lives, but providence had so ordered it, and told us
that he could not deny but that many of the things that
we desired were good, and they intended to have many
of them done, but we went in a mutinous way, and
disobeyed the Generals Orders; but withall he told us
that we should not be put off with dishonourable terms,
because we should not become a reproach to the common Enemie: but we desire all unbyassed men to judge,
whether ten shillings a man, and a peece of paper for
seven years Service, be honourable terms: the paper
being good for nothing but to sell to Parliament mens
Agents, who have set them a work to buy them for
three shillings, or four shillings in the pound at most;
and we are forced to sell them to supply our wants, to
keep us from starving, or forcing us to go to the high
way, by reason they will not pay us one penny of our
Arrears any other way but by papers, that so they may
rob us and the rest of the Souldiers of the Armie of
their seven yeers Service, to make themselves and their
adherents the sole possessors of the late Kings Lands for
little or nothing: and for ought we know, the moneys
they buy our Debenters withall, is the money the Nation cannot have any account of. But this their dealing
is not onely so to us, whom they pretend disobeyed
their commands; but they dealt so basely by other Souldiers who never resisted their unjust Commands, as we
beleeve no age can parallel: For in the first place, they
turned them off with two months pay. Secondly, they
have taken away three parts of their Arrears for Free-
quarter, though the Country (whose victuals, grasse and
corn they eat) be never the better; and do also force
them to sell their papers at the rate aforesaid. And deer
fellow-Souldiers, think not, because you are in Arms a

little longer then we, that you shall speed better then we, which they have disbanded before you; but be assured, that when they have their own ends served on you, as they have already on us, you shall have as bad conditions of them, and may be, worse, if it be possible, then we have had before you; and may also reward you for your good services, by raising a company of mercenary Rogues to cut your throats, as they did trayterously to cut ours at Burford.

But to return, from this sad and long digression: by this their serpentine craft, and our own over credulous innocency, we were overthrown, and our hopefull beginnings for the rescue and deliverie of our selves and the nation from thraldome, blasted and destroyed; and then utterly to break and dash in pieces our spirits, and in us all Assertors of the Freedoms of England, and to put an utter inconfidence and jealousie for ever amongst such upon all future engagements, they made that wretched Judas Den, to that end their pandor and slave: they pretendedly spare his life after his condemnation to death, although now upon good grounds and intelligence, (yea partly from his own confessions as is noted before) we doe beleeve that from the beginnings of our proceedings, he was their appointed Emissary (as well as the forementioned Quartermaster) to be most zealous and forward of any man for us, the better to compasse our ruine and lead us like poor sheep to the slaughter; they enjoyne Den, to preach Apostacy to us in the Pulpit of Burford Church, to assert and plead the unlawfulnesse of our engagement, as much as before the lawfulnesse to vindicate, and justifie all those wicked and abhominable proceedings of the Generall, Lievetenant Generall and their officers against us, howling and weeping like a Crocadile, and to make him a perfect Rogue and villain upon everlasting Record, to which like the most abhorred of mankind to bring about their pernicious ends upon the people, he willingly submitted, and to this end published a Recantation paper fraught with lies, infamies and most Trayterous assertions of an arbitrary power evidently tending to the introduction thereof upon this Nation in the persons of the cheife Leaders of the Armie, and in that paper at the advantage of this wicked and treacherous overthrow of ours endeavoured to bury our sollemn Engagement at Newmarket heath in our ruines, as if long since cancell'd and of no longer force or obligation, pretending that by petition we had call'd home our councell of Agitators and so dissolv'd our engagement at New-market heath, And so the Army absolved from all further observation thereof.

Now to this, is to be considered, that the said engagement was radicall upon the grounds of common freedom, safetie, and securitie to the Nation, and upon that account and to that end onely undertaken and solemnly made, and all righteous othes, vows, and covenants are indissolveble and of force till their full and perfect accomplishment; the Apostacy and defection of no man, though of him or those that vowes, or makes such oaths or engagements can absolve or untie them; and this no man that hath any spark of Conscience or Christianitie in him can deny. Therefore it was most deceitfully and corruptly urged, that the same power that gave it a being dissolved it; for till the vowes of that engagement be paid unto the people, it standeth firm and obligatorie, till then the gates of hell are not able to prevail against the being and obliging power thereof; and we are sure none can say, the genuine ends and intents of that engagement are yet obtained, but a thousand times further off, then at the making of that vow: besides, as that engagement enjoynes, what securitie or satisfaction to their private or publick rights, both as Souldiers and commoners, have we or the rest of our fellow souldiers yet received from a councell consisting of two Souldiers chosen out of every Regiment, two Commission officers with such Generall officers onely as assented to that undertaking, when or where was it? Indeed had such a Councell so concluded, and we the souldiers by our unanimous testimony and subscription (as we did to our engagement) testifie our satisfaction, there might have been some plausible pretence for its dissolution; but to this day it is evident to the whole world that no such thing hath been, and this was the expresse letter and intent of that New-market engagement; and to urge a petition for recalling the Agitators is a blind excuse; for put the case that there hath been such an one, and that of generall concurrence yet could it not detract or any way diminish from that righteous engagement; though the defection and subscription were both of Generall, Officers and Souldiers, yet the foundation of that Vow standeth sure to us all, it is immovable till its own proper end, *viz*. the accomplishment of the righteous end therein contained, affix its period: which we earnestly desire, may be conscienciously and seriously laid to heart by all our fellow-souldiers in solemn covenant with us; for there is a God that over-seeth, and one day (when there will be no Articles of War to prevent) will call us to a strict reckoning for the breach of our faith and vows one to another, and the Nation, and account with us for all the blood, ruine, misery and oppression that thereby hath ensued, and still dependeth upon that most monstrous Apostacie. That pretended Petition at that day will be found to be but a broken reed to lean upon, it will nothing abate of the guilt: and how-ever it is now highly urged to wipe off all worldly dishonour from the iron Rulers of our Age, we are not such strangers to the Army, if any such Army Petition were, as not to know it: Sure wee are, no such Petition can be produced from any single Troop, Company, or Regiment, much lesse from the Armie. And though some such endeavours were for the promotion of so wicked and vile an enterprise, and now as evilly made use of; yet it never fell under the cognizance of the Army, neither yet of any single entire Regiment, Troop or Company; and the Engagement by the Army was made as an Army, by unanimous consent, and therefore no otherwise dissolvable, but unanimously as an Army and that neither otherwise then righteously, after the tenour and true intent of that Engagement, as we have clearly evinced, and therein have discharged our Consciences: See further upon this Subject a late Book of Aug. 1649 Lieut. Col. John Lilburns, Intituled, *An Impeachment of High Treason against Oliver Cromwell and Henry Ireton Esquires* page 4, 5. See also the 40, 41, 42, 43, 81 pages of the second Edition of his Book of the eight of June 1646 Intituled *The Legall Fundamentall Liberties of the People of England, asserted, revived and vindicated.*

Thus we have truly stated the case of our late proceedings and differences betwixt our Officers and us, and hope sufficiently to beget a right understanding and approvement, especially with all honest and conscientious people, of the equity of our late undertakings: however to those that are and shall come after, we have published and left upon record a perfect view and Prospect of our condition, that if the present Perusers shall not, yet happily that those that are to come may be thereby provoked to consideration thereof, and equall resentment with us of the righteous ends of that now betrayed, deserted, Engagement of the Army, which we chiefly desire and expect at the hands of our Fellow Souldiers, that they may not longer like their Leaders be numbred amongst such as will not be limited or circumscribed within any Bounds, Engagements, Oaths, Promises, or Protestations, but levell, break, frustrate and throw off all, (as if no tyes betwixt man and man were to be on mankind) to bring about the corrupt ends of their ambition and avarice, as not only in this case of ours, but in all others of their publike undertakings since the beginning of the Armies Engagement is clearly manifest, and yet all their successes, and advancements over the People, gaind by their perjury, fraud, equivocations, treacheries and deceipts they ascribe to the immediate approving hand of God, and zeal over their delusions with the glorious exercise of Religious formalities to the eye of the People, by which a thick mist, as thick as the Egyptian darkness is lately come over the eyes of the greatest pretenders to true puritie and Religion, and many conscientious people therewith bewitched into the favour and approvement of their alone Jesuitical, wicked, desperate and bloody wayes, even to the opposition and persecution of the most faithfull and constant promoters of, and sufferers for, the just freedoms of the Nation.

But in case our fellow Souldiers will not remember their vows, but still slight and desert the same, their sin be upon their own heads, we have discharged our selves; yet considering they may again possibly incline to their countries redemption (as labouring more under ignorance then willfulnes) we shall offer them and all others that bear good will to the Nation, what in reason and Equity is most conducing to a safe and well grounded peace amongst us, and which by its greatest Adversaries cannot be denyed but to be righteous and just, though contradictory to the lawless Lordship and ambitions of their Officers.

And first, We desire it may be considered, that our Hostile engagements against the late King, was not against him as out of any personall enmity, but simply and singly against his Oppressions and Tyranny on the People, and for their removall, but the use and advantage on all the successe God hath been pleased to give us is perverted to that personall end, that by his removall the Ruling sword-men might intrude into his Throne, set up a Martiall Monarchie more cruell, Arbitrarie and Tyrannicall then England ever yet tasted of, and that under the Notion of a Free State, when as the People had no share at all in the constitution thereof, but by the perjurie and falseness of the Lieutenant Generall and his Son in Law Ireton with their Faction was enforced and obtruded by meer conquest upon the People, a Title which Mr John Cook in his Book Intituled *King Charles his Case &c.* there confesseth to be more fit for Wolves and Bears then amongst men, and that such Tyrants that doe so govern with a rod of Iron, doe not govern by Gods permissive hand of approbation, and in such Cases its lawfull for a People to rise up and force their deliverance, See page 8, 10.

Now, rather then thus to be vassallaged, and thus trampled and trod under foot by such that over our backs, and by the many lives, and losse of our blood from us and our fellow-souldiers, have thus stept into the chair of this hatefull Kingship and presumption over us, in despight and defiance of the consent, choice and allowance of the free-people of this Land the true fountain and original of all just power, (as their own Votes against the Kingly Government confesse) we will chuse subjection to the Prince, chusing rather ten thousand times to be his slaves then theirs, yet hating slavery under both: and to that end, to avoid it in both, we desire it may be timely and seriously weighed.

That whereas a most judicious and faithfull Expedient to this purpose, hath, as A Peace-offering been tendered to the acceptance of the free people of England, intituled, *An Agreement of the People,* dated May 1 1649, from our four faithfull Friends, now close prisoners in the Tower of London, we cannot but judge, that that way of Settlement, to wit, by an *Agreement of the People* is the onely and alone way of attonement, reconciliation, peace, freedom and security (under God) to the Nation; it being impossible by way of Conquest to allay the feud, divisions, parties and Quarrels amongst us, which if not stopt, will certainly devour us

314

up in Civil and domestick Broils, though we should have none from abroad; for the Sword convinceth not, it doth but enforce; it begetteth no love, but fomenteth and engendreth hatred and revenge; for bloud thirsteth after bloud, and vengeance rageth for vengeance, and this devoureth and destroyeth all where it cometh. And though our present Rulers have setled themselves, and their conquest-Government over us; yet are we farther from peace and reconciliation then ever: the discontents and dissatisfactions amongst the people in the Kings time, which at length burst into desperate Warr was not the hundreth part so great as the discontents that are now; and if so much did follow the lesser, can better be expected from the greater? never were there such repinings, heart-burnings, grudgings, envyings and cursings in England as now, against the present Governours and Government; never such fraction and division into parties, binding, biting, countermining and plotting one against another for preheminency and majority then now; and of all this nothing is the cause, but this way of force and martiall obtrusion: And can it be imagined such counterplottings, repinings and divisions can be with safety and peace? it is impossible: Insurrections, tumults, revoltings, war and commotions are the proper issues of the wayes of such violence, and no better is to be expected: none but intruders, usurpers and tyrants can be for the way of force; such as would be but servants to the people, and not make the people their servants, cannot but abhor it, and lay down their glory at the feet of the people: these (that now ramp and rage over us) were they other then Tyrants, could do no lesse: they draw near it indeed in words, but are as far as hell from it in actions; they vote and declare the People the supreme Power, and the originall of all just Authority; pretend the promotion of an Agreement of the people, stile this the First yeer of Englands Freedom, intitle their Government a Free State, and yet none more violent, bloudy and perverse enemies thereto; for not under pains of death, and confiscation of lands and goods, may any man challenge and promote those rights of the nation, so lately pretended to by themselves: if we ask them a Fish, they give us a Scorpion, if bread, they give us a stone. Nothing but their boundlesse, lawless wils, their naked swords, Armies, arms and ammunition is now law in England; never were a people so cheated, so abused and trod under foot; enough to inrage them (as once the children of Israel against Adoram) to stone them to death as they passe the streets; which some could not certainly escape, were it not for the fiery sword, vengeance that surrounds them, which at the best is but the arm of flesh, for their shelter and protection, and may fail ere they are aware: all sorts of people watch but for their opportunity, and if it once come like a raging sea on Pharaoh and his host, they will swallow and devour them up alive: and sure, this kind of constitution of Government thus by force in despite of the people obtruded and setled, thus grutched, cursed and hated, will never bring any peace, quiet or rest unto this Nation, it will be but as a continuall fire in their bones: therefore this conquest Constitution is not the way of Englands peace: There is but two wayes, by Conquest, or Agreement; by fire and sword, or by compact and love; and both these are contrary to each other as light is to darkness, and take their rise from contrary ends; and the way of love must needs be of God, for God is love, and all his ways are love; therefore we are bold of all other ways and Expedients whatsoever, to commend only this way of love, of popular Agreement to the publick consideration for a well founded and safe setled peace: and upon this account, and no other, can any security or enjoyment be expected to any publick transactors in this English Theatry, whether Prince or others. We beleeve, he that now judgeth otherwise, will at the length, it may be, when it is too late, finde himself as much deceived, as he that lost his head against his own Palace gate.

Therefore considering there can be no sure building without a firm foundation, and for prevention of further homebred divisions and backslidings into blood, we desire our fellow Souldiers for their severall Regiments of Horse and Foot to chuse their respective Agents to consider of this way of Peace, that yet at length they may be instrumentall in saving (as now they are in destroying) this Nation; but considering what unsetledness, and wavering from their principles, hath appeared among them, and how slender grounds we have of their return from Apostacy, we heartily desire that all serious and well-affected people, that have any bowels of compassion in them to an afflicted, distressed nation, any sence of piety, justice, mercy or goodness in them, any hatred to oppression or remorse of spirit, at the afflicted, or desire of deliverance, or freedome from their worse then Egyptian bondage, that they would lay the miserable condition of the Nation to heart and unite themselves in their endeavours for a new, equall and speedy Representative; and we humbly offer this motion as a just expedient to that end that they would chuse two or three or more faithfull persons from their severall and respective Counties of the Land to come up to London to demand the freedom and release of the Owners and Publishers of the foresaid *Agreement* unjustly detained in Prison by Wil and Force, to debate and consult with them &c. of some way if possible to accomplish the said Agreement, before a deluge of Intestine insurrections and Forraign Invasions from Ireland, Scotland, Swethland, Denmarke, France, and Spain, sweep us away from the Land of our Nativity; and for our parts we doe declare, that though we have been thus abused and defeated, we have still the hearts of Englishmen in us, and shall freely (if there be occasion) spend the Remainder of our strength and blood, for the redemption and purchase of an *Agreement of the People,* upon the foresaid principles, the which for the satisfaction of such as have not seen it, We have hereunto annexed the forementioned draught of the said *Agreement* of our 4 imprisoned Friends in the Tower of London, as containing those things our souls like and approve of as the most exactest that our eyes have seen, and commend the effectuall promoting of it to the serious consideration of all the true hearted friends of this miserable and distressed Nation, and rest

The Nations true Friends and hearty Wel-wishers while we have a drop of blood running in our Veines.

signed at London this 20 of August 1649, by us

John Wood   Robert Everard   Hugh Hurst
Humphry Marston   William Hutchinson   James Carpen

in the behalf of ourselves, and by the appointment of the rest of our forementioned Friends of the three forementioned Regiments.

FINIS.

XVI

The Just Defence of John Lilburn

[In 1652 Lilburne was banished by the Long Parliament. After it was dismissed by Cromwell in April 1653 he argued that his banishment was no longer valid and presently returned to England. In June he was arrested and held to await trial. Between then and his acquittal in August he wrote a number of justificatory pamphlets. This, one of the last, forms a short autobiography. Though acquitted on August 20th, he was not released and was held for some time on the island of Jersey. Later Lilburne became a Quaker and, though not entirely freed, the conditions of his detention were greatly eased. He died in 1657. Though dated by Thomason August 23rd, 1653, *The Just Defence* must have been finished before his acquittal.
H. and D., pp. 450–464.]

THE
JUST DEFENCE
OF

John Lilburn,

Against
Such as charge him
with Turbulency
of Spirit.

Job. 5. 15.
But he saveth the poor from the sword,
from the mouth and from the
hand of the mighty.

ALTHOUGH it be a small thing with me now, after many yeers of sufferings, to be judged of any, or of mans judgement, knowing how apt men are to judge things hastily before the time, before the Lord come, who will bring to light the hidden things of darkness, and will make manifest the councels of the hearts, yet considering how vehemently at present my life is sought after (as for a long time it hath been) and that those who so earnestly desire my blood, wanting matter in true law to compass it, have by their politick Agents, filled almost every mans mouth with clamours against me, that I have ever been, and continue a man of a turbulent spirit, always opposing, striving, and flying in the faces of all authorities, restless, and never satisfied whoever is uppermost; yea, though those whom I my self have labored by might and maine to advance and bring into power: and that therefore it is very requisite I be taken off, and that otherwise England must never look to rest long in peace; yea, so turbulent, that if there were none in the world but John Lilburne, rather then want one to strive withall, forsooth, John would certainly quarrel with Lilburne. Finding that this, how slight and unjust soever, hath prevailed more then true Christianity would admit, and threatens my life more then any matter that is against me, most men of judgement evidently seeing that nothing is laid to my charge, worthy either of death or bonds; I take my self obliged to vindicate my conversation from all such wicked & causless aspersions lest by my silence I should seem guilty, and to have nothing to plead in my defence.

All therefore who have any of the true fear of God in them, may please to take notice, that as they ought to judge nothing before the time, so are they to be careful not to judge according to appearance, but to judge righteous judgment: the reason is, because the appearance of things, the gloss and outside is usually made by politicians, the Arts-men and Craftsmen of the world, for maintenance of their corrupt interests; these will be the sole interpreters of men and things, raising, by art and sophistry, such mists before mens eyes, as what therewith, and by changing themselves into the shape of Angels of light, deceive (were it possible) the very elect: but whosoever judgeth according to their Vote, is certaine to judge amiss, may soon be a slanderer, and soon after a murtherer; and if he stop not quickly, go to hell with them, which is the end of all such as love and make a lye, especially such lyes as whereby mens lives are put in danger.

For thus dealt the false prophets with the true, and by their craft and policy led many people to destroy them; and so likewise dealt the Scribes and Pharisees with the Lord Jesus himself, giving out he was a winebibber, a friend of Publicans and sinners, that he cast out devils by Beelzebub the prince of devils: and that for no other cause, but that he published doctrines destructive to their interest of glory and domination.

And just so dealt they with the Apostles and Disciples of our Lord, as may be seen Acts 4. and throughout the whole body of the Scriptures: and as Heb. 11. 37. were stoned, were sawn asunder, were tempted, were slaine with the sword, wandered about in sheep-skins and goats-skins, being destitute, afflicted, tormented, of whom the world was not worthy; they wandered in desarts, and in mountaines, and in dens, and caves of the earth. And all these in their several times were reviled and reproached as turbulent persons, as Paul and Silas were in Acts 17. 6. And when they found them not, they drew out Jason and divers brethren unto the rulers of the City, crying, These that have turned the world upside down, are come hither also, whom Jason hath received, and these do all contrary to the decrees of Caesar, saying, There is another King, one Jesus.

And thus in every age ever since hath it been, as witness all the volumes of the books of Martyrs, and the Chronicles of almost every nation; and thus sometimes upon a religious, and sometimes upon a civil account, and very often upon both in one and the same persons: the most faithful servants of Christ in every country where they lived, being ever the greatest enemies to tyranny and oppression, and the most zealous maintainers of the known laws and liberties of their Country, as was John Hus in Bohemia, Jerom of Prague, John Wickliff in England, the Martyrs in Queen Maryes dayes, the Hugonots or Protestants in France, the Gues in the Low-Countrys; all not only esteemed Hereticks by the Church, but rebels and traytors to their several States and Princes.

And to come home to our selves, and to our own knowledge, none have in the least opposed the illegal practices of those that for the time being have been uppermost, but as they have been given out to be Hereticks and Schismaticks; so also to be factious and seditious, men of contentious and turbulent spirits: and this for no other cause, but for standing for the truth, and contending for the known laws of the land; the prosecutors and cryers out of turbulency, proving ever unjust persons and oppressors; and the oppressed and sufferers, though through the policies of wicked men they have been supposed to suffer as evil doers, yet a short time hath proved they have suffered for truth and right, and were both faithful to God, to their consciences, and truest friends to their native countries, and to the laws and liberties thereof, which rightly understood, give check to all such unjust and evil practices: So that if men would but consider whence the cry ariseth, and that it cometh ever from those that do the injury, and is done purposely to fit and prepare such for destruction as oppose their unjust designs, that whom by law they cannot destroy, first to kill their reputation, and to render them odious; that so what violence or bloody injustice is done unto them, may be digested, if not fully approved. I say, were these truths considered, well-meaning people would not be so easily deluded and drawn in to cry, as these politicians cry; nor so easily under the notion of turbulent spirits give up in sacrifice the lives and bloods of their dearest and best friends, to the lawless lusts and wills of ambitious men, untill none are left that dare utter one word in defence of known rights, or once open their mouths in opposition of arbitrary and illegal proceedings.

For wherein can it be made appear that I ever have been, or am of a turbulent spirit? true it is, since I have had any understanding, I have been under affliction, and spent most of my time in one prison or other; but if those that afflicted me did it unjustly, and that every of my imprisonments were unlawful, and that in all my sufferings I have not suffered as an evil doer, but for righteousness sake; then were they turbulent that afflicted and imprisoned me, and not I that have cryed out against their oppressions; nor should my many imprisonments be more a blemish unto me, then unto the Apostle Paul, who thought it no dishonour to remember those that somewhat despised him, that he had been in labours more abundant, in stripes above measure, in prisons more frequent, in deaths oft.

And truly, though I have not wherewith to compare with those glorious witnesses of God, that in the Apostles times sealed the testimony of Jesus with their bloods, nor with those that in the ages since, down to these times, who have with the loss of their own lives brought us out of the gross darkness of Popery, into a possibility of discerning the clear truths of the Gospel; yet as I have the assurance of God in my own conscience, that in the day of the Lord I shall be found to have been faithful, so though the policies of the adversaries of those truths I have suffered for, do blinde many mens understandings for a season concerning me, yet a time will come when those that now are apt to censure me of rashness and turbulency of spirit, will dearly repent that ever they admitted such a thought, confess they have done me wrong, and wish with all their hearts they had been all of my judgement and resolution.

There being not one particular I have contended for, or for which I have suffered, but the right, freedome, safety, and well-being of every particular man, woman, and child in England hath been so highly concerned therein, that their freedome or bondage hath depended thereupon, insomuch that had they not been misled in their judgements, and corrupted in their understandings by such as sought their bondage, they would have seen themselves as much bound to have assisted me, as they judge themselves obliged to deliver their neighbour out of the hands of theevs & robbers, it being impossible for any man, woman, or child in England, to be free from the arbitrary and tyrannical wills of men, except those ancient laws and ancient rights of England, for which I have contended even unto blood, be preserved and maintained; the justness and goodness whereof I no sooner understood, and how great a check they were to tyranny and oppression, but my conscience enforced me to stand firme in their defence against all innovation and contrary practices in whomsoever.

For I bless God I have been never partial unto men, neither malicing any, nor having any mans person in admiration, nor bearing with that in one sort of men, which I condemned in others.

As for instance, the first fundamental right I contended

for in the late Kings and Bishops times, was for the freedom of mens persons, against arbitrary and illegal imprisonments, it being a thing expresly contrary to the law of the land, which requireth, That no man be attached, imprisoned, &c. (as in Magna Charta, cap. 29) but by lawful judgement of a Jury, a law so just and preservative, as without which intirely observed, every mans person is continually liable to be imprisoned at pleasure, and either to be kept there for moneths or yeers, or to be starved there, at the wills of those that in any time are in power, as hath since been seen and felt abundantly, and had been more, had not some men strove against it; but it being my lot so to be imprisoned in those times, I conceive I did but my duty to manifest the injustice thereof, and claime and cry out for my right, and in so doing was serviceable to the liberties of my country, and no wayes deserved to be accounted turbulent in so doing.

Another fundamental right I then contended for, was, that no mans conscience ought to be racked by oaths imposed, to answer to questions concerning himself in matters criminal, or pretended to be so.

The ancient known right and law of England being, that no man be put to his defence at law, upon any mans bare saying, or upon his own oath, but by presentment of lawful men, and by faithful witnesses brought for the same face to face; a law and known right, without which any that are in power may at pleasure rake into the brests of every man for matter to destroy life, liberty, or estate, when according to true law and due proceedings, there is nought against them; now it being my lot to be drawn out and required to take an oath, and to be required to answer to questions against my self and others whom I honoured, and whom I knew no evil by, though I might know such things by them as the oppossors and persecutors would have punished them for, in that I stood firm to our true English liberty, as resolvedly persisted therein, enduring a most cruel whipping, pilloring, gagging, and barbarous imprisonment, rather then betray the rights and liberties of every man; did I deserve for so doing to be accounted turbulent? certainly none will so judge, but such as are very weak, or very wicked; the first of which are inexcusable at this day, this ancient right having now for many yeers been known to all men; and the latter ought rather to be punished then be countenanced, being still ready to do the like to me or any man. I then contended also against close imprisonment, as most illegal, being contrary to the known laws of the land; and by which tyrants and oppossors in all ages have broken the spirits of the English, and sometimes broken their very hearts, a cruelty few are sensible of, but such as have been sensible by suffering; but yet it concerns all men to oppose in whomsoever; for what is done to any one, may be done to every one: besides, being all members of one body, that is, of the English Commonwealth, one man should not suffer wrongfully, but all should be sensible, and endeavour his preservation; otherwise they give way to an inlet of the sea of will and power, upon all their laws and liberties, which are the boundaries to keep out tyrany and oppression; and who assists not in such cases, betrayes his own rights, and is over-run, and of a free man made a slave when he thinks not of it, or regards it not, and so shunning the censure of turbulency, incurs the guilt of treachery to the present and future generations. Nor did I thrust my self upon these contests for my native rights, and the rights of every Englishman, but was forced thereupon in my own defence, which I urge not, but that I judge it lawful, praise-worthy, and expedient for every man, continually to watch over the rights and liberties of his country, and to see that they are violated upon none, though the most vile and dissolute of men; or if they be, speedily to indeavour redresse; otherwise such violations breaches, and incroachments will eat like a Gangrene upon the common Liberty, and become past remedy: but I urge it, that it may appear I was so far from what would in me have been interpreted turbulency, that I contended not till in my own particular I was assaulted and violated.

Neither did I appear to the Parliament in their prime estate as a turbulent person, though under as great suffering as ever since, but as one grievously injured, contrary to the Laws and Rights of England; and as one deserving their protection and deliverance out of that thraldom wherein I was, and of large and ample reparation, as they did of Mr. Burton, Mr. Pryn, and Dr. Bastwick; and which their favourable and tender regard to persons in our condition, gained them multitudes of faithful friends, who from so just and charitable a disposition appearing in them, concluded they were fully resolved to restore the Nation to its long lost liberty without delay.

Being delivered by them, and understanding their cause to be just, the differences between them and the late King daily increasing, I frequently adventured my self in their defence; and at length, the controversie advancing to a war, I left my Trade and all I had, and engaged with them, and did what service I was able, at Edge-hill, and afterwards at Branford, where after a sharp resistance, I was taken prisoner; and refusing large offers if I would renounce them, and serve the King, I was carryed a pinioned prisoner to Oxford, where I endured sorrows and afflictions inexpressible: yet neither by enemy nor friend, was ever to that time accounted turbulent, though I there insisted for my Rights as earnestly and importunately as ever, and as highly disdained all their threats or allurements; and again found so much respect from the Parliament, as when my life was most in danger, to be once more preserved by them; though then not so freely as at first, but upon the earnest and almost distracted solicitation of my dear wife, violently rushing into the House, and casting her self down before them at their Bar: for now their hearts were not so soft and tender as at first: but so far was I then from this new imputation of turbulency, either in City, Country, Parliament, or Army, that I had every ones welcom at my return; and my Lord General Essex to express his joy and affection to me, though he knew me a noted Sectary (a people he was so unhappy to disaffect) that he gave me no less then betwixt 200 and 300 l. in mony, and offers of any kindness; which I shall ever thankfully remember to his just honour.

But Col. Homsteed, and all non-conformists, Puritans, and Sectaries being daily discouraged and wearied out of that Army; and the Earl of Manchester Major General of the associate Counties, giving countenance unto them, I put my self under his Command, my then most dear friend, as much honored by me, as any man in the world, the now Lord General Cromwel, being then his Lieut. General: what services I performed whilst I continued under their command, will not become me to report; I shall onely say this, that I was not then accounted either a coward, or unfaithful; nor yet of a turbulent or contentious spirit, though I received so much cause of dislike at some carriages of the said Earl, as made me leave the service, and soon after coming for London, discovered so great a defection in the Parliament from their first Principles, as made me resolve never to engage further with them, until they repented and returned, and did their first works: from which they were so far, as that there had not been any corrupt practice formerly complained of, either in the High-Commission, Star-Chamber, or Councel-Table, or any exorbitancies elsewhere, but began afresh to be practised both by the House of Lords, and House of Commons, without any regard to those Antient fundamental Laws and Rights, for the violation of which, they had denounced a war against the King.

Nor did they thus themselves, but countenanced and encouraged the same throughout the Land, illegal imprisonments, & close-imprisonments, & examinations of men against themselves, everywhere common; and upon Petitions to Parliament, in stead of relief, new Ordinances made further to intangle them, and all still pointed against the most Conscientious peaceable people, such as could not conform to Parliament-Religion, but desired to worship God according to their own Judgements and Consciences; a just freedom to my understanding, and the most just and reasonable, and most conducing to publick peace that could be; and in the use whereof, I had in some yeers before, enjoyed the comfortable fruition of a gracious God and loving Saviour; and which occasioned me, so soon as the Controversie about liberty of Conscience began, to appear with my pen in its just defence, against my *quondam* fellow-sufferer Mr. Pryn, as a liberty due not onely according to the word of God, which I effectually proved, but due also by the fundamental Laws of the Land, which provide that no man be questioned, or molested, or put to answer for any thing, but wherein he materially violates the person, goods, or good name of another: and however strange the defence thereof then appeared, time hath proved that it is a liberty which no conscientious man or woman can spare, being such, as without which every one is lyable to molestation and persecution, though he live never so honestly, peaceably, and agreeable to the Laws of the Land; and which every man must allow, that will keep to that golden rule, to do as he would be done unto.

And though my ready appearing also for this my native Right, and the Right of every man in England, gained me many adversaries (for men will be adverse to the best and justest things that ever were, till through time and sound consideration, the understanding be informed) yet neither for this was I accounted turbulent, or of a contentious spirit.

My next engagement was as a witness against the Earl of Manchester, upon Articles exhibited by his Lieutenant-General Cromwel; wherein I being serious, as knowing matters to be foul, opened my self at large, as thinking the same was intended to have been thorowly prosecuted: but the great men drew stakes, and I was left to wrestle with my Lord, who, what by craft, as setting his mischievous Agent Col. King upon my back, and the Judges of the Common Pleas, and upon that the power of the House of Lords, as got me first an imprisonment in New-gate, and after that in the Tower. Against which oppression, for urging the fundamental Laws of England against their usurped and innovated powers, I then began to be termed a factious, seditious, and turbulent fellow, not fit to live upon earth. For now by this time, both House of Lords and House of Commons were engaged in all kindes of arbitrary and tyrannical practices, even to extremity. So that I must pray the judicious Reader well to mark the cause for which I was first accounted turbulent, *viz.* for urging the fundamental Law of the land against those that thought themselves uppermost in power, and above the power of Law, as their practices manifested; and he shall finde, that for no other cause have I been reputed so ever since to this very day; and that it shall be any mans portion that doth so.

About this time, the Army began to dispute the command of Parliament; and that as they largely declared, because the Parliament had forsaken their rule, the fundamental Laws of England, and exercised an arbitrary and tyrannical power over the consciences, lives, liberties, and estates; and instanced in me and others, who had been long illegally imprisoned. These now espousing the publike Cause, and that their only end was, that the ancient Rights and Liberties of the people of England might be cleared and secured, not onely prevailed with me, but thousands others in London, Southwark, and most places thorowout the Land, so to adhere unto them, as notwithstanding great preparations against them both by Parliament and City of London, yet they prevailed without bloodshed. A friendship they should not have forgotten.

Obstacles being thus removed, I who with many others, had adhered to them, daily solicited the performance of the end of this great undertaking and engagement, *viz.* the re-establishment of the fundamental laws: but as it appeared then in part, and more plainly since, there being no such real intention, whatever had been pretended upon this our solicitation, the countanances of the great ones of the Army began to change towards us, and we found we were but troublesome to them, and accounted men of turbulent and restless spirits; but at that time the Agitators being in some power, these aspersions were but secretly dispersed.

We seeing the dangerous consequence of so suddain a defection, from all those zealous promises and protestations made as in the presence of God: and having been instrumental in their opposition of the Parliamentary authority, and knowing that in our consciences, nor in the sight of God, we could not be justified, except we persevered to the fulfilling of the end, The restauration of the Fundamental Laws and Rights of the Nation; and I especially, who had spilt both my own and other mens bloods in open fight, for the attainment thereof, look'd upon my self as no other or better then a murtherer of my brethren and Country-men, if I should onely by my so doing make way for raising another sort of men into power, and so enable them to trample our Laws and Liberties more under foot then ever. Upon these grounds, I ceased not day nor night to reduce those in chiefest power into a better temper of spirit, and to perswade them to place their happiness not in Absoluteness of domination, but in performance of their many zealous Promises and Declarations made with such vehemencie of expression, as in the presence of God, and published in print to all the world; urging what a dishonour it would be to the whole Army, to have their faith so broken and violated, that though they might succeed in making out power and domination to some few of them, yet God could not be satisfied, nor their consciences be at peace. This was my way to most of them for a long time: but I may truely say, with David, They plentifully payd me hatred for my good will; and for my good counsel, (for so I believe time will prove it, though now they seem to ride on the wings of prosperity with their ill-gotten wealth and power) they layd snares to take away my life.

And in order thereunto, I with others being at the prosecuting of a Petition, one of their officious Spyes lays an accusation against me at the House of Commons bar; where clayming a Tryal at Law for any thing could be alleadged against me, and denying their Authority as to be my Judges, and for maintaining that I ought not to be tryed in any case but by a Jury of my Neighbourhood; For this doing, I was sent again prisoner to the Tower, where I continued for many months; and then again accounted a factious, seditious, and turbulent fellow, that owned no Authority, and that would have no Government; the cause being still the same, for that I would not renounce the Law my birthright, and submit to the wills of men in power, which as an English man I am bound to oppose.

But new Troubles appearing, and the great ones being in supposition they might once more need their dissatisfied friends, after a sore imprisonment, I obtained my liberty, and so much shew of respects, as to have the damages (alotted for my sufferings under the Star-chamber sentence) ascertained: but not the least

motion towards the performance of publike engagements, but only as troubles came, as about that time
they did appear, upon the general rising & coming in of
Hamilton, Goring, and the like, then indeed promises
were renewed, and tears shed in token of repentance,
and then all again embraced as Friends, all names of
reproach cease, turbulent, and leveller, and all; and
welcome every one that will now but help; and this
trouble being but over, all that ever was promised
should be faithfully and amply performed: but no sooner
over, then all again forgotten; and every one afresh
reproached, that durst but put them in minde of what
they so lately had promised: yea, all such of the Army,
under one pretence or other, excluded the Army, and
so nothing appearing but a making way for Absoluteness, and to render the Army a meer mercenary servile
thing, sutable to that end, that might make no conscience
of promises, or have any sense of the Cause for which
they were raised.

Perceiving this, I with others having proved all their
pretences of joyning in an Agreement of the People to
be but delusion, and that they neither broke the Parliament in pieces, nor put the King to death, in order to
the restauration of the Fundamental Laws of the Nation
whatever was pretended, but to advance themselves;
I having been in the North about my own business while
those things were done, and coming to London soon
after, and finding (as to the Common Freedom) all
things in a worse condition, and more endangered then
ever, made an application to the Councel of the Army
by a Paper, wherein were good grounds of prevention:
but some there making a worse use thereof, interpreted
the same a disturbance of the Army, earnestly moving
they might get a Law to hang such as so disturbed them;
affirming they could hang twenty for one the old Law
could do.

Whereupon, we applyed our selves to the new purged

Parliament, with a Paper called *The Serious Apprehensions:* unto which obtaining no answer, I endeavoured to have gotten hands to another Paper to be presented to the House, which was printed under the title of *The second Part of Englands new Chains discovered;* wherein was laid open much of what since hath been brought upon the Nation of will and power; which at this day deserveth to be read by all that conceive me to be of a turbulent spirit, wherein they will finde the cause still the same, *viz.* my constant adherence to the known rights of the nation, and no other.

Upon this, I was fetched out of bed and house by a party of horse and foot, in such a dreadful manner, as if I had been the greatest traitor to the laws and liberties of England, that ever was; the souldiers being raised onely against such traitors, and not to seize upon men that strove for their restoration; but now the case was altered, and I must be no less then a traitor, and so taken, and so declared all over England, with my other fellow-sufferers, and all clapt up prisoners in the Tower, and after a while close prisoners, and then not only aspersed to be factious and turbulent, but Atheists, and Infidels, of purpose to fit us for destruction.

And though after a long and tedious imprisonment, they could never finde whereof legally to accuse us for any thing they put us in prison, yet scrap'd they up new matter against me, from the time they gave me liberty to visit my sick and distressed family; a thing heathens would have been ashamed of (but who so wicked as dissembling Christians?) and upon this new matter, small as it was, what a Tryal for my life was I put upon? what an absolute resolution did there appeare to take away my life? but God and the good Consciences of twelve honest men preserved me, and delivered me of that their snare; which smote them to the heart, but not with true repentance; for then had they ceased to pursue me: but just before that my Tryal, it is not to be forgotten, how a Declaration was set forth by the then Council of State, signifying my complyance with young Charles Stuart, just as now was published in print upon the very morning I was brought to the Sessions-house: yea, and the same papers brought into the now Parliament, of purpose to bespeak and prevent the effect of those Petitions then presented in my behalf, and to turn the spirits of the House against me: so that nothing is more evident, then that the same hand still stones me, and for the same cause; and that I may be murdered with some credit, first they kill me with slanders: but as they in wickedness, so God in righteousness, and the Consciences of good men in matter of Justice, is still the same; and I cannot doubt my deliverance.

God and the Consciences of men fearing him more then men, freeing me from this danger, I endeavoured to settle my self in some comfortable way of living, trying one thing and another; but being troubled with Excise, wherein I could not sherk like other men, I was soon tired; and being dayly applyed unto for Counsel by friends, I resolved to undertake mens honest causes, and to manage them either as Sollicitor or Pleader, as I saw cause; wherein I gave satisfaction. And amongst others, I was retained by one Master Jos. Primate in a cause concerning a Colliery, which I found, though just, to have many great opposers, and chiefly my ingaged adversarie, Sir Arthur Haselrige, one that did what he could to have starved me in prison, seizing on my moneys in the North, when I had nothing to maintaine my self, my wife and children; this cause had many traverses between the Committee in the North, and the Committee for sequestration at Haberdashers Hall.

And so much injustice appeared unto me to have been manifestly done, that I set forth their unworthiness as fully as I was able, and at length the cause being to receive a final determination before that Committee, I with my Client and other his councel appeared daily for many dayes, proving by undeniable arguments, from point to point, the right to be in Master Primate: but Sir Arthur Haselrige a Member of Parliament and Councel of State, and a mighty man in the North and in the Army, so bestirred himself, That when Judgement came to be given, it was given by the major Vote against my Clyent, quite contrary to the opinions of most that heard it, and to my Clients and my understanding, against all equity and conscience.

Whereupon, my Client by his petition appealed to the Parliament, wherein he supposeth that Sir Arthur had over-awed the Committee to give a corrupt Judgement. And being questioned, avowed the petition to be his own, and cleared me from having any hand therein. The house were in a great heat, and quarrelled my giving out the petitions before they were received by them, though nothing was more common; but order a rehearing of the whole matter by a large Committee of Members of the house in the Exchequer-Chamber, where notwithstanding the right appeared as clear as the Sun when it shines at noon-day, to be in my Client, to all by-standers not preingaged, yet whilst it was in hearing, long before the report was made, I had divers assured me I should be banished; and when I demanded for what cause, I could get none, but that I was of a turbulent spirit. It was strange to me, nor could I believe a thing so grosly unjust could be done, and provided nothing against it.

But upon the report of Master Hill the lawyer, most false as it was, the House was said to have passed Votes upon me of seven thousand pound fine, and perpetual banishment.

And upon the Tusday after called me to their Bar, and commanded me to kneel once, twice, and again; which I refusing, and desiring to speak, they would not suffer me, but commanded me to withdraw; and the next news I heard, was, that upon paine of death, I must within twenty [days] depart the land: which though altogether groundless, yet finding all rumors concurring in their desperate resolutions, thought it safest to withdraw for a season, into some parts beyond the seas; and so I did, where I had been but a very short time, but I saw a paper intituled *An Act in execution of a Judgement given in Parliament, for the banishment of Lieut. Col. John Lilburne, and to be taken as a felon upon his return, &c.* at which I wondered, for I was certaine I had received no Charge, nor any form of trial, nor had any thing there laid to my Charge, nor was never heard in my defence to any thing.

Nevertheless, there I counted in much danger and misery for above sixteen moneths, my estate being seized by Sir Arthur: at length understanding the dissolution of the Parliament, I concluded my danger not much if I should return; and having some incouragement by my wife, from what my Lord General Cromwell should say of the injustice of the Parliaments proceedings, and of their (pretended) Act, I cast my self upon my native country, with resolutions of all peaceable demeanor towards all men; but how I have been used thereupon, and since, the Lord of heaven be judge between those in power and me; It being a cruelty beyond example, that I should be so violently hurried to Newgate, and most unjustly put upon my trial for my life as a Felon, upon so groundless a meer supposed Act, notwithstanding so many petitions to the contrary.

And now, that all men see the grosness of their cruelty and bloody intentions towards me, and having not consciences to go back, they now fill all mens mouthes, whom they have power to deceive, that I am of so turbulent a spirit, that there will be no quietness in England except I be taken off.

But dear Country-men, friends, and Christians, aske them what evil I have done, and they can shew you none; no, my great and onely fault is, that (as they conceive) I will never brook whilst I live to see (and be silent) the laws and rights of the Nation trod under foot by themselves, who have all the obligations of men and Christians to revive and restore them. They imagine, whilst I have breath, the old law of the land will be pleaded and upheld against the new, against all innovated law or practice whatsoever. And because I am, and continue constant to my principles upon which I first engaged for the common liberty, and will no more bear in these the violation of them, then I did in the King, Bishops, Lords, or Commons, but cry aloud many times of their abominable unworthiness in their so doing; therefore to stop my mouth, and take away my life, they cry out I never will be quiet, I never will be content with any power; but the just God heareth in heaven, and those who are his true servants will hear and consider upon earth, and I trust will not judge according to the voice of self-seeking ambitious men, their creatures and relations, but will judge righteous judgement, and then I doubt not all their aspersions of me will appear most false and causless, when the worst I have said or written of them and their wayes, will prove less then they have deserved.

Another stratagem they have upon me, is, to possess all men, that all the souldiers in the Army are against me; but they know the contrary, otherwise why do they so carefully suppress all petitions which the souldiers have been handing in my behalf? indeed those of the souldiers that hear nothing but what they please of me, either by their scandalous tongues or books, may through misinformation be against me; but would they permit them to hear or read what is extant to my vindication, I would wish no better friends then the souldiers of the Army; for I am certaine I never wronged one of them, nor are they apt to wrong any man, except upon a misinformation.

But I hope this discourse will be satisfactory both to them and all other men, that I am no such Wolfe, Bear, or Lyon, that right or wrong deserves to be destroyed; and through the truth herein appearing, will strongly perswade for a more gentle construction of my intentions and conversation, and be an effectual Antidote against such poisonous asps who endeavour to kill me with the bitterness of their envenomed tongues, that they shall not be able to prevaile against me, to sway the consciences of any to my prejudice in the day of my trial.

Frailties and infirmities I have, and thick and three-fold have been my provocations; he that hath not failed in his tongue, is perfect, so am not I. I dare not say, Lord I am not as other men; but, Lord be merciful to me a sinner; But I have been hunted like a Partridge upon the mountains: My words and actions in the times of my trials and deepest distress and danger have been scanned with the spirit of Jobs comforters; but yet I know I have to do with a gracious God, I know that my redeemer liveth, and that he will bring light out of this darkeness, and cleer my innocency to all the world.

FINIS.

XVII

Leveller Organisation

[The three following letters illustrate aspects of Leveller organisation at different stages of their history.]

THREE
LETTERS
TO

The Agitators
The Kentish Levellers
Corporal Parkinson

Letter from Lt. C. to
The Agitators

[This was written in May 1647 at the height of the Army's resistance to disbandment and illustrates the excitement and hopes aroused by the crisis as well as the extent of the underground organisation that had been created. Professor Woodhouse identifies Lt. C. as Edmund Chillenden, a former associate of Lilburne and at this time a leading figure among Army Levellers. His zeal was short-lived — at Putney he was one of Ireton's few supporters and at Ware he was put in charge of the arrested Levellers.
Woodhouse, p. 400.]

Gentlemen,

MY BEST respects. I rid hard and came to London by four this afternoon. The House hath ordered and voted the Army to be disbanded, regiment by regiment. The General's Regiment of Foot on Tuesday next to lay down their arms in Chelmsford Church, and they do intend to send you down once more Commissioners, to do it, of Lords and Commons. They will not pay more than two months' pay, and, after we be disbanded, to state our accompts and be paid by the excise in course. This is their good vote, and their good visible security! Pray, Gentlemen, ride night and day. We will act here night and day for you. You must by all means frame a petition in the name of all the soldiers, to be presented to the General by you the Agitators, to have him, in honour, justice and honesty, to stand by you, and to tell

Skippon to depart the Army, and all other officers that are not right. Be sure now be active, and send some thirty or forty horse to fetch away Jackson, Gooday, and all that are naught. And be sure to possess his soldiers: he will sell them and abuse them; for so he hath done, he engaged to sell them for eight weeks' pay. Gent., I have it from (59) and (89) that you must do this, and that you shall expell them out of the Army; and if you do disappoint them in the disbanding of this regiment, namely (68), you will break the neck of all their designs. This is the judgement of (59) and (89); therefore, Gent., follow it close. The (52) are about (42), which copies I send you. And let me tell you (41) and (52) in (54) are all very gallant. I pray God keep us so too. Now, my lads, if we work like men we shall do well, and that in the hands of (53). And let all the (44) be very insistant that the (55) may be called to a (43), and that with speed. Delay it not. And by all means be sure to stir up the Counties to petition for their rights, and to make their appeal to (55) to assist them. You shall hear all I can by the next. So till then I rest.

     Yours till death,

                          102

From 51. 11 at night.

Letter to
Kentish Levellers

[This is one of several documents printed in a hostile pamphlet, *A Declaration of Some Proceedings of Lt. Col. John Lilburn And his Associates* (February 1648). There is no reason to doubt its authenticity. It dates from the time when the most serious efforts were being made to build a permanent party with solid local organisation.
H. and D., pp. 102–104.]

Worthy Gentlemen, and dear Friends,

OUR BOWELS are troubled, and our hearts pained within us, to behold the Divisions, Distractions, heart-burnings, and contentions which abound in this distressed Nation, and we are confounded in our selves upon the foresight of the confusion and desolation, which will be the certain consequence of such divisions, if they should be but for a little time longer continued; there are now clouds of bloud over our heads again, and the very rumors and fears of Warre hath so wasted Trading, and enhaunsed the price of all food and cloathing, that Famine is even entring into your gates; and doubtlesse, neither pen nor tongue can expresse the misery, which will ensue immediately upon the beginning of another Warre; Why therefore O our Country men, should we not every man say each to other, as Abraham to Lot, or Moses to the two Israelites, Why should we contend each with other, seeing we are brethren? O that our advice might be acceptable to you, that you would every man expostulate each with other, and now while you have an opportunity, consider together wherefore the contention hath been these six or seven years! Hath it not been for freedome and Justice? O then propound each to other the chief principles of your freedome, and the foundation of Justice, and common Right, and questionlesse, when you shall understand the desires each of other, you will unite together inviolably to pursue them.

Now truely in our apprehensions, this work is prepared to your hands in the Petition, which we herewith send to you; certainly, if you shall all joyne together to follow resolutely, and unweariedly, after the things contained in that Petition, the bloud and confusion which now threaten us may be prevented, and the sweet streames of Justice will run into your bosomes freely without obstruction; O that the Lord may be so propitious to this tottering Nation, as to give you to understand these things which belong to your Peace and welfare!

Many honest people are resolved already to unite together in that Petition, & to prosecute the obtaining it with all their strength; they are determined, that now after seven years waiting for Justice, Peace, and Freedome, they will receive no deniall in these requests which are so essentiall to their Peace and Freedome; and for the more effectuall proceedings in this businesse, there is a Method and Order setled in all the Wards in London, and the out Parishes and Suburbs; they have appointed severall active men in every Ward and Division, to be a Committee, to take the speciall care of the businesse, and to appoint active men in every Parish to read the Petition at set meetings for that purpose, and to take Subscriptions, and to move as many as can possibly, to goe in person when the day of delivering it shall be appointed; and they intend to give notice of that time to all the adjacent Counties, that as many of them as possibly can, may also joyne with them the same day; and the like orderly way of proceeding is commended to severall Counties, to whom the Petition is sent, as to Hartfordshier, Buckingham, Oxford, Cambridge, Rutlandshier, &c. And we cannot but propound to you the same Method, as the best expedient for your union, in pursuing after a speedy settlement of your Peace and Freedome, therefore in brief we desire,

1. That you would appoint meetings in every Division of your County, and there to select faithfull men of publick spirits, to take care that the Petition be sent to the hands of the most active men in every Town, to unite the Town in those desires of common right, and to take their subscriptions.

2. That you would appoint as many as can with convenience, to meet at Dartford, the 23. of this present January, being Lords day, and we shall conferre with you about the Matters that concerne your Peace, and common good and Freedome.

Wee shall at present adde no more but this, that to serve you, and our whole countrey in whatsoever concerns its common peace and wellfare, is, and alwayes shall be, the desire and joy of

Your most Faithfull Friends and Servants which came from London from many other friends upon this Service,

John Lilburn.
Wildman.
John Davies.
Richard Woodward.

Dartford, this 9. of Jan. 1647.

Mr Samuel Otes
to Corporal Parkinson

[This letter, with its enclosure, shows how even in the 1650's rank and file Levellers had not entirely given up their efforts to rebuild their organisation. Colonels Okey and Saunders were forced out of the Army in 1654 for protesting against the Insrument of Government.

John Nicholls, Original Letters and Papers, pp. 132–133.]

From Aberdeene, Dec. 2nd, 1654.
Brother Parkinson,

I HAVE obtayned mercie to love yow, though I of late obtayne mercie to see yow, and I doe not know whether I shall ever see your face any more in Scotland, for I entend ere long to goe for England, if God will, and I think I shall not come a good while into Scotland. Brother, I am in great heavines to think how wee have made the hearts of the righteous fade, which our Father, the Jehovah of Hosts would not have made fade, by not answering there expectations; for wee have promised to make them a free people, and that they should have free and successive parlements, but performe neither; for Coll. Okey hath bin in trouble, and Coll Sanders is now upon his tryall, for aserting of and pleading the things we have fought and prayed for. And, brother, wee are moved now to make some address to the Generall Monck, and soe to the Protector, for to desire those things which wee should have had long agoe, and wee should have sent to your troops, but that yow ly so farre northward to intreat yow to have mett us by a Christian freind from your regiment; but wee thought it was too troublesom. Nevertheless I have sent you an accompt of a letter sent to twelve or fourteen regiments, to intreate there prayers and Christian advice, and wee hope God will put us in a way to offer something to the Generall Monck and the Protector. Sure its a sad thing that wee should build again the things we have destroyed. Wee shall make ourselves trespasers. Brother, pray present my Christian love to all the good soules, our bretheren: and I pray you shew this letter to the regiments, to our friends, and set them to work for us in prayre to the Father; to whom I committ thee, and all the rest with thee, and rest thy loving brother in the Lord

Samuel Otes.

For Corporall Parkinson, in Captain Evensons troope, in Commissary Generall Whaleys regiment, at his quarters, or to Mr Watsons clarke to the troope, these.

ENCLOSURE

Dearly Beloved Brethren,

The most high God hath sett it upon our harts, and wee judge it ought never to be forgotten by us, the emmenent mercies and deleverances the Lord of Hosts hath made us subjects of, and instruments in. He hath called us forth in our generation to asert the freedomes of the people in the preveledges of Parlement; for which hath been expended vast treasures, spilt much blood, put up to heaven many prayers, powered out teares, and sent doune from heaven many signall salvations; for the accomplishment of which end there lyes upon us many vows, declarations, and soleme apeales to the most high. And now the price of all that blood and treasure, the answere of all those prayrs, the accompt of all those teares, the improvement of all those salvations, the performance of all those vowes, and declarations to God and the people, and the vindication of our censerity in those apeales, call aloud upon us seriously to consider whether wee have obtayned our ends, and may quietly sit down satisfied in the present state of publick affayres, and with a good conscience look the King of Terrors in the face, as having faithfully served our generation; or whether, except wee do somewhat more, the guilt of the blood of soe many thousands, the miseryes of a wasted Commonwealth, the breach of vowes and trust, the prayrs and cries of the saynts, and the hypocrisie of our professions, will not lie heavy upon our consciences, bodyes and estates, till we return to our dust, and afterwards sink us downe to the bottomlesse pit. Wee therefore being pressed in our consciences, doe desire a meeting with yow, or whom ye shall appoynt, to the end aforesaid. If a sence answerable to ours bee not upon your harts, and that yow slight this our advice, yett wee shall have comfort in this, that we have so much discharged our dutys towards yow. Wee remaine

Your affectionate faythfull freinds,
Aberdeene Dec. 1654.
The place appoynted is the greene dragon in the Cannygate in Edinbrough, the first day of January, at foure of the clock in the evening. Enquire for John Loveland. To our Christian freinds in Coll Whaleys regiment.

Briefly,
ABOUT THE EDITOR

In the years 1921–1924, A. L. Morton (born in 1903) was a student at Cambridge University, where he studied English literature and history. It was then that he encountered the ideas of socialism, and in 1929 he joined the Communist Party. The Depression years were marked for him by periods of unemployment interspersed with odd jobs outside his profession of teaching. For a time he worked as a journalist, contributing to a variety of periodicals. From 1933 to 1936, he was a staff member of the London *Daily Worker*. He wrote *A People's History of England* in 1936–37, a pioneer work which established him in the forefront of British Marxist historians. A list of his published works appears on page four of the present volume.